SILVER SHOALS

BY THE SAME AUTHOR

Somewhere Else
The Accidental Angler
Silt Road: The Story of a Lost River

SILVER SHOALS

Five Fish That Made Britain

Charles Rangeley-Wilson

Chatto & Windus
LONDON

1 3 5 7 9 10 8 6 4 2

Chatto & Windus, an imprint of Vintage,
20 Vauxhall Bridge Road,
London SW1V 2SA

Chatto & Windus is part of the Penguin Random House group of companies
whose addresses can be found at global.penguinrandomhouse.com.

Penguin
Random House
UK

First published in the United Kingdom by Chatto & Windus in 2018

penguin.co.uk/vintage

A CIP catalogue record for this book is available from the British Library

ISBN 9781784740863

Typeset in 11.5/15.5 pt Adobe Caslon Pro
by Integra Software Services Pvt. Ltd, Pondicherry

Printed and bound in Great Britain by Clays Ltd, Elcograf S.p.A.

Penguin Random House is committed to a sustainable future for our business, our
readers and our planet. This book is made from Forest Stewardship Council®
certified paper.

MIX
Paper from
responsible sources
FSC
www.fsc.org   FSC® C018179

To Orri Vigfússon
fisherman and conservationist
10 July 1942 – 1 July 2017

This island is made mainly of coal and surrounded by fish.
Aneurin Bevan

The fishermen know that the sea is dangerous and the storm
terrible, but they have never found these dangers
sufficient reason for remaining ashore.
Vincent Van Gogh

CONTENTS

PROLOGUE: HOME

FISHER'S END

I've looked out over the North Sea, on and off, for much of my life.
I can see it now from where I'm typing at the back of the house.
The wind is blowing hard from the north this evening and already
waves are breaking over the outer sandbanks. The sea is almost
glowing, both beautiful and menacing. The sight of the pounding
water and a flickering light over the waves that keeps on vanishing
for moments at a time reminds me of a story I read about fishing
boats out on the sandbanks in a big storm, how once the boats broke
anchor and got up on the sand, they were finished. The sea, so it
went, rushes in 'from an unhindered sweep of 600 miles' and makes
matchwood of any boat unlucky enough to drift on to the hard
sand-flats. The story was told by Frank Castleton, one of the last
fishermen from my local town, King's Lynn, who could still remember
– as an old man in the 1980s – its fishing community. Frank described
what he saw the morning after that storm, the four smacks that had
gone down and how 'all that was left of them were the sternposts,
with a few bits of planking hanging to them and odd scraps of gear
such as stoves lying forlornly around'. Though he didn't intend it
this way, Frank's description was a metaphor, I thought, for what
had happened to him and his community.

Carved wooden bench-ends from St Nicholas' Chapel in what
used to be the fishing quarter of the town – Fisher's End – depict

the glory days of the King's Lynn fishery when Frank's ancestors sailed each spring in square-rigged fishing boats to the seas around Iceland, and returned in the autumn loaded to the gunwales with cod which they had salted and dried on that distant shoreline. The bench-ends are 600 years old and for five and a half of those centuries King's Lynn was a thriving fishing port: as were Lowestoft and Great Yarmouth, Grimsby, Scarborough, Bridlington, Berwick and dozens of other towns along the east coast of England and Scotland. There's not much left of fishing in many of those places now: a brown-shrimp fishery in Lynn, a herring-processing plant in Great Yarmouth; just these 'odd scraps lying forlornly around'.

In King's Lynn only a few houses remain in Fisher's End, along with street names and family names on gravestones scattered through the churchyard, or the phone directory. To walk around there now you would never guess that the place-name described a history. Apart from anything else, no one calls that part of the town Fisher's End any more. The original Fisher's Fleet where those early Renaissance fishing boats moored, granted in perpetuity to the Lynn fishermen by Elizabeth I, now lies under the tarmac behind Enterprise Rent-a-Car and the ABC Car Wash. An ivy-wrapped level crossing marks the spot where the channel once passed under what used to be Pilot Street, but is now called John Kennedy Road.

Most of the little fishermen's cottages that surrounded the Fleet were done away with when King's Lynn's authorities cleared away the town's 'slums' in the 1930s and the 1960s, when the sailors, sailmakers, fish merchants, mariners, harbour pilots, fishermen, fisherwomen, fishwives, ropemakers, boatbuilders, twine-spinners and cord-wainers who lived there were rehoused throughout the town. Only two small cottages are left, known by their old name of True's Yard. Somehow they survived the demolition and in the 1980s a trust was founded to buy and preserve them as a memorial to the vanished community. Side by side they stand in the shadow of the fishermen's chapel, one-up one-down, their bedrooms barely big enough for the bedsteads, and the kitchens dwarfed by a single dresser and chair. It was six kids to the bed the last time anyone lived in them, Mum on the floor behind a curtain and Dad downstairs on the rag rug in the winter – the rug with a red diamond at its centre to ward off the Devil – or on a fishing smack in summer. But King's Lynn's fishing industry was already on the way out by then.

For a long time the town's mainstay was North Sea herring, not Icelandic cod, just as it had been for many other east-coast fishing towns. But by the 1950s the herring shoals had been drastically overfished and demand had fallen away almost completely: freezer technology, excise wars and finally the Bird's Eye fish finger – invented, ironically, just around the coast in Great Yarmouth – all contributed to the slow, drawn-out expiration of the town's fishing industry. Fish fingers somehow seemed to suit the dulled, post-war British palate. For a while the less fish-fussy Greeks and Italians offered a respite and in the 1950s British Rail even laid on a special herring train from Norfolk to Italy. But the creation of the Common Market was the final nail in the coffin: new tariffs killed much of the rest of our trade to the continent, especially to Germany. After that not even a new generation of superfast gutting machines could keep herring prices keen enough or the east coast's failing industry alive. Nor could selling herrings for pet food, the remarketing of them as 'Edinburgers' to unimpressed Americans, or finally the desperate attempt by the Herring Industry Board to turn the fish into a tasty snack bought from a vending machine.

King's Lynn's story wasn't unique. The decline of its fishery is echoed all around the eastern English coast and that story is echoed all around the British coast. Overfishing and later the conflicted and conflict-making ways we have (or have not) responded to the environmental and cultural crisis caused by overfishing, along with changing tastes and a changing, damaged, environment have together almost done away with formerly vibrant and vital parts of our national culture and identity: fish and the fishermen who catch them.

Inland, along our rivers and lakes, the story is just the same: salmon and eels are the two species of fish most often mentioned in the Domesday Book, William the Conqueror's audit of the financial worth of his newly conquered kingdom. For the Normans, the wealth of these English fisheries was a large part of the spoils of their invasion. Now, at the start of the twenty-first century both salmon and eels are on the edge of survival. The salmon is already extinct throughout large parts of its native British range, close to extinction along the English south coast and under threat more or less everywhere. The eel – which scientists estimate once accounted for as much as a third of our freshwater fisheries' biomass – is now classified as Critically Endangered by the International Union for Conservation of Nature ... the same precipitous status as the tiger and albatross. As these iconic fish vanish so does the cultural history that surrounds them: a double impoverishment.

For my whole life I've been fascinated by fish, rivers and oceans, by the landscapes of which these habitats and life forms are a distillation and by the human history that is shaped by and has shaped them all. If I'm sure we'll one day look back on these most recent decades as some kind of turning point in the inter-relationship between our human and natural histories, I can't say which way we will have actually turned. The cod fishery of the Grand Banks collapsed in the 1980s and has never recovered. The cod fishery in the North Sea almost collapsed in the 1990s and is now showing some signs of life ... but only after immense hardship endured by the British fishing industry. In the late 1980s salmon were being pillaged in utterly unsustainable numbers from their high-seas feeding grounds and their close-to-shore migratory routes. Now there is no commercial high-seas salmon fishing, the netsmen of

Greenland and the Faroes have stopped catching salmon and have been supported into new enterprises, as have the drift netters of the English, Irish and Scottish coasts. But the survival rates of salmon at sea are apparently no better and perhaps are even worse. Eel numbers fell off a cliff in the late 1970s and have stubbornly refused to recover. And then in 2012 and 2013 the number of young eels returning to Europe from the breeding grounds of the Sargasso Sea broke all records. For both fish and fishing there are signs of life, signs of death. Quite how we navigate our way to a genuine and sustained recovery of both, there's the question.

In 2008 I went to Japan to make a film about the Japanese and *their* relationship with fish and fishing. It seemed a good way into a culture that is in many ways so very different from ours, because at least we have that in common – fish and fishing, a vital part of both our island stories. That point was well made when, on a train running from one coast to another, I started chatting to my travelling companion, Aki, about what the film should be called. We went through a few not-so-good titles, none of which stuck. 'I have an idea,' said Aki after a moment of staring out the window: 'Call it "Fish … and … Japs".' We didn't use it, of course, though we all wanted to. Aki, in his potentially controversial haiku of a title, had captured exactly the cultural commonality that was the unstated background to the whole film. He'd never been to Britain, but he understood us in terms of our national supper, fish and chips. And as I toured Japan over those six weeks – spending time with champion koi breeders, with chefs and fish merchants, with salarymen who fish for carp in swimming pools, or head off into the mountains in their Subarus at the weekend to fly-fish for cherry salmon, with old ladies who free-dive for shellfish and old men who go to sea in little fishing boats to catch whitebait or fugu-fish, or young men who go to sea to spear whales – I realised that just the same kind of story could be told about where I came from. Only for one reason

7

and another the obvious vitality of that Japanese story – and for now I will skip past the ecological complexities of the rapacious Japanese appetite for all things fishy – is dimming in our islands' version. As in Japan, our iconic fish are endangered, our seas are overexploited, our rivers are polluted, our oceans are getting warmer. But as *we* wrestle with what to do about these problems, the cultural history that is a large part of what makes the natural history matter is fading too. The more I thought about this the more it bothered me: in a busy landscape subject to a multitude of environmental pressures, the continuing vitality of cultural history might seem like just another pressure, while in truth it helps to keep effective conservation alive. Finally, in the summer of 2015, I set out on a journey, north, south, east and west around the British Isles, out to sea and inland, looking for both – the natural history and the cultural – hoping to discover how we might hold on to one … without losing the other.

There are many species of fish indigenous to the British Isles. The quotidian brown trout means more to me than any other because there's nothing I enjoy more than fishing for it or exploring the places which this obsession takes me to. After that, and only a fraction after, there's the Atlantic salmon. Then pike, perch, grayling and sea bass – I like fishing for all of them. In British rivers or lakes there are also bream and tench, barbel, roach, rudd, dace, chub, bleak, eels, gudgeon, minnow and miller's thumb. Around the coast there are the various sharks – mako, porbeagle, blue, thresher, whale – as well as the sharklike tope and dogfish; the various species of ray with their beautiful names like cuckoo, sandy, starry and thornback; there are skate, white, common and long-nosed; there's the 'gadiforme' family of cod, haddock, whiting, pollack, hake, coley and ling; there are plaice, sole, monkfish, anglerfish, garfish, wrasse, John Dory, mackerel, bream, weever fish, shad, anchovy, sand eel, conger eel, flounder, dab, mullet (thick-lipped, thin-lipped, golden and grey); there are even sunfish and swordfish and tuna. The list is long.

Amongst all these species of fish, however, there are a handful so culturally embedded that their history is our history. These are the fish I wanted to write about: cod, salmon, herring, eels and the immigrant carp. Every one of these but carp is on a knife-edge of viability.

Cod (I could add haddock, but cod and haddock are so often said in the same breath, caught in the same nets and cooked in the same batter, they can be looked at almost as one entity) are the staple component of our beloved fish and chips, which, as Aki implied, defines us as a nation. Fish and chips fed the Industrial Revolution, fish and chips (never rationed) helped us survive two world wars. Further back in history, cod was the slimy creature on which our ascendancy from a pugnacious maritime nation was built.

Herring were called 'silver darlings', no doubt because herring are as lovable as fish get with their large, doleful eyes and pouty lips. But also because in their glittering millions herring were worth a fortune. If Amsterdam was built on the bones of herring, then so too was much of our now beleaguered east coast. Fishing-port towns from the Orkneys and Shetland south to East Anglia, have all prospered or fallen on hard times in tune with the fate of this diminutive fish.

In the Middle Ages the eel also had a currency status reflected in its common name: we called eels 'fish-silver'. They were a slippery, medieval bit-coin and the wealth eels gave us built cathedrals. Nowadays, the juvenile eel is still a virtual currency, but an illegal one. The black-market trade serving billions of young European eels to the dining rooms of the Far East may undo the species altogether. Meanwhile the eel continues to be just about the most mysterious fish there is. No one has seen eels spawn or hatch in the wild, and vast tracts of their life cycles are still subject to speculation. This otherwise marvellous mystery has a downside: eel numbers appear to be crashing and no one really knows why.

The salmon is the sacred fish of Celtic myth for a reason: the huge journeys it undertakes, its athleticism and beauty are awe-inspiring. Along our south coast, which was never covered by glaciers, salmon are amongst our oldest native vertebrates. They have been British for millions of years. But as the North Atlantic gets warmer, and our rivers fill with agricultural run-off, this fish that has ennobled our island since long before humans lived here is inexorably disappearing from the British Isles. The time-scales involved might span many human lifetimes, but the pace of change is accelerating alarmingly.

The immigrant outlier in this cast of endangered but culturally important fish is the corpulent creature that the seventeenth-century pastoralist writer Izaak Walton described as the queen of our rivers. There were no carp in British waters before the late fifteenth century, but browse the bottom shelf of WHSmith and you'll find twice as many magazines dedicated to angling for this arriviste, or to keeping it in ornamental ponds, as to any other fish, salmon included. The carp was brought over in the Middle Ages as a miracle food-fish and something of a novelty for listless aristocrats. Many to most of the ancient ponds in the English landscape have the keeping of carp in their origins. Centuries later steam-powered trawling and the railways which ushered unprecedented volumes of cod to inland Britain might have tipped carp off a menu they were only just clinging to anyway, but then carp found a new place in the hearts of obsessive British anglers and a whole new chapter began. Carp are a big part of British history, but beyond that carp also tell a more important story of what we have done to our landscape, rivers and seas. They are the one fish in this history not in any danger at all: carp will be all we are left with if we don't look after the fish that belong here.

SILVER DARLINGS

The vulnerability of our fish and fisheries is revealed in all these fish histories, but is nowhere more starkly shown than in the story of the herring, where I started and ended my journey, close to home.

It's October as I write this and bright shoals of herring, those that are left, will be migrating through that rough sea I am watching. Not that anyone is out there catching them any more. Which is strange to think, given that herring fishing almost defined the east-coast ports of England and Scotland, and that Great Yarmouth – just around the coast from me in Norfolk – was in the early years of the twentieth century considered 'the herring capital of the world'. So many fishing boats, 'drifters' as they were called, operated here in the heyday of the fishery that it was said that you could cross from one side of the River Yare to the other by walking across their decks. You'd almost believe it too, looking at the photographs from that time, the endless masts and funnels and the tangles of rigging and the drifters moored three abreast on both banks, row on row shrinking to a vanishing point lost in the haze. You can see the names on some of them – *Ocean Dawn, Ma Freen, Lydia Eve* – and the registration codes which described the peripatetic fair of the east-coast herring season. There's YH47, YH89 and YH297, all Yarmouth boats. But also a KY322 which would be from Kirkcaldy, a PD145 from Peterhead, a FR25 from Fraserburgh, a BCK67 from Buckie and an INS530 from Inverness. Fishermen from all parts of the coast joined in the autumn herring festival off the East Anglian coast. It was the crescendo of the herring year: a festival of fishing, processing, packing and shipping those 'silver darlings' that had ticked clockwise around the compass as the months passed, driven as it was by the mysterious life-cycle and migratory routes of herring.

That herring season began in early spring when Yarmouth and Lowestoft boats would in their turn have been seen off the north-west coast of Scotland. As the months passed and the herring moved, so did the fishermen and not only the fishermen but the entire infrastructure of the industry – the herring girls, the porters, the curers – from the Western Isles, Stornoway and Lochmaddy, across the sea to the mainland ports of Mallaig and Oban. Then to Orkney and the Shetland Isles, Kirkwall or Lerwick in early summer, and on again to Fraserburgh and Peterhead and the seas around the Moray Firth. Through August to September the fishery migrated southwards to Seahouses and Bridlington, to Grimsby, Hull and Scarborough, a few weeks in each port and on, restlessly chasing the restless herring until in autumn they arrived at the East Anglian coast, a few boats to King's Lynn, but most to Lowestoft, Gorleston and Great Yarmouth where the annual herring fair reached its zenith.

In fact those *Clupea harengus* caught by the million in October and November off Great Yarmouth were not the same *Clupea harengus* caught earlier in the year further north. Nor were the Moray fish the same as those from the west coast. Although herring mix en masse in the open sea, feeding on zooplankton in vast gyroscopic sweeps of the ocean, they also subdivide into distinct races or tribes, each with its own spawning areas and migratory routes.

Across the wider North Atlantic there are Icelandic herring, White Sea herring, and Norwegian herring. There are Baltic herring too. While in the North Sea and around the British coastline there are Shetland and Orkney herring, Buchan herring, Banks (or Dogger) herring and Downs (or Southern Bight) herring.

There's even a Blackwater herring unique to the Thames Estuary, a smaller, fatter and paler fish than its North Sea cousins, with one less vertebra. These little Blackwater fish were always a more diffi-cult sell at Billingsgate, at least until the North Sea herring fishery collapsed in the 1950s. Then, in a microcosmic echo of a wider history, the Blackwater herring fishery followed the exact same trajectory in a fraction of the time: it grew into that late 1950s void, bloomed towards record catches in 1972 and then collapsed only a few years later with a complete closure of the fishery in 1979.

If the Blackwater fishery was an echo of a bigger history, so the herring fishery itself stands as a metaphor for all our fish and fisheries. A vibrant industry that shaped an entire coastal community collided fatally with history, greed, mismanagement, politics and environmental change to the point where there was simply nothing left. As tragically, when the natural resource collapsed, so did the human communities that had depended on it.

I suppose our fatal tendency to have fished for herring as if there were infinite numbers of them must be partly explained by the fact that there appeared to be: herring shoals were once vast beyond imagining, a mile or more wide, containing millions of glittering fish. How could the inhabitants of the Western Isles, the Orkneys and Shetland and the eastern coastline have refrained from surfeiting on this virtual miracle of a fish when the miracle occurred at the same place and at the same time, year in, year out, and in such profusion?

This apparition was the herring's own fatal tendency: the annual spawning run, when herring are fat with the goodness of the sea and easy to catch. Most fish have a single reproductive season: salmon spawn in the winter, for example, North Sea cod in the spring. The strange characteristic of herring that created this year-round nomadic fishery is that one or other of these localised tribes of herring will be found spawning in more or less every month of the year. Evolution devises many ways to ensure the survival of a species. This staggering of the spawning run must be one way in which the herring, which is beset by predators throughout its life, tries to ensure its own. Another must be to reproduce with such fecundity that the eighteenth-century French naturalist Georges-Louis Leclerc, Comte de Buffon, famously deduced that were a single herring suffered to multiply 'unmolested and undiminished' for twenty years it would yield a progeny greater in bulk 'than ten such globes as that we live upon'; and if 'all the men in the world were loaded with herrings, they would not carry the thousandth part away'.

This superabundance of herring was such that early naturalists like Buffon thought the fish came from the Arctic, that only under the ice caps could they 'multiply beyond expression' as they appeared to do and that it was the sheer bulk of their number that forced portions of that northern population to migrate south. Thus the enormous body of herring was split into its constituent parts by the merciless attentions of its predators and appeared on the shores of Britain with such regularity: it was a poetic, if far-fetched, narrative.

In fact it was the herring's appearance at our coast that signalled their multiplication beyond expression, because herring migrate inshore to spawn on gravel and marl banks in shallow, choppy, tide-swept water. They shed their eggs – some 20,000 to 70,000 will fall from a single female fish – in such profusion that the entire seabed becomes draped in a sticky ectoplasmic carpet, layers deep and acres wide. Significantly, the North Sea herring perform this reproductive phenomenon almost exclusively off the British coast. Buchan herring spawn around the Western Isles and the west coast of Scotland in spring. Shetland herring spawn off Shetland and Orkney and the north and eastern Scottish coasts in early summer; Banks or Dogger herring spawn off the eastern English coast in late summer and early autumn; and Southern Bight or Downs herring spawn off the south coast through the winter.

Before the days of echo-sounders fishermen had to rely on instinct and a keen ear or eye to detect the arrival of the herring. They'd describe some ineffable change in the air, or how the water would fall calm under an oily film, or how the surface was flecked with millions of silver scales, or how the sea hissed as bubbles rose like upturned rain from the fishes' swim-bladders. Buffon describes how the shoals arrived in such bulk 'as to alter the very appearance of the ocean', how the water 'curls up before them as if forced out of its bed' and how in bright weather the herring shoals 'reflect a variety of splendid colours like a field bespangled with purple, gold and azure'.

These are descriptions that animate the sense of the miraculous and explain the exhortations which were often made, centuries ago, to coastal communities to lead blameless lives and conduct themselves in ways pleasing to God. The arrival of the herring shoal was a sign of God's pleasure and in far flung coastal communities, a lifeline to survival or even prosperity.

But God was not always pleased. Or the herring were capricious. Because from time to time over the centuries herring shoals which had seemed as reliable as the rising sun, have simply disappeared. In the late thirteenth century the Pomeranian fishery, which had operated in the southern Baltic for 400 years, faded to nothing. The herring fishery in the southern part of the North Sea collapsed in 1360. The fishery off Scania disappeared in the late fifteenth century. Medieval minds searched for reasons and found them in immorality and superstition.

When the herring run on the Isle of Man failed in 1649 the bishop there rebuked his clergy for selling ale so that 'many of the people became not only tipplers, but infamous for drunkenness'. He composed a prayer to be read in all the churches 'that it may please God to restore and continue to us all the blessings of the sea'. God heard him and the herring returned in 1667 even if they vanished again in 1711. The disappearances of herring from Heligoland in 1425 and 1753 were blamed on the woman who had swept the fish from the street after a high tide had dropped them there, or the boys who had taken a 'king herring' (a mythical fish, the head of each shoal) and whipped it before putting it back in the sea, or the fishermen who dropped a crucifix when they saw the vast herring shoal they had hoped to summon by carrying it.

Adultery, violence or murder were also blamed if the herring runs failed: 'It is a General Observation all Scotland over, that if a quarrel happen on the coast where Herring is caught, and that blood be drawn violently, then the Herring go away from the Coast without returning during the season,' wrote Martin Martin in his *Description of the Western Isles of Scotland* published in 1703.

In Norway, where they set watch on the rocky coastline looking out for the annual arrival of the herring, the lookouts had to take care that the herring did not see them first: if they did the fish would turn away and never come back.

Post-Enlightenment naturalists looked for more rational explanations: in his 1833 account of the parish on Lewis, Reverend Robert Finlayson wondered if the failure of the herring fishing might have something to do with the constant reaping of seaweed along the coast. Marcus Bloch, the eminent eighteenth-century German naturalist and ichthyologist, attributed the infamous failures of herring runs in Norway, Sweden and Prussia to the disturbances caused by relentless fishing pressure there during the spawning season. Both men were probably partly right, even if two centuries later we still do not know exactly what causes herring runs to vanish. The temperature of the sea and the air above it, the depth and patterns of oceanic thermoclines, weather fronts and storms, as well as the relative abundance of the zooplankton on which herring feed – which is also governed by the same factors – all these things appear to influence the fish's migratory routes, abundance and oceanic distribution. Contemporary observations from the time when the herring stocks collapsed in the southern North Sea in the late fourteenth century describe stormy, unstable weather patterns that persisted for decades: we now know that these marked a transition from the Medieval Warm Period to the Little Ice Age. We also know that oscillations in temperature that span centuries are underscored by higher-frequency fluctuations such as the Atlantic Multidecadal

Oscillation and exacerbated by recent man-made trends of global warming. It is likely these all make an impact, suggesting (with the exception of recent global warming) that these disappearances were natural.

But there is compelling evidence to suggest that the herring collapses of the past, way back into the Middle Ages and long before the recent acceleration of climate change, were also influenced, perhaps caused, by us. In that sense 'sinful' mankind was partly to blame, though not because of adultery or bloodshed, so much as farming and overfishing. The Pomeranian herring collapse of the thirteenth century followed widespread forestry clearance and agricultural development in the catchments that fed into that part of the Baltic: changes on this scale probably affected nutrient levels in the sea, causing eutrophication (over-enrichment of the water) and also the siltation of the herring's spawning grounds. The delicate nature of this habitat and its proximity to shore, whether in the Baltic or the North Sea, makes the herring particularly vulnerable to the careless activities of man. The changes we have made over the centuries to the coastline of the North Sea, the land reclamations but also the untold billions of tons of sediment that will have poured into it from the destabilised watersheds of Britain and the continent must also have had a significant impact. As Charles Clover points out at the start of his seminal book *The End of the Line*, the North Sea was not always a muddy brown. Too much of what was once farmland is swilling around in it.

All these anthropogenic changes are implicated, but one thing stands out and Marcus Bloch had his finger on it: too many fishermen catching too many fish. All around the North Sea, Iceland, Norway and the Baltic, peak catches have preceded collapses in the herring fishery, over and over again. And there has never been a bigger collapse than that of North Sea herring in the mid-twentieth century, which was indeed preceded by a gluttony of fishing on an almost incredible scale. There is only so much damage you can do to herring stocks fishing under sail, hauling nets by hand, the way herring had been caught for hundreds of years. But the mechanisation of the Industrial Revolution accelerated the pace and intensity of the British fishery and later the whole North Sea fishery beyond all recognition.

By the turn of nineteenth century, when this step change began, we had been watching for four long centuries, apparently helplessly, the Dutch fleet plunder our herring stocks. 'It hath been since the beginning of the Dutch fishery,' wrote James Solas Dodd in his 1603 Brexit manifesto *Towards a Natural History of the Herring*, 'that this nation hath looked with an evil eye upon their invading of our property.' Dodd's complaint was that the Dutch had cornered a market in a fish that ought – by geographical proximity, if nothing else – to have belonged to British fishermen almost exclusively. And the Dutch had grown conspicuously wealthy in doing so. Dodd's lament made no difference.

That we had lost the market in the first place was perhaps our own fault. For hundreds of years before the Dutch annexation of this 'British' fish in the fourteenth century, the British had owned the North Sea herring fishery, and Dutch merchants had bought their herrings directly off the boats of Scottish and English fishermen. Trade was sufficiently brisk by the twelfth century that Yarmouth had its own herring fair, hosting merchants from all over the Low Countries, France and Germany. But with riches came conflict. The Yarmouth merchants began to place conditions of trade on their guests. They developed a system of *hosting*, ostensibly to help trade but in practice a protectionist racket whereby visiting merchants were assigned to townsmen who provided accommodation and business assistance in return for a slice of the goods the visitor traded. That slice went up and up. The trickery didn't end there: Yarmouth merchants tried to corner the market by funding drifters in return for that crew's entire seasonal catch, or by 'forestalling' (the origin of the word) the drifters at sea and buying that morning's haul. They threatened violence to any fishermen who sold direct to foreign merchants instead.

Edward III's *Statute of Herring* in 1357 was an attempt to curb the worst excesses of the market in general and Yarmouth merchants in particular. But by forbidding the sale of herring anywhere but the town itself – a ban on forestalling – the British Crown did more harm than good. Herring spoil quickly and the delay of taking them to shore rendered the fish less attractive to foreign buyers. Yarmouth ignored the statute anyway and kept on with its own internal edicts, swelling the coffers of the town, lining the pockets of its merchants and bailiffs.

The result was that the Dutch deserted the fair altogether and invested instead in their own fleet of fishing boats (called busses) and service vessels to speed the herring back to Holland. It was worth the investment, especially when in 1397, the Dutch discovered their own, superior way of curing herring, one which proved immensely popular in Europe, especially Germany. For the next few hundred years the Dutch, through the diligence of their preparation and the consistency of their product, more or less owned the market. By the late seventeenth century there were 3,000 Dutch fishing busses and 50,000 Dutch fishermen catching, salting and packing herring within sight of the British coast. High-quality Dutch-cured herring furnished the dining tables of Europe while the inferior British herring went only the other way to feed slaves in the Caribbean at a third of the Dutch-cure price.

Having cornered the market it seemed only the Dutch had the wealth and the know-how to exploit it. How could the comparatively artisanal and haphazard British fishery compete when the Dutch busses alone cost tens of thousands of pounds? For a while in the eighteenth century the British government tried: they built and equipped a fleet of British busses and offered a bounty for each barrel of salted herring. This initiative was much praised at the time, but it didn't really work and the herring subsidy was singled out by Adam Smith in *The Wealth of Nations* 1776 as an exemplar waste of money. It had promoted inefficiency, he wrote, with fishermen chasing the bounty more than the fish.

Real change came only when a handful of far-sighted and benevolent Scottish gentlemen formed the Highland Society with the particular aim of developing rural Scottish industries from the ground up. One of its members, John Knox, wrote a paper with the catchy title *A Discourse on the Expediency of Establishing Fishing Stations and Small Towns in the Highlands of Scotland and the Hebridean Islands*, in which he advocated the development of purpose-built fishing villages around the remote Scottish coastline, each with cottages and gardens, schools and churches, storehouses, boat sheds and jetties. The first real success was at Wick where there were plenty of herring but where the boats had to work off storm beaches and cliff edges. And what a success! Thomas Telford's Pultneytown harbour, designed for 400 boats, was full to overflowing within a few years of its completion in 1811.

With most British herring still shipped to the West Indies, the British abolition of the slave trade in 1807 (and finally of slavery itself in 1831) might have undone the work of the Highland Society if, a few years later in 1819, the Arts Society of London had not sponsored a competition to develop a rival to the Dutch cure. One J. F. Donovan from Leith claimed the fifty guineas prize money having employed Dutch spies to help him. The secret was simply to remove the gills and the guts before curing.

The Scots then added a secret of their own, one that the Dutch with their long-range fishery could not so easily copy. The Scots curers found that salt – if applied too early – softened the fish. It made for an infinitely better product to gut and pack a hard, fresh fish only a few hours from the sea: but this was possible only where the port was close to the fishing grounds – at Wick, for example, or Peterhead or Fraserburgh, Lowestoft or Great Yarmouth. Or any of the British ports and none of the Dutch ones. Thus the Crown Brand Scotch Cure was born and the Dutch monopoly on the valuable north European market ended. Soon every Scottish and then British barrel was inspected for quality and having passed was stamped with the date of the cure, the name and address of the curer and fishery officer and finally the Crown Brand: a seal of quality that conquered and secured the continental market. When the government removed the tax on salt in 1832 – dropping its price from £30 to £1 a barrel – the brakes really came off.

Over the succeeding decades one innovation after another boosted the fishery's profits and productivity. In 1850 James Patterson of Musselburgh invented a loom that could weave cotton into fishing nets: these were lighter, larger and longer than the hemp nets they replaced, and this evolution alone is estimated to have increased catches fourfold. In the same year the introduction of a manual capstan helped ease the back-breaking strain of hauling the nets aboard, while in 1876 the invention of a steam-powered capstan or 'iron-man' replaced the labour of seven men with one machine.

All of these allowed for bigger boats and bigger catches. By 1897 the British were landing over a quarter of a million tons of herring a year, the British fishery was growing 10% year on year, and yet the steam-drifter years that marked Great Yarmouth's heyday had only just begun.

The steam-powered drifter took the already enhanced capacity of a sailing drifter, with its cotton nets and iron-man, and multiplied it several-fold. In 1899, two years after Lowestoft's prototype steam drifter *Consolation* had reset the bar for the sheer numbers of fish a single boat could land, there were sixteen registered in England.

Within a few years there were several hundred, while the Scots, who were a year or two late to the stream-drifter party, soon made up for it by building and registering even more boats than the English. Within a decade over 1,000 boats sailed in autumn off the East Anglian coast: an armada of herring drifters scrabbling for sea room under a sky blackened by smoke.

Year after year the records tumbled. In 1911 the herring fishery in East Anglia alone amounted to almost 1 million 'crans' of fish, a cran being made of ten 'hundreds', a hundred being thirty-three 'warps', and one warp being four herrings. In other words a cran was 1,320 herrings, and that season's catch amounted to over 1 billion fish! So many that fishermen wondered if a haul that enormous could ever be repeated.

But the run of good catches simply persuaded more and more fishermen to invest in steam. The fishery grew and grew until in 1913 a simply enormous fleet of 1,100 Scottish herring drifters joined 600 English boats on the East Anglian coast. Here, over the next few weeks, they landed 824,000 cran at Yarmouth and 536,400 at Lowestoft: 1,795,728,000 herring! On Monday 12 October alone, thirty-three drifters landed over a quarter of a million herrings ... each.

Imagine the quayside: an undulating mass of baskets piled high with fish, of barrels honeycombed into mountainous stacks, of dray horses and carts, sacks of coal, sacks of salt, and mile upon mile of cotton nets strung out to dry. Threaded through it all were the jostling crowds of flat caps and headscarves: buxom women in black aprons and galoshes, forearms sparkling with herring scales; and wiry fishermen in their 'gansey' sweaters, hefting baskets of fish from deck to quayside, or pausing for a smoke. Imagine the noise too, the cry of seagulls, the frenzied shouting and bustle of the fish auctions, the steam whistles and engines, the hammering of barrel makers.

It was a gold rush, with herrings the gold. Every house became a boarding house and boarding houses were full throughout the town, three girls to a bed and the bedrooms lined with dust sheets and newspaper to provide some measure of protection against the eternal stink of herring. With 1,000 drifters and each drifter crewed by ten fishermen, and with every post at sea matched by ten on shore, this herring carnival utterly transformed the town. It took more than fishermen to make the herring industry go round. There were the 'herring girls', a trade that had started life in the remoter parts of Scotland when girls travelled to the Western Isles, Shetland and Orkney to work through the summer gutting and packing herring. There were the coopers too, who made the barrels the herring were packed in. Both worked for the curers, the merchants – usually Scottish – who ran the packing and preserving enterprise. There were ransackers – usually men – who worked in warehouses riffling through the miles of cotton nets looking for tears. And there were the beatsters – usually women – who worked in the same warehouses, repairing them. There were coalies, stokers, canners, hauliers and drivers, a whole host of other trades that serviced the fishery. Pubs sold more beer in those few weeks than they did for the rest of the year. The post offices sent and received more parcels. Banks, the Salt Union and five different railway companies all opened temporary branches at the quayside. Fancy-goods stores thrived on payday.

*

If the outbreak of war in 1914 was a disaster for Europe it was also a disaster for this resurgent British herring fishery. By 1914 the Klondike Trade to Germany – named after the Canadian goldrush of the late 1890s – was the biggest part of the herring trade by far. Suddenly we were at war with our major market. The British government requisitioned most of the fleet to use as naval vessels and the North Sea became a very dangerous place for those few left fishing. Meanwhile Holland and Norway remained neutral, the Dutch were able to reclaim the market they had lost in 1819, and the Germans invested in their own fleet in an effort to become self-sufficient in fish.

When the war ended both the German and Russian markets had changed entirely: Lenin forbade the trade in Scottish herring, while the German Mark was worthless. One Wick-based curer is said to have papered the walls of his house in German banknotes. It got so bad that in 1923 the islanders of Lewis almost starved. Boats which had cost £5,000 were worth £150 and many fishermen emigrated to Canada.

Somehow the industry limped on. The government stepped in with quasi-nationalisation and the creation of a Herring Industry Board. The board decommissioned a sizeable part of the fleet, spent money on advertising, on herring cookery demonstrations and cookbooks. But the British were notoriously reluctant to eat herring and the board tried with only mixed success to open markets elsewhere.

The Second World War was more bad news for markets, if not for stocks of herring: both wars had allowed a recovery. But when fishing resumed again in the late 1940s and into the 1950s it was on a different technological footing, with the herring bound for a wholly different end. Taking a lead from the Norwegians, in 1947 the board opened its first herring-processing factory with the aim of turning herrings into animal fodder and their oil into ice cream and margarine. In that year only 3% of the British herring catch was processed in this way, but within five years it was almost half. Meanwhile fishing methods were changing. The Scots had discovered 'ring-netting' which could pretty much encircle and scoop up an entire shoal, while the Scandinavians developed a trawling method known as the Larsen trawl, judged as 'deadly' by one curious East Anglian herring company.

These changes had a drastic and decisive impact on herring stocks. Herring bound for curing and the dining table had to be a certain size and caught and handled carefully: the Crown Brand fishery of the early 1900s was at least self-limiting in this way. Herring bound for animal fodder, however, could be any size and mangled in the process of capture, it made no difference. The Scandinavians were now catching herring on a terrifying scale, trapping juvenile fish along with anything else that got in the way of their trawl nets, all bound for reduction factories. Desperate to keep up, French and Belgian trawlers started on the herring spawning grounds with predictably disastrous results. In its 1960 report, the Herring Industry Board reported there was nothing to suggest that 'nature is succeeding in counteracting the effects of man's onslaught on the North Sea herring stocks on all stages of their growth'.

By now there were only two drifters on the register of boats in Great Yarmouth, but fourteen nations were involved in the exploitation of the herring fishery in seas that were open to all. Great Yarmouth's heydays were long since over yet North Sea catches *peaked* in 1965 and then nosedived in the years that followed. In spite of the repeated warnings of the International Council for the Exploration of the Sea that herring stocks were collapsing, the North East Atlantic Fisheries Convention had no mandate to protect the species without the agreement of all fourteen nations – who could not agree. None believed the others would implement the same restraint and all could see that to rein in catches would lead to bankruptcy and unemployment not only amongst the herring fishermen, but also all the packing and processing and pet-food industries that served it. Herring were culturally so important to these countries their governments tended to listen more to the fishermen and commercial interests than to the Cassandra scientists. But herring, like cod, exhibit what is known as the 'basin effect' in response to depleting numbers: their population retracts. Spatially the herring might be less widely distributed, but the stock

25

where you find it is as dense, giving a false impression – should you fill your nets there – of overall numbers. Besides, as catches fell, the price of herring went up: this, ironically, allowed the North Sea fishery to keep operating all the way to and over the edge of the cliff.

To our credit the British had sounded warning bells for some time. It was only on 1 January 1977 when countries all around the North Sea started to declare their own Economic Exclusion Zones (EEZ) that Britain was able unilaterally to ban herring fishing within its own waters (the EEZ is an area of sea around a nation's coastline exclusively theirs: the US and then Iceland had set the precedent). In a replay of history another conflict with the Dutch followed. Declaring the herring season open, two Dutch fishing boats sailed into the British EEZ and were seized by the Royal Navy. Somehow the incident focussed minds enough for the scientific argument to finally be heard and win the day. By the end of June 1977 the North Sea herring fishery had closed.

Through greed and ignorance we had more or less wiped out one of the most abundant fish in the North Sea and had driven one of its most vital and culturally important fisheries off a cliff too. Since that time stocks have recovered and faltered and recovered again. Markets have changed drastically. The British public has lost what taste it ever had for herring and the Norwegians have managed to pick up on trade lost by other nations. Across the wider North Sea, herring fishing has resumed under tighter control. In 2016 ICES was able to recommend a lifting of the Total Allowable Catch (TAC) to over half a million tons, describing the stocks as 'very strong'. But the British are now allowed to take only a small part of this TAC.

The Scottish herring fishery has recovered to some extent, and in 2013 was certified 'sustainable' by the Marine Stewardship Council. Their catch might be a fraction of what it was in those distant boom years, but the market is much the same: high-quality cured and smoked herring sent to the Netherlands and Germany.

The East Anglian herring fishery has not recovered. Today there is only one steam drifter at Yarmouth, *Lydia Eve*. But it's a museum not a working boat. There is one herring smokehouse still operating in the town, HS Fishing 2000, where they smoke herrings caught by Norwegians and export them to northern Europe. And by all accounts there are only two or three fishermen still working the sea there, when once there were thousands. Even these few are hard to find.

SURVIVAL AT SEA

I set out on my fish odyssey in August 2015, starting at home in East Anglia where I hoped to discover what was left of all that heritage, all those herring. I began by hunting around online using any combination of search terms I could think of. Nothing. Search after search came back with only a selection of gloomy local news stories dating from 2008: Great Yarmouth's last working fisherman was hanging up his oilskins and nets having been driven to the wall by ever more restrictive EU quotas. The various stories all alluded to the once-great herring fishery, but *Eventide*, the boat pictured, was not a drifter and herring were not even mentioned in the list of fish that Jason Clarke had recently put to sea to catch. His cod quota would not feed a cat, he said. Next month Jason would be starting work on a boat servicing the wind farms that were springing up around the East Anglian coast. His brother Richard had already left and was enjoying this new line of work. It was steady with a predictable income.

If Jason really was the last Yarmouth fisherman I had missed any chance of anchoring my history in some living present. He had alluded to a handful of part-time fishermen who worked out of nearby Caister and after another search I found another story, also gloomy, but a name too. The headlines were from 2014 this time, and Dick Thurlow, a lifeboatman and part-time herring fisherman, was lamenting an imminent EU ban on drift netting that would spell the complete end of fishing for herrings off East Anglia. The EU's ban was aimed at limiting the bi-catch of dolphins and turtles taken in huge drift-nets in the Mediterranean, but would affect these few Norfolk boats too. It would, said Dick, be the end of the fishery: no more fresh herrings caught off the coast of Norfolk.

It was all bad news, but at least this story implied there had been *some* herring fishing going on until very recently.

I tried calling the lifeboat station in Caister. Every call cut through to an answerphone that said the mailbox was full. I tried searching the phone book. There was no R. Thurlow, but there was a Thurlow, also in Caister. This one didn't even have an answerphone. I tried again and again, alternating with the lifeboat station, day after day until the other Thurlow picked up.

'He's my cousin,' said the voice when I explained I was looking for Dick. 'I've got his number somewhere.' He went off to look and came back to say he couldn't find it. 'I had it once. But he's not here now, anyway. He's working in Scotland.'

'In the energy industry?' I asked, despairingly.

'Yes, that's right. He's skippering boats for an oil company.'

I gave up on the idea that I'd ever find a herring fisherman in East Anglia and decided instead to head north where there was still some sort of viable fishing industry. I was already in touch with Mike Park – secretary of the Scottish Whitefish Producers Association (nothing to do with herring) – and he had put me in touch with Dave Milne only a few days before, saying that Dave was a friendly skipper who probably wouldn't mind taking a curious writer out on his boat. Dave was a trawlerman, not a herring fisherman. But perhaps I'd get somewhere with herring while I was up there pursuing my next story – cod and haddock.

I wrote to Dave asking if I could drive up to Peterhead and chat to him about the state of commercial sea-fishing today, cod and haddock in particular and maybe go fishing with him and spend some time with the crew at work. Dave was at sea and I'd been warned he picked up email only intermittently. But I heard back later that day. He was out chasing his quota hard, he said (the boat had been damaged and in dock for a frustrating five weeks), and he didn't really know when he'd be back. Then he wrote again later the same day. They'd hit fish in between emails and filled the hold.

'Charles,' he wrote, 'it looks like we'll be sailing (again) Thursday. You will need a sleeping bag and a pillow and could you confirm asap so I can order more food? And Charles. You'll need to do a Sea Survival Course. Can you fix that in time?'

Suddenly things were unspooling in a hurry. I was still in a bookish research mode and hadn't yet psyched myself up for a week on a trawler. I knew I'd have to go at some stage but a pal of mine had spent time filming on a trawler and had terrified me with stories of giant waves, claustrophobia and seasickness. Right then I wouldn't have minded an unavoidable excuse. How often could they possibly run courses in Norfolk? One or two a year? Perhaps I was fine. For now.

Clive Monk, a local rep for the Eastern Seafish Training Association, emailed me that afternoon. 'Following your recent message I can confirm I have booked you a place on our Sea Survival Course being held at Go Scuba near Norwich on Wednesday. Directions are attached. Please bring swim shorts, T-shirt and towel for the pool session.'

I wrote back – 'Thanks very much, Clive' – without quite meaning it. I had Tuesday to pack – notebook, camera, pillow, water – book a room on the route north and work myself up into a lather of trepidation. Trawling is, they say, the most dangerous job in the world.

*

'You must be Charles,' Clive said standing at the doorway to a hut in a sandy forest. 'And you're writing a book about fish?'

I explained what I was up to.

'There's a guy in there you should meet. He'd tell you a lot about Norfolk, the herring fishery, all that kind of thing.'

'He's not called Dick, is he?' I asked, laughing away the possibility.

'That's right. Dick Thurlow. D'you know him? Anyway, in you go. Grab a cuppa. We'll be starting in a minute.'

Inside the incongruously landlocked hut that is Go Scuba were a dozen men of all ages. I nodded hello to the room and took a seat. The man next to me held out his hand. I shook it and asked, 'Dick Thurlow, by any chance?'

'Might be. Who's asking?' he said.

'You have no idea how hard you are to find.'

It turned out Dick was home from Scotland for a few days and had come here to get his 'refresher ticket' while he was down: the course was something they all had to do from time to time.

I told Dick why I'd been trying to get hold of him. He shrugged and said that he'd given up on herring, that there was no money in it any more, that the rules and regulations had suffocated it all. I said it was a shame and that I would have liked to go out fishing with him. He still fished for herring, he admitted, though it was more a hobby now. He came back every autumn if he could and went out with his cousins and brothers. Just to be out there, like old times.

'Here. Take my number and give us a call in October. We'll get you out there somehow.'

Round-the-room self-introductions revealed that most of the guys here were from the energy, not the fishing industry. One young lad in his twenties was part-timing on a small fishing boat out of Brancaster, the next village along the coast from me. Another man – in his forties I guessed – had worked on trawlers all his life and was still trawling. I suppose I was surprised, pleasantly so, that he was black *and* a fisherman *and* from Norfolk, especially when he spoke like Bernard Matthews. He said he was here for a refresher and rolled his eyes. Most of the room nodded. Then, slowly it became obvious that all of them had *once* been trawlermen, only now with the almost total demise of the East Anglian fishery they were skippering boats for the east-coast wind farms, running ferries, crewing on pleasure barges in the Thames. These were the descendants of Frank Castleton, on 'refresher tickets' to keep the insurers happy. Our instructor was called Simon. He'd been a crab fisherman at Cromer.

And then there was me. Writing a book about them. Or at least about what had happened to them, and the fish they were no longer catching. As such I may well have been the only one in the room who hadn't seen and heard all this before: the videos of crews being winched to safety, of a broken-backed trawler sinking in five minutes flat, the flares, and survival-food packets, the various types of life jacket, the whistles, radios and beacons, the rafts which pop open as the boat goes down, which you have to find in the dark and the cold as you're tumbled over and over by the forty-feet waves that sunk your boat in the first place. I was certainly the only one not yawning, or laughing or getting prompted by someone else's first-hand anecdote of disaster into telling their own story of how they had narrowly cheated Davey Jones's locker. I was listening carefully, trying to take it all in, trying to ignore the gallows humour.

But even I could sense the cavernous gap that must exist between the choreographed safety procedures rehearsed in this warm, dry classroom where you could laugh your way into a safety suit only to find it was on backwards, and the wet and windy reality of going under at night in December somewhere between Peterhead and Oslo. Was this why trawlermen don't learn to swim? As if to underline this disconnection, we took to a swimming pool in the afternoon. Two-dozen pasty limbs padded from the changing room to the poolside of the house next door. I was later told these live sessions used to be conducted at sea. But too many people had drowned or got close to it, so they were moved inshore and finally onshore. And now our 'live' session was to be taken in a heated, indoor, domestic swimming pool.

First up we had to launch the raft, a large cylindrical canister about the size of a sofa. With a 'one, two, three, heave', splash ... the cylinder was in the water. A sharp pull on its rope and the canister popped open with a violent bang and an extended hiss and as if by magic a giant doughnut with a tent on top appeared, bobbing on the fractured mirror of the pool. Somehow it was a comforting sight even here, where we were miles from the sea and safe as houses. I could only imagine what it must look like when you need it most.

Since together we represented a crew we all had to clamber in, one after the other, find a space with our backs to the edge and then help the next man. This must be like being swallowed by a whale, I thought as I floundered face first onto the wet plastic and into a world of bobbing, pneumatic wobbliness. The raft could take twelve – in theory. But soon the space had filled to a density that would have been only barely tolerable under the actual life-or-death circumstances it was supposed to replicate. The temperature climbed. I counted. There were eight of us. Four more waited poolside. Bloody hell!

When finally we were all crammed in – the appropriate simile being 'like sardines' – Simon leaned in from the comfort and solidity of the tiled edge and patiently, long-windedly even, took us through the raft's features, the food reserves in little plastic pouches, the whistles and lights and the seasick pills which you ought to take no matter who you are because, as Simon needlessly explained to the dozen of us crammed together in our claustrophobic waterbed, 'you don't want anyone being sick in here'.

'How do you take a piss?' someone asked.

'Over the side,' said Simon. 'Same as the other thing.'

But no one could move, let alone clamber to the side and relieve themselves. I was trying to imagine what a few hours on a violent sea might be like when I noticed the disconcerting sound of hissing bubbles, the groans and squeaks as if from a deflating balloon. I had thought the increasing claustrophobia I felt was a trick of the mind, that I was only imagining the raft getting smaller and lower in the water, and that we – who had been far, far too closely packed to start with – were slowly drawing closer together. I asked if the noise was normal. Someone said he was sure it wasn't.

'We're sinking,' said one of the sangfroid skippers as if he'd known all along, only didn't care.

'I thought that was you farting, only I was too polite to comment.'

'Last man out is a dead man.'

Simon insisted on the seaworthiness of the thing, that these rafts could float perfectly well with only one ring inflated. No one was listening. We were on a sea-survival course and with half an excuse to abandon ship we plunged one by one into the pleasantly warm pool where we bobbed about like naughty schoolboys intent on mild insurrection. The raft farted incontinently.

There were a few other tests and procedures – we each took it in turns to jump in with a life jacket, to drag one another the full length of the pool, and to turn the capsized raft back upright – but the main event of the afternoon was lifting a stricken colleague to safety. The idea was simple enough. First off, one man has to clamber from the pool into the empty raft. Since the raft is slippery, there is little to grab on to and even less to push off, this is not easily done. But he gets there in the end and, once inside, the first man then helps the second and once there are two aboard it is much easier to heft in those that follow: in this exercise a series of supposedly comatose, semi-drowned colleagues. So, we took it in turns to clamber in or play dead or heft, the idea being that each of us should play each part in the cycle once through. I was back in the pool when it was the turn of the largest man in our party to be rescued. I hadn't got his name but he was a porter at one of the fish docks. He was six-foot-four top to toe and round about and it was soon obvious our well-built porter would need more than just the two colleagues either side of him and the two above. One after the other the unemployed boatmen in the pool joined the frothing, Keystone Cops heave, all elbows in faces and shoulders under buttocks, spluttering and gasping for air until finally our colleague landed on the floor of the raft like a giant tuna. A loud cheer echoed around our indoor, luxury pool.

Now that it was the porter's turn to heave, I expected that the next man would be hauled aboard with ease. I hadn't mentally prepared myself for the way the laws of physics would throw this particular rescue. Our 'unconscious' sailor was duly fetched to the side. He was light enough. Two men pushed and two men pulled. But one half of the pulling team now weighed about the same as all the others put together and much more than the far side of the already limp raft. One moment they were there, an ordered structure of rescue. The next they were gone. All five vanished as the raft flipped up and consumed them whole like the closing top jaw of an enormous grouper fish. Imminent rescue to total disaster in the blink of an eye. It was, in a swimming pool, one of the funniest things I have ever seen. Out there, on the North Sea in the dark, I might not have laughed so hard. I might not *be* laughing so hard.

Late in the afternoon I drove away from the dusty car park of Go Scuba, my towel and swim shorts laid out to dry across the back seats of the car and next stop Gretna Green's Day's Inn. Then tomorrow, Peterhead and a trawler called *Adorne*.

I. NORTH

SEA FRET

Peterhead was much, much further than it looked on the map. Perth, Dundee, Forfar, Stonehaven. The A90 went on for ever, and there was a speed camera every fifty yards to curb any thought I might have had of shrinking the dual-carriageway purgatory. But the sky was a high and infinite blue. Rolling fields of wheat hardly stirred under the shimmering air. Tea-stained rivers glinted brightly. And I had the Waterboys on the car stereo – 'Oh I wish I was fisherman, / Tumbling on the seas'. It was good weather and good music to go fishing to. Then somewhere around Aberdeen a sea fret rolled in. My car was swallowed in the haze and briefly, so were my spirits. I too had the fisherman's blues. What was I letting myself in for? There's something about the localised misery of a sea fret that really frays the soul. But only if you're under it all day. The tobacco gloom pawed at my windscreen for a mile or two more, daring me to turn back, then cleared in a burst of sunshine by the cliffs beneath Longhaven where the North Sea reappeared, glittering and calm. If she stayed like that I'd be fine, I thought. No *mal de mer*, no giant waves to sweep me overboard. A bright fishing boat, low in the water and chugging for home, split the emptiness like a zip in a sequin cloth. As I drove into town, Peterhead's mauve-stoned and austere Victorian architecture was chiselled by the northern light into a shimmering, cubist townscape, all primary colours and deep shadows. At the harbour, fishermen leant on boat rails, chatting. Crates clattered, gulls cried their plaintive, marine cries and the soft gurgle of diesel engines echoed back and forth across the oily water. A scent of fish and grease and rust marbled the salty air.

Having found the fish market, but no trawler marked *Adorne*, I went in search of yellow wellies to replace my green ones. I did not need yellow wellies now, of course. But I'd been spooked by the memory of my grandmother's superstitions and thought that I might as well complete the genuflection ...

Two days earlier a pal of mine had mentioned in passing that I shouldn't wear green on a trawler. I hadn't paid much attention. I was too consumed with everything else I was doing in a hurry. But when I stopped for the night at Gretna Green services on my way north, I opened Redmond O'Hanlon's book *Trawler* and hadn't got past the first page before he was being told the same thing: 'Don't bring green!' I shut the book remembering my Irish gran blaming my grandfather's cold on green curtains. I remembered her standing at the door to her flat, armed with a brush and a pot of white paint, ready to paint over the door the building committee had deemed should be green like all the others. I remembered my aunt telling me her uncles had been trawlermen in Wicklow and finally I knew from where my gran had derived her morbid and unshakeable suspicion of green. Fishermen! Why green? I didn't know. But when you live every day in fear of death, which in a trawler can come at any moment – an unexpected wave, a foot in the netting – superstition takes an unshakeable hold. The last thing I wanted to do was curse the voyage. Yet everything in my holdall was green. Green coat, green trousers, green wellies. I emailed Dave, the skipper, but hadn't got a reply by breakfast. So, I diverted through Perth anyway and bought a blue overcoat and trousers. No wellies, however. All theirs were green too. Peterhead was my last resort.

Then somewhere around Aberdeen Dave replied: 'Don't worry about the green,' he wrote. 'We don't care what you wear, so long as you wear something!'

Oh well. These fishermen, perhaps uniquely, weren't superstitious after all. I was £200 poorer, but at least I wouldn't be a Jonah … except now, *I* was superstitious. And so here I was, in Peterhead, on a rendezvous with Dave's trawler *Adorne*, and finishing what I had started in Perth in front of a huge rack of yellow fishermen's wellies. I rationalised this mildly irrational behaviour by remembering my green wellies lacked steel toecaps. These yellow ones would be much better should someone drop a fish crate on them. And I'd been right to suppose that Peterhead might be the last place on earth to stop selling yellow wellies. You can fill your boots with them – so to speak – at C&L Supplies, if you can find the anachronistically Dickensian store tucked down a side street and up an anonymous flight of stairs where, having chosen your boots, you must climb yet more stairs to buy them from a man who sits behind an oak desk and writes 'paid by hand' on your receipt and logs the purchase – also by hand – in a ledger.

'Good luck with your trip,' he said as I left.

Adorne was still nowhere to be seen. So, I parked by the harbour front and walked the length of the quay to the Dolphin Café. I found a corner table by the harbourside window and settled down with a mug of tea, a bacon sandwich and my notebook. Then I saw across the water – moored under the looming black tower of the North East Flake Ice Company – the trawler that would be my home for the next week. The *Adorne*. Her deck empty, she sat quiet and unhurried. I still had time for my tea and sandwich. I sent Dave a text to say I was in Peterhead, eating tea across the way, but otherwise I was ready to go.

Trade was brisk in the Dolphin Café. Locals seemed to know the place as a good chippy. In ones and twos they strolled down from town in their shirtsleeves and left with fish suppers wrapped in white parcels and stacked in the ubiquitous thin, blue bag of the British chippy.

What had I been I thinking? I'd driven miles to sail in a trawler, to go catch cod and haddock and here I was eating a not very good bacon sandwich. I really should have ordered a plate of our national dish. Apart from anything else I love a good fish supper. My wife Vicky and I have marked our tenth and our twentieth anniversaries and a few in between with fish and chips and a bottle of fizz on the beach. Food doesn't get better than good fish and chips eaten in the fresh air. Although 'good' is not as easy to find nowadays as it ought to be. Too many chippies sell frozen fillets that go all watery in a fryer. I guessed I'd get on to why in my next few days at sea with Dave. But even if standards are slipping, and even if there aren't as many chippies now as in their 1930s heyday, fish and chips is still *the* iconic British dish. George Orwell reckoned the comforting solidity of fish and chips saved the nation from revolution. Churchill thought the meal helped us defeat Nazism. He called fish and chips our 'Good Companions'. In both wars, Lloyd George and then Churchill thought fish and chips so vital to national morale they exempted the meal from rationing. And during the confusion of the D-Day landings 'fish and chips' became the code for identifying fellow countrymen: one would say 'fish', the other would answer 'chips'.

Strange to think then, how a deep-fried slab of cod and fried slices of potato is now as British as red telephone boxes, unarmed police, *Doctor Who* or Her Majesty the Queen, when in reality we derived one part of the equation from Jewish émigrés, the other from Belgium, and nobody had even thought to place one alongside the other until quite late in the nineteenth century.

We had fried fish before that fateful marriage: Dickens refers to a 'fried fish warehouse' near Holborn in *Oliver Twist* (1837–9), and it does not feel as if he is describing a novelty. Some years before this,

Sephardic Jewish refugees had brought their way of cooking fish, deep-fried in batter, to London. It had quickly caught on. The renowned Jewish con artist Sarah Russell, who among other things sold 'magnetic rock-water dew' from the Sahara as an elixir of youth (it was just London water), also sold plaice or dabs fried in a turmeric batter at her 'hot potato and fried fish shop' at 4 Clare Market in Westminster, next to the Fountain pub. The 'hot potatoes', at a ha'penny each, were already popular with the poor and working classes. But they weren't yet chips.

Meanwhile the Belgians had the fried chip: Dickens, again, refers to 'husky chips of potatoes fried with some reluctant drops of oil', this time in *A Tale of Two Cities* (1859), though here he is describing a scene in Paris. There is a dubious French claim to the invention. But it is more likely that chips came from Belgium. Here in 1680-something, so the story goes, a desperate but nameless mother, unable to get fish because the Meuse was frozen, carved potatoes into the shapes of little fish and fried them for her children. So, there was something fishy about them from the start. By the early nineteenth century the fried chip was insanely popular throughout Belgium and France and one way or another the innovation migrated and caught on here, just as the fried fish had.

But the fried chip and the fried fish weren't placed side by side on the same plate until about 1860. Even then there is considerable partisan rivalry about who (and therefore which city) is first respon-sible for the nation-building act of culinary genius. The southern claim goes to Joseph Malin, a Jewish immigrant who started selling fish and chips in Bow in 1860 when he was only thirteen years old. His family were rug weavers and to boost income they also sold fried chips from the front of their house. Joseph hit on the idea of buying fish from a local fried-fish shop and of selling the two together as he toured the streets with a tray hung round his neck. Later he opened a fish and chip shop in Cleveland Street near St Mary-le-Bow

Church. So the story goes. The dates are controversial. Some say none of this happened until 1865. Those 'some' being from Oldham. Because there's a northern claim too, this time for John Lees, who began selling fish and chips from a wooden hut in Mossley Market in 1863 and later also opened a fish and chip shop under the sign 'Lees's Chip Potato Restaurant: Oldest in the World'. I don't suppose there's any settling that argument, but however, or wherever, fish and chips started, very quickly the happy marriage became the nation's favourite hot, comforting, filling, affordable and nutritious meal. The development of steam-powered trawling and the railway network made all the difference. Steam-powered trawling massively increased the catch rate. And faster trawlers also made it back to shore more quickly than they ever had under sail; meaning fresher fish, further inland. Trains running from ports like Whitby and Grimsby were able to deliver these fresh 'wet fish' landings to industrial centres in the heart of England, places like Manchester, Leeds, Sheffield and Nottingham, to feed the tens of thousands of hungry people working in factories.

Fish and chips helped us build our industrial might, helped us build the British Empire, helped us prevail in two world wars. And here I was with a bacon sandwich! While I shamefully ate it anyway, I also noticed that for every fish supper going out the door there were two of something else. Fishermen and dock workers drifted in and out, still in working gear, wet and oily, and ordered … sausage and chips, chicken and chips, pie and chips. Anything but fish and chips. Forgivable for them I suppose. After a week, even a lifetime of hauling and gutting thousands of cod and haddock, the thought of actually eating one might pale. I had no such excuse. And if anywhere was going to sell a good fillet, it would have to be the café next to Peterhead fish dock, surely? I promised myself and my conscience that I'd make up for it when I returned to shore. I'd have a slap-up at the same table … if I came back in one piece.

*

Dave called to say he was unloading his catch and that I could get my stuff aboard whenever I was ready. I eked out the last of my tea. People do this all the time, I said to myself. Weeks at sea, one after the other, are just a normal working life for them. Deep breath. Last sip. I stood up and walked out into the soft, warm evening.

On the deck of *Adorne* two figures winched boxes from deep in the trawler's hold, craning them to a third who waited on the quay with a trolley jack. Once the stack was four or five boxes high this man levered them up and, shoulders back, belly out, snatched the load round in a fast circle and pushed it on through the misted plastic curtains which covered the doorway to the market itself. I followed him inside. It was as cold as a winter's day in there, but the men were flushed with exertion, sweating and stern-faced. They worked in pairs, hefting the boxes one by one to ground level, where they dragged them hissing across the wet, icy floor, and arranged them by species and size. Row after row of hake, haddock and cod. Big, coal black eyes stared out of every box. Thousands of eyes shrouded in ice.

Dave came over, looked at his fishy glove and hesitated. We shook hands anyway.

'So, this is what you've come to write about, Charlie,' he said, dragging a crate of large cod to its berth alongside a dozen or more containing fish of the same size. The biggest cod I'd ever seen. Cod as long as the fish crates.

'I guess so,' I said. 'Big fish.'

But Dave didn't stop to talk. There was more pressing business at hand than a writer stowaway.

Back outside, the unloading job continued. I hung about looking and feeling a little spare, then went back to the car to fetch my stuff. I plonked my holdall on the quay, decorated the top with two embarrassingly new and bright yellow wellies and waited. Eventually the younger of the pair took a break from the winch and came over. His English wasn't great – he looked Filipino – but he gestured for me to pass my bags down – the tide was out and the boat was some way below the quay – and then jump after them on to the deck.

'Frankie,' he said tapping his chest. 'I show you.'

I followed Frankie into the bowels of the boat. One flight down we passed what must have been the galley. The space looked impossibly tiny. The telly was on, though no one was watching it and the air was hot and thick with the smell of frying and cigarettes. Pairs of yellow wellies lay scattered here and there, each man's oilskins peeled down and round the boots like banana skins. Pairs of blue gloves hung off the ladder steps, the handrails, the sink. This was the scramble gear, I reckoned, ready to be put on in the blink of an eye.

One flight further and we were below water level. There were no windows and the air was stuffy with the smell of sweat, socks and deodorant. Frankie pointed to my home: a wooden box, the size and shape of a coffin, in which were stuffed an old duvet and pillow and a few curled up newspapers. There were eight bunks like this – though two were unoccupied and had become storage cupboards for life jackets and crates of Coke – each accessed through a narrow, wooden slot. Inside the inhabited bunks were iPads and headphone cables, sleeping bags, pictures of home, of kids and wives and girlfriends. In the centre of the room was a large Formica table with drawers underneath, all half open and stuffed to the brim, the tabletop covered in luggage, T-shirts, shorts, towels, more crates of Coke, bars of Fruit and Nut. Round the back of the table and under the bunks was a vinyl bench, though it too was covered with more of the stuff that filled the empty bunks and the stuffed drawers and the tabletop. Whatever hadn't found room in any of these places was on the floor.

'Okay?' asked Frankie.

'Okay,' I said.

Frankie went back up, leaving me to sort myself out. I stood on the bench and looked inside my bunk. The mattress was grey with the unwashed liquor of a trawler – sweat, oil and fish – and tucked around its mouldy edges were socks, a pair of pants and yet more curled up newspapers, all disconcertingly soggy. I did not want to get caught in the act of being a bit soft, but while the boat was quiet and deserted I took my chances and pulled the whole lot out, wiped down and dried the inside of the coffin, threw the newspapers and socks in the bin. I was stuck with the mattress but the other side was not so grey, so I flipped it over and stuffed it back inside on to a layer of fresher *Scottish Herald*. The cleanish duvet made one more layer and on top of that went my unzipped sleeping bag, with a pillow on top. I made some room for my bags on the shelf by the bunk and climbed inside. Not so bad. My holdall was in reach and so therefore was my lifeline of books, seasick pills, toothbrush, clean pants. I might just do this, I thought. I might make it.

Through the stillness I could hear an occasional clang, or dull shout from the hold. With nothing else to do I dug out my camera and climbed back upstairs to photograph the men at work. I took snaps of the fish crates, of the porter disappearing through the curtains into the fluorescent interior of the market, of the men in blue overalls and orange oilskins shivering in the chill of the hold. When I stopped I was standing next to Frankie and Jake.

'Hi,' I said.

Frankie smiled. Jake didn't. There was a long pause.

'You must be Charlie,' Jake said eventually.

'Yes,' I said.

Jake turned back to the winch, shouted something to the men below. They shouted something to each other. Then one shouted back up. I didn't get a word of it.

'Thank fuck,' said Jake, more comprehensibly. The unloading was over.

'And you've come here to write about this ... ' he paused for emphasis ' ... fucking awful job.'

'Yes. I suppose I have,' I laughed.

FISH BONES

The job, the fish, the history.

We are at a turning point – or a *potential* turning point – in our relationship with fish and more widely the natural world. A great fisherman, Bernard Venables, once wrote that life starts and ends with water, that if the condition of our water is not right, the condition of society is not right either. The metaphor easily and obviously extends to the fish that live in it. We depend on fish and fishing for employment, food, for cathartic pleasure and escape and – vitally – as a barometer for the health of the planet. In recent decades that barometer has plummeted alarmingly. We have exploited our cod and other high-seas fisheries to the very edge of viability, if not virtual extinction. This is not hyperbole: the Canadian government issued a moratorium on cod fishing on the Grand Banks in the early 1990s, a fishery that had been the life force of community and industry on the Canadian east coast and in Newfoundland for 500 years.

Fishermen, scientists, government had all thought the sea so infinitely fecund its cod would never run out. But a graph of the Grand Banks catches reads like the trajectory of a plane crash: it climbs and climbs through the decades, 1850s, 1860s, 1870s and so on, goes into a sort of skyrocket ascent in the 1950s, free-falls in the 1970s (this was a warning that went unheeded), levels off for a few years (this was read as a recovery) and then just nosedives to oblivion. The moratorium was intended to be temporary: long enough to allow the stocks to recover. But they never have. Scientists have been watching for a quarter-century now. A flicker on the cardiograph in the last few years is a sign of hope: a 69% increase in stocks between 2007 and 2010 could almost make a headline. Until you realise that is 69% of not much and we're still hardly at 10% of what used to be there. Ongoing research is just starting to get to the root of what went wrong, though it's kind of obvious when you think about it: the demise of cod led to an explosion in the numbers of the fish they ate and this turned everything on its head. Zillions of smaller fish smothered any cod recovery by eating all the food young cod need to get large enough to start eating them! Meanwhile jellyfish and various other species drifted in to the void. Cod were literally fished out of the food web. At the same time, 35,000 Canadian fishermen, packers and dockers lost their jobs. Five centuries of culture, identity and history hit the buffers just as much as the cod did. Fishermen left the industry, or they emigrated, or they drifted around, listless and unemployed. A lucky few retrained and went back to sea to catch the crabs and shrimps that were booming now there were no cod to eat them. Otherwise, that east coast was changed irrevocably.

In the last ten or fifteen years our fishing industry has gone through something of the same crash, the difference being we may – just – have averted an equivalent disaster to the extinction of the Banks. Even then, stalling short of oblivion has brought real pain and hardship to the likes of Jake and Dave. And they are the ones still fishing. Many more have lost their livelihoods.

So yes, I had driven up to Peterhead to write about this 'fucking awful job'. Cod and fishing are a big part of our culture too and the ties go back further than fish and chips. When the *Mary Rose* sank in the Solent in 1545, she took down with her, along with 400 unfortunate mariners, a trove of cannons and longbows, Tudor fiddles and pewter plates ... and dozens of baskets and barrels of salted cod.

Their bones tell a story.

In 1412, 133 years before the *Mary Rose* sank, the Icelandic *Nyi Annáll* records 'there came a ship from England east of Dyrhólmaey, people rowed out to them and they were fishermen of England'. The English mariners had followed the scent of the air-dried cod known as '*stokfisk*' from Bergen in Norway to Iceland and discovered the Norwegian–Danish fishing grounds. Iceland is a long way from King's Lynn or Newcastle, but it was worth the journey. The medieval fisherman caught his cod with hand lines, jigging a lure over the side of the boat until a greedy cod took hold. The density of cod on the Icelandic shelf eclipsed our North Sea stocks, and Iceland's cold summer winds were an integral part of the curing process. Cod was a valuable commodity at a time when the Catholic grip on Europe compelled an almost insatiable demand for fish, and for cod more than any other type of fish because cod meat has almost no fat: it can be cured with salt or brine and dried into a light, leathery husk that is easy to pack and transport and it lasts forever. To eat dried cod, just add water: it was the medieval Pot Noodle.

The Norwegian–Danish King – Eric III – was not keen to share his fast-food riches, however. Nor were the Hanseatic League – a coalition of merchants and guilds clustered around the Baltic and the North Sea – who jealously guarded their monopolies. The Hansa had barred English merchants from trading at Bergen, sending the English in search of their own supplies. And stakes were high in the rush to this cod gold: only a few years earlier the Hansa had bound and thrown overboard ninety-six English fishermen they had caught fishing in Norwegian waters.

King Eric sent emissaries to Henry IV in England, but Henry claimed that the English had fished off Iceland for years and did nothing to stop his East Anglian fleet. Before long, dozens of boats were making annual fishing voyages from England to Iceland, where they set up shore-camp and fished the summer long: 'making use of everything as if it was their own', so the Icelanders complained. Isolated and impoverished, the Icelanders were more or less defence-less against this mercantile assault. For almost a hundred years the English ruled the place more effectively than its true Norwegian and Danish overlords. The fishery they established is memorialised in those bench-ends from St Nicholas' Chapel.

Neither the Danish–Norwegian government, nor the Hansa, thought much of this English raid on their resources. Skirmishes and tensions were inevitable. Things came to a head when the English built a fortified base on the Westman Islands off the Icelandic coast and kidnapped the Danish governor, Hannes Paulsson, when he tried to assert his authority there. Paulsson was spirited across the water to England where he wrote a long list of complaints: the English had stolen children, he said, or enticed their parents to give them away for trinkets, they had sacked farmsteads, burnt churches, settled royal property and built fortresses without permission.

From time to time over the following decades the Danish–Norwegian monarchy tried to reprieve the virtual annexation by imposing a fishing licence, but the English weren't always inclined to pay it. So, in 1467 a frustrated Danish king withdrew the licence completely. The English carried on regardless. A new governor – a native Icelander called Björn Þorleifsson – tried again to prevent them. English merchants upped the stakes from kidnapping to murder. They tossed his body into the sea, stole gold and silver from his wife and burnt down his house. In Icelandic folklore she is said to have avenged the death by beheading a dozen Englishmen. In reality, much more serious conflict followed.

Seizing the moment and emboldened by their closer ties with the Danish Crown, the German Hansa began to muscle in to the void created by this thuggish English diplomacy. Didrich Pinning, a German sea captain, was appointed governor. He made a respectable attempt to impose order and a truce between the English and the increasing number of Hansa fishermen and merchants. But it didn't really work. The English were used to behaving as if Iceland was theirs and regarded the Hansa as a threat, and vice versa. They murdered one another, seized ships, stole cargo. It was a lawless cod-rush played out on the frigid waters of the Atlantic.

Then, in 1532 a full-on battle broke out in a small harbour called Básendar on the Reykjanes peninsula: hundreds of fishermen, merchants and farmers attacked each other with cannons and cross-bows. The English lost. Two were beheaded to avenge old grievances and two more were tortured until they were almost dead. The English surrendered one of their ships and forty tons of dried cod, then the defeated remnants of the ragtag fisherman army were sent packing. They retreated to Grindavík, a former stronghold, but fuelled by a century's worth of grievances, an even more bolshy rabble of German fishermen and Icelanders led by the royal bailiff chased them down. Fifteen more English fishermen were killed in the skirmishes that followed, the crew of one ship drowned and all the remaining Englishmen were expelled.

It had become war in all but name. So, to effect some kind of peace a treaty was signed whereby the king of Denmark and the Norwegian Council allowed both Hansa and English vessels access to their Icelandic fishery, in return for dues. But the truce was loaded against the English from the start, specifically prohibiting *duggarar* – decked fishing boats which only the English possessed – 'because they rob both property and people from this poor country and thus reduce the tax of our gracious Lord the King and the tithe of our God'.

The English held on in dribs and drabs. But eventually they lost control even of Grindavík and in 1558 the Danes confiscated the final English stronghold on the Westman Islands, the construction of which had started all the trouble.

It was odd, perhaps, that the pugnacious English should have meekly withdrawn after so much blood had been spilled. That retreat can be explained by those fish bones from the *Mary Rose*. Several were from the North Sea, the Orkneys or Shetland, where there was also a trade in dried, salted cod. Many came from Iceland: among the last – for the time being – from that outpost. But one of the *Mary Rose* fish was from the far side of the Atlantic, near Newfoundland, the next chapter in England's cod story.

Zuan Caboto – or John Cabot as he was known in his adopted Bristol – had 'discovered' Newfoundland only half a century before in 1497 whilst searching, on behalf of Henry VII, for a shortcut to Asia. Though he claimed the land for England, the Basques had known about the cod fishery there for some time. At first the English did not rush to exploit it: they had Iceland. After 1532, all this Icelandic strife suddenly looked like too much trouble. Newfoundland might have been a longer voyage, but the English now had the fleet and the know-how to stage long-distance cod raids. They left Iceland to the Hansa, who were soon eased out by Denmark anyway, and transferred attentions to this new cod mine on the far side of the Atlantic.

It was a seasonal operation at first, as it had been in Iceland. Ships arrived in spring, sailed home in late summer, with every start-of-season a scramble for shore room. But the English had learned all about occupation. Before long they left winter crews behind to guard and maintain their infrastructure: the landing stages and cook rooms, the huts and the 'horses' of stones on which they dried the fish. It must have been the short straw for those who stayed, facing east over an ice-bound sea and at their backs nothing but hostile wilderness and Beothuk natives. But these winter guardians soon got the run of the place and, possession being nine-tenths of the law, the English began to ease aside their Spanish and Portuguese rivals.

Back in the Old World, war with Spain was an ever-present threat. Here England was in a double bind. Spain was an important market for English cod, but Spanish trade all but fell apart in the 1560s. Queen Elizabeth had tacitly encouraged English privateers to harass the Spaniards on the high seas, and while the English gentlemen pirates like Sir Francis Drake did rather well at it, some government ministers saw a weakened fishing trade as a real threat to our national security. William Cecil wrote to Queen Elizabeth: 'selling of fish out of the realm hath of present no great vent: remedies must be sought to increase mariners by fishing'. Cecil wanted to stimulate an internal market to keep the fishermen in business, fishermen who could be recruited to the navy at short notice. If you've ever wondered why Wednesday is also a fast day, blame a looming Spanish invasion and the 1563 Navigation Act. Wednesday became another Friday. Devout Englishmen ate more fish. The fishermen kept on sailing. The navy had its reserves.

When war finally broke out in 1585 – the Spanish had seized English ships caught trading in a Spanish harbour – the English knew exactly where to hit back. The Privy Council authorised a campaign against Spanish fishermen in Newfoundland. Sir Bernard Drake – sea captain and distant cousin of Francis – sailed there with the news: it was time to put our feisty fishermen to the test. 'Drake's Sweep' as it came to be known was the first stage in what was, effectively, a battle for mastery of the Atlantic. With the help of the institutionally combative English fishermen, Drake harried, plundered, burned and scuppered the Spanish fishing fleet until there was more or less nothing left of it. Fate overtook him when he died of the same gaol fever that did for most of the Spanish and Portuguese prisoners he dragged back to Exeter. But in the larger scheme of things the campaign was a lethal blow to the Spanish. They left Newfoundland alone and after the other Drake prevailed in his rout of the Armada, they never really went there again. English fishermen and their ships played their part in that more famous battle too: many remained at home in 1588 when Bristol, Bideford, Dartmouth,

Plymouth, Topsham, Bridport, Exmouth and Poole – all West Country fishing ports – had their share of the fight.

The Spanish had overreached themselves. The English, whose tactics were only ever a waspish harassment whenever and wherever, now had complete control of Atlantic trade in general and the transatlantic cod fishery in particular. In so many ways, then, the British Empire was born on the deck of a fishing boat. The rest, as they say, is history.

Yet Britain's cod conflicts have never quite ended. Newfoundland and the Grand Banks were contested with the French on and off for the next 400 years. Cod grounds were discovered to the south too, along the coast of New England. Disputes over cod fishing and cod markets in large part fanned the flames of United States independence. As evoked in Mark Kurlansky's well-known book *Cod*, the history of cod fisheries and markets is the history of nation-building and imperialism. Having defeated an armada with a fishing fleet, it didn't take the British long to realise the strategic significance of cod, not only as a resource the access to which preserved a reservist force of fishermen mariners, but the Royal Navy also sailed on cod rations: dried fish was deemed so vital to British naval ascendancy that the Crown restricted trade and banned the sale of cod direct to European ports.

Then, a century or so down the line, the British discovered fish and chips and *we* began to eat cod as never before. Not because of holy days and fast days, not salted and cured, but fresh off the boat, propelled by railway to the nearest fryer, wrapped in yesterday's news, all to fill the tummy of the working man with something hot, cheap and tasty. Demand for the meal which powered British industry drove a cod rush of a different kind: trawlers powered by steam and diesel. The North Sea could not provide it all and as stocks close to home dwindled, here was an echo of England's first forays to distant fishing grounds in the 1400s: what came to be known as the first, second and third Icelandic Cod Wars, but what should really have been called the second, third and fourth.

By the time the British discovered their love of fried cod, the world had changed, even if Iceland hadn't. From the time of the English retreat in 1532 until the middle of the nineteenth century, the Danes had kept Iceland in something of a commercial lock-down. Foreigners went fishing there: the Dutch, the French when they were elbowed out of the New World. But now Britain wanted more cod than it could catch and – with the humiliating defeats of Básendar and Grindavík buried under 500 years of history – they went back. The Icelanders were as little impressed this time as the last. And as unable to resist. British trawlers – more powerful than any the Icelanders had seen until now – muscled in along their coastal shelf, displaced the more artisanal Icelandic fleet and began to fish the hell out of the place. For a while the Icelanders tried to compete. They bought British boats and by 1915 had a fleet of twenty steam trawlers of their own. Luckily for them – and the cod – the Great War was some kind of respite against what was starting to look like the next phase in the pillage of the North Atlantic: already the British boats were catching three times what they had been used to in the steadily diminishing Newfoundland fishery.

When the British trawlers returned after 1918 there might have been fewer of them – many had been casualties in the war or had been permanently requisitioned by the Admiralty – but with radios, electricity and echo-meters, they were more efficient than ever before. At that time a nation's private waters extended only as far as three miles offshore. Even into that modest, private margin the British made incursions. The Icelandic coastguard – code-named 'Grandmother' by the Brits – tried its best, but they were competing against all this war-honed technology. The Brits radioed each other warnings – 'Grandmother is well', 'Grandmother is beginning to feel bad' – and with their faster boats made a mockery of Iceland's attempts to police its own back yard.

The Second World War brought another reprieve. For six years the Icelanders even kept Britain in fish and chips. Fish prices soared and a formerly impoverished, but now emboldened Iceland climbed into a new world order. Icelanders were now keenly aware of the value of their cod asset and weren't about to let the British grab it back. Though the concept of private coastal waters was somewhat contentious and the principle of an international sea almost sacrosanct, American president Harry S. Truman let the brakes off when, in seeking to safeguard oil assets, he asserted America's rights to its own continental shelf. In the shadow of this move Iceland claimed an extra mile for their exclusion zone. And got away with it. Even so, catches still plummeted and the Icelanders knew why: too much fishing pressure and too many foreign trawlers, many of them British.

In a series of belligerent and plucky moves, Iceland extended its territorial limit from three to twelve miles (1958), from twelve to fifty (1971) and finally to 200 miles (1975). Each time the British protested mightily and tried to carry on fishing. The Icelanders armed their coastguard boats with wire cutters and if a trawler refused to give up the game, they lost their nets. The Icelanders rammed British trawlers. British trawlers rammed them back – which suited the Icelanders because while the British were ramming they weren't fishing. From time to time the Royal Navy mounted a guard, but this imposed such restrictions on the trawl pattern as to render the fishing almost pointless. At one point shots were fired. A British trawler was hit. Several were confiscated. Miraculously, no one was killed.

In that sense things had improved since the year 1532. But in another sense things were the same: the British lost. They had simply underestimated the determination of Icelanders to protect their resources. Thus by the middle of the 1970s Britain was thrown back on its own.

What was left of them. Because the same story of overfishing, declining catches and brief wartime respites had played out in our own back yard too, only to worse effect. We'd been raiding Iceland's stocks, and ransacking our own. Raiding theirs *because* we'd ransacked our own.

A SEA OF INFINITE FISHES

Fishermen had noticed the decline almost as soon as Joseph Malin first put a fried fish next to a fried chip in 1860. Things had moved on since the Middle Ages. Long lines – set with hundred of hooks – had replaced hand lines and now trawled nets had replaced both. Catch rates soared. The trawling and transport technology that enabled a rush of fresh cod from the bottom of the sea to fryers in Britain's industrial heartlands became the serpent that ate its own tail. Railways created the demand. Trawling responded. Even under sail, which might seem a benign, almost artisanal way of fishing, bottom-trawling was too effective from the outset. Traditional longline fishermen regarded the newfangled methods with hostility. By 1863 their concerns about overfishing precipitated a Royal Inquiry. Commissioners visited eighty-six ports and took statements from 700 witnesses drawn from all quarters of the fishing industry. B. Simpson, ex-longliner from Spurn Point, had this to say: '20 years ago we used to get 600 or 700 head of fish a day there; now they cannot get above 20 head, or 3 or 4 score at the outside.' T. Fell, longliner from north-east England, the same: '20 years ago a boat would get 58 or 60 stone of cod, haddock and other fish. Today they average sometimes 12 or 15 stone. Sometimes a boat will go out and only get 2 or 3 stone.' And so on.

Opposing sectors of the fishing industry gave contradictory testimony and there were no fisheries records to back up the old-timers' claims. Besides, the industry was changing at such a pace the commissioners could hardly but fail to underestimate the impact of modifications to techniques and gear. They may also have had half an eye on the growing commercial importance of this new kind of industrialised white-fish harvest: cheap food for the working masses. Either way, the commissioners' conclusions, which no doubt read as the sober advice of thoughtful men in 1866, seem like nothing more than hubris today: 'The allegations that trawling in the open sea has exhausted any trawling grounds, and that trawlers have been obliged to leave trawling grounds on account of exhaustion are devoid of foundation,' they wrote. Far from restraint, they recommended the 'unrestricted freedom of fishing'.

Twenty-odd years later at a conference in London called to address unextinguished concerns about overfishing, the Darwinian naturalist Thomas Huxley was still backing the claims that trawling had no impact: 'I believe that it may be affirmed that, in relation to our present modes of fishing, a number of the most important sea fisheries, such as the cod fishery, the herring fishery, the mackerel fishery, are inexhaustible.' Not everyone was so blinkered: the zoologist Edwin Lankester, wielding what looks like nothing more than common sense, countered Huxley's belief in the magic properties of the sea: 'It is a mistake to suppose that the place of fish removed on a particular fishing ground is immediately taken by some grand total of fish, which are so numerous in comparison with man's depredations as to make his operations in this respect insignificant.'

So the debate went on in the corridors of academia. How did fishermen respond to the declining stocks? They used more gear, set more nets, spent longer at sea and travelled further to find their fish.

A second commissioners' inquiry followed in 1885: more ports were visited, many more witness statements were recorded. This time the weight of evidence was compelling. Not that it did much good. The commissioners were more or less forced to conclude that in places stocks had declined, *not* that trawling was responsible. Instead, they recommended a reform of scientific study and the start of national record-keeping. Thus lower catch rates and stock estimates had become normalised before the bar had even been set.

It's easy to lose touch with how things used to be when only the memories of old fishermen bear witness. But a few records that pre-date national statistics give at least some documentary evidence: these suggest a decline of some 66% over a quarter-century between 1867 and 1892. In 1900 the English biologist Walter Garstang published *The Impoverishment of the Sea* showing how the catch rate of plaice had decreased in spite of an increase in fishing effort: arguments that discredited Huxley and his apostates. Still some scientists persisted. In 1898 William McIntosh had espoused his theory of infinite fishes in *Resources of the Sea*. He delivered strident, defiant lectures and was courted by the trawling industry as just the right kind of authoritative voice.

It took a world war to show the impact of trawling in terms that could not be ignored – although McIntosh did his best. In 1914 the average daily landings of a trawler had fallen to 716 kg. By 1918 when the fleet cranked into action again, landings had bounced back to 1,546 kg. For four years trawling effort had declined to almost a quarter of its pre-war level, while the stock of fish in the North Sea more or less doubled. It had been, in the words of Edward Russell, a Scottish biologist and newly appointed director of fishery investigations for the British ministry, 'the Great Fishing Experiment'. It had made the point.

Two years after the war ended – with catch rates falling again – a young naturalist called Michael Graham started work at the same Ministry of Agriculture and Fisheries' Laboratory in Lowestoft. Graham was an eccentric – he rode a horse to work in the dark of winter with a red light on the port side of his bowler hat and a green on the starboard – but also a man of passionate conviction – he also rode his horse back and forth over the slag heaps covering his beloved Lancashire countryside, knowing that trees would sprout in the hoof prints. He was something of a naturalist polymath, but for two decades in the 1920s and 1930s his attention was focussed on every detail of the cod's existence and its exploitation. His first paper, *Modern Theory of Exploiting a Fishery, and Application to North Sea Trawling*, explained his ideas in an intriguing mix of elegant English and bewildering mathematical formulas. Graham had noticed a strangely inverse relationship between fishing effort and yield: that our ability to catch fish had reached such a level of efficiency as to become counter-productive; that as fishing technology and fishing know-how improved and as effort increased, catches no longer kept pace. There were simply fewer and fewer fish in the sea. The paper was an attempt to formulate, as he described it, the opinion of many fishermen and scientists, that fishermen *and* fish would be better off if we gave 'the fish a chance to grow ... and a better chance to breed'.

Russell's argument in *The Overfishing Problem* was that stocks like cod, haddock, hake and plaice were being 'overfished' not just in an abstract sense, but because the intensity of the fishing effort was depressing the overall size of the fish population *and* the average size of the fish. This wasted the resources of the fish, and of the fishermen who had to work harder and harder for the same reward. Ultimately, he reasoned, they would fish themselves out of a job. Michael Graham summed it up in his Great Law of Fishing: 'Fisheries that are unlimited become unprofitable'.

To Russell and Graham, the end of the Great War had been a wasted opportunity to reassess the way we fished and both men were keenly aware that in 1939 another chance had come to correct what had been missed in 1918. There was no time to lose. 'We used to think,' wrote Graham, 'that fishermen should moderate their efforts for the sake of posterity, in order that there should be a living in the sea for their sons, whereas we now see quite clearly it is essential for the sake of their own living, that they should band together to exercise the virtue of moderation.'

Here I was on the deck of a Scottish trawler hoping to find out what had happened to that moderation, what had happened to that 'living in the sea', what had happened to the sons.

Though I'd hardly noticed their arrival, the crew were now on board. People had appeared as if from nowhere and were bustling about the deck unhitching ropes, tying stuff down. Suddenly we were ready to sail. Dave eased past me on to the bridge. I followed him and tried to work out where I could stand and not be in the way. While I was doing this I got in the way. So I moved a bit and got in the way again. Someone opened the stairwell door into my back and I stepped aside into the space they wanted to go through. And so it went. Not getting in the way is the occupation of the unoccupied on a trawler. And there are few places it can be done. Your bunk. The bench in the galley – though often I was in the way there, too. And a small patch of the bridge between the computer screens and the old mapping drawers. I didn't know it then, as we eased away from the quay, but I'd spend most of the next seven days rotating between these three spots, or occasionally leaving them to do something more interesting, only to find myself in the way.

'Best stand over there,' said Dave.

'Are we off?' I asked, feeling I ought to send a text home before I lost reception.

'In a while. Got to pick up ice first.'

We puttered through the harbour from the market to the icehouse. It was almost dark outside. Late evening now. The spotlights and streetlights of the harbourside shone through the bridge windows, glistening on the condensation. A smell of frying drifted up the stairs.

'You've come up to write about cod, but I'm afraid we'll be trying to avoid them this week,' said Dave as he unhitched his oilskins.

'Have you caught your quota already?' I asked.

'No. Not all of it. But we have to catch haddock. We've got hundreds of tons of haddock to catch, and they're just not coming on this year. Lots of small fish. Maybe it's the cold.'

This was only the second time Dave had gone to sea since earlier in the summer. 'The boats are picking things up in the harbour,' he said to explain why they'd been out of the water so long. 'And this one's really bad for it. There's tyres and all sorts of other shit in here and when the water's low stuff gets stuck round the propeller. Sometimes you can clear it, so one of the lads ran out and gave the prop a spin and that bent it completely! That was us scuppered for five weeks.'

And *Adorne* is getting more and more costly to keep on the water. She was built in 1986 and fitted with a Dennis engine. The problem, Dave explained, is that Dennis engines were too good. They never broke down, so no one ordered any parts and eventually Dennis went out of business. Now *Adorne*'s spares cost a fortune. Dave spends over £100,000 each year, just servicing her.

'So, I've ordered a new one now,' he said, cheerfully.

'Engine, or boat?'

'Boat.'

'Wow. That's a big decision.'

'Yes. It's the time we've been waiting for really, with stocks so good. We've been through some very hard years. But it looks better now. I've got maybe ten years till I retire and it would be good to get a little ... comfort.' He smiled.

Already this meandering chat had suggested that *my* fishing trip – fishing for the story – might throw up the unexpected. Dave was avoiding cod because he was getting close to the top of his quota, and the previous week, judging by what I saw being unpacked at the market, had pushed him yet closer. 'With stocks so good'? This was news.

Because everything I knew about the subject had told me that North Sea cod were on the edge of oblivion. The moderation that Michael Graham had hoped for never came. In 1945 the world had had no appetite for the wisdom of Russell and Graham, for their suggestions of limited days at sea, of maximum global tonnages, of minimum mesh sizes. While the British government did at least argue for a limit to the sizes of the various fleets operating in the North Sea and Atlantic, no other country would sign up to the restriction. In fact the 1946 fisheries conference became a model for all those that followed: short-term, partisan interests prevailed over long-term sustainability and international co-operation. Total allowable catches, closed seasons and exclusive rights in certain areas – radical ideas that might have saved our seas – were all rejected.

Worse still, the formulas that Graham and his team of maths geniuses had devised as a rationale for reducing fishing effort were used as a justification for *increasing* effort. Convinced that there was a point at which fish populations could be most efficiently and sustainably exploited, Graham had come up with a theoretical concept he called Maximum Sustainable Yield. Ancient and well-established fish populations, so he speculated, yield a less-than-maximum potential crop to fishing because a large part of those populations consists of old and slow-growing fish. Replacing these older fish (by fishing them out) with a greater number of faster-growing, smaller fish, so the theory went, maximises the potential yield. The fishery can then be held at this optimum state of productivity through efficient, but controlled fishing pressure. It was all theory, but how governments liked the theory! Graham had been aiming at the concept of controlled and limited pressure, but in practice Maximum Sustainable Yield became a target, rather than a cautionary limit.

This was the fisheries world into which the European Economic Community was born. Proliferating fleets, chasing diminishing

returns and no single government – let alone a coalition of governments each looking after number one – prepared to make the tough
decisions that might avert disaster.

Ever since I'd read Charles Clover's 2004 book *The End of the
Line* and learned about the dire status of the world's fisheries in
general, and North Sea cod in particular, I'd been careful to order
haddock at the chippy, or ask if the cod was from Iceland. I'd read
the bleak headlines: 'Just 100 cod left in the North Sea' was a 2012
byline so catchily doom-laden, the story had run all over the news.
It had echoes of the disastrous tale of the Grand Banks.

Latterly, quotas have been part of the EU's way of urgently trying
to avoid that fate. Kind of. Some say they're also a way of divvying
up a diminishing resource and of ignoring science while doing so,
which is how we got into that sorry state in the first place. Quotas
are the amount of fish of a given species that a boat is *allowed to
land and sell* (remember the italics). Dave has a quota for X amount
of cod, Y amount of haddock, Z amount of hake and so on. Dave's
quota comes out of the Total Allowable Catch (TAC) that the UK
is given annually, which in turn is a share of the TAC of all the
member states of the European Union put together. These TACs
are set in December each year by the EU Council of Ministers, and
they're based on the advice of its own scientists and also – ideally
– of independent bodies like the International Council for the
Exploration of the Sea.

It all sounds simple enough. In practice it has been anything but.
Quotas and TAC are the primary tools of the EU's Common
Fisheries Policy (CFP), a framework of fishery management
conceived in the early 1970s. Despite four rounds of reform on each
tenth anniversary since then, the CFP is often described as Europe's
worst policy. If preserving fish stocks is a measure of its success, it
has indeed been a disaster. There's cheating, some almost state-
sponsored. There's inconsistent policing. It's unworkable. Quotas are

too generous to fishermen and unsustainable, or based on poor science and political expediency, depending on who you talk to. Just one easy Internet search in the days before I left revealed a polarised narrative over the years, of conservationists calling for quota cuts, while fishermen called for quota increases. The fishermen need to make a living. The conservationists want to preserve stocks. I guess I had inclined to believe the conservationists as much as I tried to sympathise with the fishermen.

Maybe Dave's 'with stocks so good' was just *his* way of looking at it.

OUT TO SEA

We filled up with ice – an elephant's trunk spraying icy snow into the hold – then chugged back through the harbour, across the bay and out to sea. Dave eased a lever forward as we rounded the storm wall, the engine note dropped an octave then picked up as we kicked out into the swell. A swell in the sense that the sea was not – quite – flat. I felt the gentle rise and fall, but I doubt anyone else did, and here by Dave's open window and doped up on seasickness pills I reckoned I could cope well enough if the weather stayed this calm. The harbour lights grew distant, flickered and finally went out. It would be seven days before I saw land again. Seven days if things went well, if Dave found fish.

We chatted off and on, touching briefly on subjects I knew I'd want to go back to once I had my voice recorder and notebook and sea legs: the pain of the decommissioning years, the difficulty of hiring young men into the industry, the nefarious practices of foreign fishing fleets, and at home the 'slipper skippers' making money out of fishing while watching the telly, the closest they get to water being when they fill the kettle. The evening wore on and I could tell after a while that Dave wanted peace and quiet. Then the door opened and a new face appeared.

'Would you like something to eat, Charlie?' It was Richard, second mate and the boat's chef.

I hesitated.

'Aye,' said Dave. 'You'd best get something inside you.'

I followed Richard below deck. The rest of the crew were sitting around the two small galley tables, smoking and watching the football.

'Do you like the football, Charlie?' asked Jake, stubbing one ciggy out and lighting another.

'Sure,' I said, lying. 'Not too much up on it though. Who's playing?'

Silence. If I knew anything at all I'd know who was playing by looking at the screen. I looked. No idea.

'I'm more into rugby,' I said, hoping this might help.

'League?' asked another new face – Michael – sideways on the bench, feet up, blowing smoke over the top of his iPad.

'Er. Not so much. Union. I watch league for sure. Once in a while.' This was a lie too. I don't know why anyone watches rugby league.

Silence. These were either unconvincing or the wrong answers and we all knew it.

Richard punctured the quiet and told me to grab a plate and help myself from the trays of sausages, chips, beans and coleslaw. I was almost hungry, so I tucked in, or tried to make a show of it anyway.

'Get some food in yer belly, Charlie.'

'Er ... It might not be in there for long, Jake. So, I'm ... you know ... going slowly,' I said.

'It's all in yer head,' he said, tapping his temple.

At the far side of the table another member of the crew, tall and thin, his face carved by worry, was shaking his head ... and worrying. This was Jakey.

'How far we going?' he asked.

'Nae far,' said Richard.

'Fuck.'

'Dave said something about forty, or fifty miles,' I chipped in, thinking this would be both helpful and good news. There was, deep inside my vault of various fears, the illogical idea that the closer we stayed to shore the better.

'Fuck,' said Jakey, again.

'Not good?' I asked.

'Not good,' said Jakey, as if at forty or fifty miles there lay a monster which would pull us under with tentacles.

I waited for a moment, thinking, hoping, he would elucidate. But he just shook his head and said 'fuck' again under his breath. He said other stuff too, but 'fuck' was the word I could most easily discern.

I soon realised that the word 'fuck' was my one and only linguistic bridge with these men, often when they were talking to me, but always when they were talking to each other. Sometimes I made out 'c**t' but mostly it was 'fuck'. I would have understood more on a French trawler. When they spoke to me, however, I could tell they made an effort, because I went from understanding nothing to picking up the general sense and even one or two words and phrases.

'What's at forty miles?' I asked.

'It's nae what's there,' said Jakey. 'It's how long it takes to get there. First sail's the longest we'll get our heads doon all week. Foor fuckin' oors.'

I could see his point. Or could have if I'd known then what I knew seven days later. He wasn't exaggerating.

I ate slowly, trying to look interested in the football, but also hoping the others would stop smoking soon. Before long the galley cleared. First Jake, then Michael, then Jakey stubbed out their cigarettes and headed down to the bunk room. Richard washed out the pans and headed down too, leaving only Frankie and Johnny, the two Filipino crew members, who'd been silently busy at the cooker, chopping vegetables, boiling rice. I thought it was some kind of hierarchical thing at first, that they ate only after the others had left.

But when Frankie sat down with an enormous bowl of rice, chicken stock, vegetables and spices I saw it was just about food. Filipino food. Scottish food. He smiled at me and tucked in. It smelt good.

We chatted falteringly. I learned that Frankie had been over here several years, was married and had children back home, and that Johnny – at twenty-something he was by far the youngest on the boat – had been here for eighteen months. I asked where home was and they both said the Philippines. They went back there once a year, if they could.

'Home when you're here,' I said, correcting my meaning.

'This is home,' said Frankie pointing downwards. 'This boat is home.'

A tunnel of dim light illuminated the foot of the stairwell in an otherwise darkened bunk house. I slid my hands down the chrome bannister and descended stair by stair, trying to assimilate things. Not so much the disorienting dark, or the thick air or the sweat-filled heat. More the head-splitting racket that thundered and echoed through the fabric of the room, shaking my fillings, my bowels, my brain. The bunk house, I could now hear, could now *feel*, was sandwiched between the engine and the propeller, and both were working at full pitch as we steamed towards our first fishing ground. With the bags I'd so carefully placed now lost in the gloom I couldn't find my torch and without that I couldn't find anything else. I couldn't think either, so I just clambered up into the bunk, fully clothed and lay there enveloped in this jarring, pounding mechanical din, wondering how in God's name I was ever going to sleep through the barrage.

Sometime around four-thirty in the morning the lights went on. Someone cried out 'Tea-oh. Tea-oh,' from the foot of the stairs. Locked inside a numbed, exhausted half-sleep I sensed movement in the room. I'd better get up too, I thought, before falling back inside my steel-foundry dreams. I woke again. It felt like only seconds had passed but the room was now deserted. I forced myself out of bed. The seasick pills and the infernal din had doped my brain. Drunkenly I pulled on my bright wellies and clambered upstairs.

The others had finished their tea and were emerging one by one from the smoke-filled galley, stepping into those peeled-banana boots and oilskins. Braces hitched, gloves on, they were out on deck, leaving me once again alone, behind the curve. I went back down for my camera, then followed.

Up on deck it was busy. Our pair boat, *Audacious*, was alongside. I'd not seen her till now, not in the harbour, nor on our night-time run to get here, though we'd been travelling together. To me the sudden, physical presence beside us of this fellow hulk of steel was strangely reassuring. We were not – quite – alone. It was dark, but with the faintest glow of light to the east I could feel the empty vastness of the sea, and how small we were in the midst of it. These sweaty, steel walls were our world. Out there was the uncaring universe.

Audacious had backed stern-on to our side, dangerously close so it felt to me as the two boats bobbed up and down on the swell, *Audacious* rising as we fell and vice versa. Two men hung off her stern, grim-faced, both smoking. Richard swung a rope and buoy round and round his head, taking aim at this moving target. The buoy sailed up and out, missed the grasp of the first man, bounced off the steel side of the trawler and fell with a splash into the sea. It was close enough, however. The other had a grappling hook ready. He dropped it and pulled, retrieved the buoy, then the rope and the two of them quickly turned and busied themselves tying it up to a link under a sagging coil of nets. Suddenly the wordless choreography was over and *Audacious* was away, her engine gunning hard as the rope snapped up and tightened. Sea-spray flickered from it like a starburst in the spotlights. A chain clanked along our deck, accelerated violently and rung itself over the side. Finally the steel hawser, wrapped on a drum like the largest fishing reel you've ever seen, began to pay out, scything viciously over the gunwale at the back of the boat. I stood there watching the lights of *Audacious* flicker through the soft dawn, mesmerised by the potent lethality of the whole operation, only to find that once again I was alone.

I stepped back into the doorway of the bridge and smelled cigarette smoke rising up the stairs from the galley. I really wanted a cup of tea, but couldn't face that curtain of smog, so I hung about Dave's space listening to him chat to the skipper – also called Dave, but known as DG – on the other boat. Our Dave spoke only occasionally, usually an 'aye' mumbled close to the microphone, just enough to trigger the next wave from *Audacious*.

'Twa gannae fuckin' gin nit, noo, nae fuckin', na wha th fuck' sawa th nog bla' fuckin' gan fur heed fur twa fucked fuckers.'

'Aye.'

'At weel a way blather fuck, gan doon ne'er waivers gan fuckin' brae hisself reecht well noo, cam doon th' fuckers gannae aback fuckin' aboot.'

'Aye.'

'Aye. Fuck it, 'n all.'

I got the impression some disaster was unfolding and asked Dave during a pause if all was okay.

'It's fine,' said Dave laughing. 'He's always like this.'

'There's only one word I can understand,' I said.

'His father was worse,' said Dave. 'His father was called Captain Fuck Fuck.'

Audacious was running parallel, about 200 or 300 yards to our starboard. Dave explained they always trawl in this arrangement. The starboard boat shoots the net, while the port boat tethers it. Then, when its *Adorne's* turn to shoot they switch sides. The net is dragged along the seabed between the two boats, a thought which bothers me no matter how much I like my fish and chips. I asked Dave about what's down there on the sea floor, what sort of reefs and habitat might exist. It's mostly sand and mud, he said. Dave was sanguine about the damage done. It's not much more than the impact of the tides, of currents and storms. It recovers quickly enough. He would say that of course. So I checked later and it seemed that the North Sea is mostly sand and mud ... although it also occurred to me that might be because we've been trawling across it for over a hundred years.

Then we hit a snag that wasn't sand or mud. I felt the change, a tremor and the sudden difference in the way the sea-swell hit the boat. The *Audacious* expletive index rose sharply.

'Not good,' said Dave.

Wordlessly, the skippers fell into an instinctive choreography. Dave dropped his speed while *Audacious* went ahead. There was a deadening brake and then sudden relief. The boat surged.

'Sometimes you can make the ropes skip,' said Dave. 'You slow one, speed the other. Change the angle. So our rope must have jumped over whatever it was.'

But the trawl was not a good one. Dave drew alongside as the first net came to the surface, a giant draw-string purse overspilling with glittering, silver fish. I could tell from his face he wasn't happy.

'No good?'

'Nah. Just lots of small cod and haddock,' he said. 'A few herrings.'

Another indecipherable conversation followed, effing this, effing that from *Audacious* Dave, a short reply from us.

'Looks like you'll be meeting the Norwegians, Charlie,' our Dave said when they'd finished. 'Because we're going to Norway.'

'Norway?' I asked, amazed, unnerved.

'Well, most of the way there anyway.' Dave pointed to a square in the middle of the Jackson Pollock squiggle of lines on his computer screen. 'We're heading here.' He might as well have been pointing to somewhere near Jupiter. We were already in the middle of nowhere and we were going further in. Much further.

I asked if we needed permission. We didn't. We have an agreement with Norway. We can fish their waters, they can fish ours.

'But last time we were there we had them onboard for eight-and-a-half hours. Some inspectors are worse than others, of course. You get to know them.'

Dave explained that the Norwegians run a different set of regulations from the Brits and police them differently. We would more than likely be given an embarkation time and place and would have to be there come what may.

'That's when you see who the inspector is,' said Dave. 'And I reckon a little bit of the Germans rubbed off on them during the occupation. If you know what I mean.' Dave laughed.

We do it differently, apparently. We intercept at random and often we don't intercept at all. Especially when the weather is bad. Which, of course, the Norwegians know full well. And when we do catch them, Dave complained, we don't fine them enough. He told me how the British inspectors had recently captured a boat which had been carrying hidden tanks in the hold, pumped full of fish. The skipper had declared a quarter of what he was carrying but was fined only about £10,000. A paltry sum compared to the value of the illegal fish and no kind of discouragement at all.

'The trouble is,' said Dave, 'it's worth the risk.'

'What's the weather look like out that way?' I asked, turning my attention to more pressing matters.

'Ach. It's fine, I'm sure,' said Dave. 'I hardly ever check the weather in summer.'

He called up a chart on a second screen. The sea was scored with crotchets, vertical dashes with smaller dashes hatched crossways at their tail end.

'It looks calm enough,' he said tapping the screen forward hour by hour. The crotchets swirled and clustered. The hatched dashes multiplied.

'Ach. Well. I suppose it stiffens up a wee bit tonight. Twenty-five. Thirty knots. But it's not so bad after that.'

BIG DIPPER

We set off for Norwegian waters. Jakey would get his ten hours' rest after all. The kitchen had cleared by the time I finished chatting to Dave. I grabbed some egg and bacon, a mug of tea and went back to bed. Once again the bunk house was dark, the engine was at full speed and the din was infernal. But somehow I fell asleep.

I woke an hour or two later and felt the swell kicking in, the boat thumping into the waves, rising hard and hanging momentarily before plunging into the next trough. I tried to sit up, but it was too weird. I lay down, suddenly clammy with sweat. This was it. I had hoped against hope we'd avoid rough seas, that my week would be blessed by a mirror calm. But summertime or not, this was the North Sea and it's rarely calm for long.

Flat on my back with my eyes closed I could hold back the nausea. But if I opened them, almost instantly I felt dizzy and fevered as one sense argued with the others. So, eyes shut, I tried to picture the waves and how my body was riding them, up and down, up and down. After a while I could feel the big waves coming. Something in the way the boat faltered for a moment, then rose. Up and up until it was hanging in space. The hull would shudder and flex, and then the boat fell and my whole body fell with it. As the stern lifted our propeller spun wildly in the thin, frothy water. Then, worst of all, as we hit the trough and climbed the next wave a ripple of bubbles would pulse along the hull, a sickening death rattle reverberating at a frequency which seemed to cut right through the steel and through me, deep into the pit of my stomach.

I was pinned to this big dipper, pounding and rolling in the dark, over and over and over. The hours ticked by. Once in a while I lifted my head just enough to force down another sip of water, but when I'd finished the bottle beside me I had no way to get any more. The five-litre container at the foot of my bunk might as well have been onshore in Peterhead. I couldn't even sit up to reach it, let alone decant from it into my drinking bottle. Nor could I climb out of the bunk to reach the tray of Coke cans on the floor. I was trapped, eyes closed in the dark. I had no idea how far into the sail we were. I couldn't even look at my watch and it would have meant nothing if I had.

Then I started to need a pee. Not urgently at first, but as the hours passed the need grew more insistent. I held on until I had no choice. I shifted to the edge of the bunk, ready to jump. It was no good. Instantly a wave of sickness rose and I threw myself back down on to the mattress. The sickness retreated.

But still I needed a pee.

I must have felt every crest and trough of every wave on the North Sea, until – after twelve hours or so – we reached the fishing grounds. The boat slowed and a cry went up from the stairwell: 'Tea-oh. Tea-oh.' The lights came on.

When I looked out all the bunks and the room itself were empty. It was time to try moving too. I hung my legs out of the bunk again and this time forced a jump before I had time to think or hesitate. I landed and steadied myself, or tried to. But the world drained instantly into the stained carpet at my feet while the nausea rose up out of it. I tried to clamber back up to my bunk, catching urgently at anything that would give me some grip. I tried and slipped, tried again and finally hurled myself back inside the swaying aperture of my sanctuary. Thank Christ! I was lying down again. My eyes were closed. I was okay. I hadn't been sick.

But still I needed a pee.

I held on for as long as I could and then tried again. I really had no choice now. Blinded by the agony of my over-inflated bladder and desperately trying not to retch, I made it to the stairs, grabbed the rail and clambered up. At the top I was thrown into the corridor. I caught hold of the rail to the next stairwell and waited for the boat to throw me back into the washroom. Once there I braced myself against the steel wall and ... oh God! The fresh breeze from the toilet porthole cooled my dizzy head and the relief was so intense that for a few seconds I thought I'd be okay. But the toilet door swung wildly and water swilled back and forth across the floor. Rows of oilskins on hooks swayed like dancing, yellow ghosts, mocking me. I wasn't going anywhere, they said. Head pounding, I rushed back at the loo and turned inside out with retching. I retched until there was nothing left, and then I retched some more.

'Are you done now, Charlie?' Michael's unsympathetic voice roused me from my loo-side stupor.

'Will someone please shoot me?' I groaned.

'I need a piss, Charlie. Gan up on deck and get some air aboot yer heed.'

I must have looked like death when I staggered into Dave's cabin. He turned and smiled, but didn't say anything. I looked about. It was dark outside. It must have been Friday night, Saturday morning. I'd lost a full day.

'I need air,' I said. 'Mind if I open the window?'

'No problem,' said Dave. He asked if I'd been keeping up with drinking water. I confessed that I hadn't, mostly because I hadn't been able to get near any. Dave laughed.

'There's a bottle there for you,' he said, nodding at his own supply.

I sipped away at the gift, hanging out the cabin window into the night. There was no horizon, just the inky night and – illuminated by the lights of the boat – those fucking waves. Vast, rolling waves, the height of the boat, or so they appeared. One moment within touching distance, the next falling away beyond sight, the boat falling with them. Outside the window sticky, migrainous diesel fumes wafted through the cool night air. But every time I turned my face back inside it was into a warm brew of cigarettes and deep-fried heat. Before long I was sick again. I hung inelegantly out of Dave's window and spewed into the night, trying to apologise between heaves.

'We've all been there, Charlie,' he said, reassuringly. 'When I first went to sea I was sick for eight months.'

'Don't tell me that,' I moaned. 'I want to know it'll get better.'

'Ach. The wind'll die down tomorrow right enough. This shallow water settles out pretty quickly. You'll be okay by then.'

'I'll be dead by then.'

'I reckon you're best off in your bunk just now,' said Dave.

I felt I might just make it back there. I took my water bottle, staggered down the stairs and posted myself through the swaying letterbox of my bunk and stayed there, without moving, for twelve more hours, sipping just enough water to stay alive. But not enough to need another pee.

When next I climbed up to Dave's bridge he turned in his swivel chair and smiled warmly, as if greeting someone who had risen from the grave.

'Well then, Charlie,' he said. 'Feeling better? You've a bit of colour to your cheeks now. And you'll not find a flatter sea than this either.'

It must have been Saturday evening. The sun was lowering in the west, sparkling off an unruffled North Sea. It was a relief to get up out of the smoky bowels of the ship. Through the foggy anaesthesia of the previous twenty-four hours I had still noticed that Dave spent little time downstairs. I asked if he smoked too.

'I cannae fuckin' stand it,' he said.

'Well we've that much in common,' I said.

Dave had been into sports when he was younger and still liked to keep himself fit. Judo. Karate. Football. Looking at the build of him I wondered if he hadn't thought about rugby. Dave smiled like it was an obvious thing to ask, but there hadn't been much rugby in northeast Scotland when he was growing up. There still wasn't. He hadn't always been the size he was now, either. When Dave was eighteen or so he was playing a lot of football and worked as an engineer. He had some trials and might have gone on to play semi-professionally, but probably no higher. He was earning £18 a week and his mates on boats were earning hundreds. His father was on a trawler too, but it was Dave's auntie's sister-in-law who got him his first work. He went to sea on a Saturday, came back on the Tuesday with £274. He didn't look back and has been at sea ever since.

'That was serious money back in the 1970s when you could buy a pair of jeans for a fiver.'

It was very physical in those early days. You'd haul the nets on board and scoop the fish by hand into boxes on the foredeck. You'd gut them out there – in all weathers – and lower the boxes one by one into the hold. Now all that takes place below deck, the fish on a conveyor. I'd seen the guys at it on the way up, all in a row in their oilskins, gutting one fish after the other. It still looked like hard work to me.

Navigation is different now. Sitting where I was, the only place out of the way on a little wooden bench under the window, I was surrounded by computer screens, blinking in pixellated hieroglyphics: screens like Space Invaders, others like Etch-a-Sketch in the hands of an overactive child. Every so often Dave would punch a button, or scroll through different windows, all a mess of lines and triangles. I couldn't make head nor tail of them.

This all makes it easy, Dave explained, dismissing my bafflement. This one shows where we are. This one the depth and the type of ground. And the little blobs floating above are fish. Simple.

There was a lot more skill in the wheelhouse back when he started when most of the stuff now animated on these computer screens was in Dave's head. He had his own charts for shoots in certain areas, but would write down as little as possible for fear it would be stolen, and would as often as not know where he was from the depth of water and the type of seabed. More formally, navigation was done with a system called Decca, developed in the war, and more complicated than latitude and longitude. Radar stations arranged around a triangle would ping out signals, the master signal at the centre and red, green and purple signals at the tips of the triangle. The boats would know where they were from the relative positioning of the radar signals.

'The red clock went from 0 to 23, green from 30 to 47 and purple from 50 to 79. Then the sectors from A to J. So, you'd maybe get D 30 and you'd maybe get 50 in the purple and that would put you there. Or maybe you'd get 33, 55 in the purple and that would put you about there.'

Decca was more accurate than its rivals and the company that made the receivers had a corner on the market. But even so the readings were often wrong, especially first thing in the morning. You'd shoot your nets, then come back and Decca would pick up the mark and it would be two miles off where it should have been.

'It's things like that you learn,' said Dave. 'But most of the stuff I held in my head. People could take my charts and they'd find nothing in them. And that's the way you wanted it!'

Dave was at his plan chest now, opening drawers I guessed he hadn't opened in years. He pulled out some old charts, and finally a map of the entire North Sea so I could get an idea where we were and the line we'd sailed along. He'd had this chart since the early days, he said, showing me that we were now into Norwegian waters and a long, long way from home.

'So, tell me about the boats you've sailed. You've ordered a new one, but you must develop an affection for them over the years.'

'Well, you do. My first one I did because I was there when it was built. My second one I did because I was involved building it. I saw the project through from keel to the finished article and I sailed in it. I made money in it. My last one was not such a great success.'

Dave's face seemed to darken slightly with the memory of it. He'd had two boats, in fact. A pair team. But one had sprung a leak and sank. Dave remembered the date and recited it like he'd never forget – 4 November 1994. He tried to carry on 'fly-shooting' with the other boat for a while, but eventually he gave up on that and ordered a big new trawler from Poland, designed to go after the deep-water coley, a cod-like fish on which there were no quota restrictions. Then, within two years of the investment, the government clamped down on that previously unlimited fishery. Dave had a big boat on which he owed money and was forced into 'blackfish', the industry term for unlicensed fish. He went to the bank to borrow money to buy quotas and get legal again, and that was when one of his crew drove the boat aground. They were steaming home to land their catch and the guy who was on watch turned off the pilot alarm. It was the biggest tide in fifty years and the boat went straight over the beach. It was horrific, said Dave, recalling the sight of his trawler marooned in a field. They had to get her off that night or they'd never have done it at all, but it took four boats to drag the beached trawler back into the sea and she was never right after that. Dave had trouble with the engine, the gearboxes and he had trouble making the boat profitable. When the decommissioning scheme came, the bank asked Dave to put up more collateral.

'They were putting in nothing,' said Dave. 'So that was the end of it. We decommissioned.'

This was after the first reform of the Common Fisheries Policy, when the commission had tried to address the massive overcapacity of European fleets. Subsidies, the accession of Spain in 1986 – whose fleet had historically been boosted out of all proportion by General

Franco – technical advances in fishing methods and fishermen competing for a limited, shared resource, had all led to a repeat, on a grander scale, of the overfishing Graham and Russell had witnessed after the two wars, the same that Walter Garstang and all those old-timer fisherman had observed at the tail end of the nineteenth century. There were far too many boats and not enough fish. 'Decommissioning' was part of the attempt to reform what was so obviously not working: in 1992 and again but more so in 2002, member states were called upon to reduce the size of their fishing fleets. Dave became a part of that drive and sold his boat up for scrap.

'It was one of the worst things I ever did, decommission my boat. It was twenty years of hard work.'

COAL, STEEL AND FISH

To see things from Dave's point of view we need to go back a bit. We all know something of the story: there's a general background awareness that in some way or other the United Kingdom's fishermen took a hit when we joined the Common Market, when they were kicked out of Iceland's Exclusion Zone and came home hoping to set up their own only to discover they now had to share theirs with the rest of Europe. Like the Irish remember Cromwell and the British Dunkirk, fishermen know every last detail.

It goes like this: the six signatory nations to the 1958 Treaty of Rome were Belgium, France, Italy, Luxembourg, the Netherlands and West Germany. We called it the Common Market. They called it the European Economic Community. The difference is key. As a 'nation of shopkeepers', the British have always seen the EEC/EU as an economic project, whereas in reality it was a political project *by means* of an economic one, and had been from the beginning when in 1950 the French foreign minister Robert Schuman drafted a plan for the unification of French and German coal and steel production under the control of one authority: 'Europe will not be made all at once,' Schuman wrote, ' ... it will be built through achievements which create a de facto solidarity'. For Schuman the pooling of economic interests between nations that had so recently been torn to pieces by war was the means to create political unity and peace, not an end in itself. Abstract distinctions but deeply relevant, as it turned out, to fish, to a Common Fisheries Policy that hasn't really worked, and to the difficulties of reforming it.

The UK did not join the European Coal and Steel Community then, nor was it present at the Treaty of Rome. Though Clement Attlee was on the ropes by 1950, he summed up Labour's instinctive hostility to the idea when he said that there was no way Britain could accept that 'the most vital economic forces of the country be handed over to an authority that is utterly undemocratic and account-able to nobody'. The Conservatives were much more positive. Macmillan asked a rising star – Edward Heath – to lead negotiations for an application to join in 1963. French president Charles de Gaulle vetoed, but by 1971 de Gaulle was dead and Edward Heath was prime minister of a new Conservative government. Heath passion-ately believed in the European project and under his lead the UK tried again.

Iceland, meanwhile, had extended its Economic Exclusion Zone to fifty miles and, along with the rest of the world, was preparing to push it out to 200. In a crowded European seascape the spectre of these exclusion zones was a profound threat to states without much in the way of coastline or access to the fertile North Sea fisheries: the six signatories to the Treaty of Rome, for example. Even those with their own coastline were threatened: the French fleet caught much if not most of its fish in waters that would soon be exclusively British. The establishment of these 200-mile zones meant that the four hopeful applicants of the early 1970s – the UK,

Denmark, Norway and Ireland – would soon control, according to internationally accepted law, the majority of the most productive fishing around the coasts of Europe. Fish were about to join coal and steel as a key building block of that 'de facto solidarity'.

On the morning of 30 June 1970, hours before the applications for membership were handed in, the pre-existing party of six passed the innocuously titled but thunderous Fisheries Regulation 2140/70. It stated that: 'Member states shall ensure equal conditions of access to and use of the fishing grounds situated in the waters referred to in the preceding subparagraph [ie. waters coming under the sovereignty of member states] for all fishing vessels flying the flag of a member state and registered in Community territory'. Basically it said that if you want to join, we all get access to your fishing grounds. For a nation whose fishing industry was such a large part of its cultural identity, this was a tough swallow and an even tougher sell for Edward Heath.

The prime minister did manage to wangle something called a derogation (a time-limited exception to the rule) and retained for the UK exclusive fishing rights within six miles of the coast and partial control from six to twelve: luckily for Heath, but unluckily for British fishermen, debates over the precise nature of the derogation threw a smokescreen over the bigger loss of the next 188 miles. Even then, there is a feeling within the fishing community that Heath was economical with the truth in order to get his way. During the debate over the second reading of the European Communities Bill, Harold Wilson asked how the derogation might be extended after its expiry in ten years: 'there is no automatic continuation of the temporary provisions (derogation) with a veto on attempts to end them', he suggested. 'With respect to the honourable gentlemen opposite,' Heath said in his reply, 'we have the right of veto.' The bill to join the EEC was passed with a majority of only eight votes. But Wilson had been right, the derogation could only be renewed by the unanimous agreement of all member states. There was no UK veto.

For a while at least, the bitterness of the pill was sweetened with the prospect of reciprocal rights in Norwegian and Danish waters. Only our timing was poor. The Norwegians, who took more time to study what they were signing up to, balked at the implications for their high-seas fisheries and voted against accession then and again twenty years later. In 2013 Iceland shied at the same hurdle. They had both seen what a mess we'd made.

Twenty years on in 1992 and now almost at the edge of the fish-extinction cliff, the commission set fleet-reduction targets that didn't work. Thirty years on at the start of the new millennium and teetering ever more precariously over the edge, the commission removed the targets and instead called on member states voluntarily to adjust the fishing capacity of their fleets 'to suit the available fishing opportunities'. Over the next few years, under these voluntary guidelines, Alpine glaciers shrank more quickly than the EU fleet, whose 2% annual diminution barely kept pace with the technical advances that were steadily improving catch rates per boat. The commission had recognised that reducing the size of the fleet was the most fundamentally important issue at stake, and yet across two reform cycles had failed to make any inroads. Real reductions depend on the will of member states – the commission observed in their response to a 2007 House of Lords progress report – to establish a balance between capacity and resources: 'we do not, however, see political will amongst most member states'.

Three decades into this 'de facto solidarity' and to the British fishermen there was very little solidarity about it ... except of course equal access to the fish. As Sweden's fisheries minister wryly observed of France and Spain, having built up the fishing fleets with taxpayers' money for forty years, it was difficult for politicians to reduce them again.

Not so in the UK. Our government reported to the House of Lords in a much more upbeat fashion: *we* had delivered a 60% reduction in the white-fish trawling effort. Even the commission singled out the 'painful' reductions in Scotland as one of the notable successes of the EU's efforts to help fish stocks recover. No matter which way up I held this House of Lords report it felt to me as if only one or two countries in this community called Europe were actually doing any housekeeping. No wonder Dave was peeved.

'So, how long have you sailed in the *Adorne*?'

'Fourteen years maybe. To be quite honest the time has just flown. I've hummed and hayed about this. It's a big challenge again, at my age of life. I'm fifty-two this year. You get to that age you should be winding down. Not going up again.'

Dave admits that his wife would rather he stopped altogether. They could sell up and get out comfortably enough. Dave could get another job. But Dave has been his own boss for thirty years and working for someone else is not his way. Besides he still enjoys the work, and after all the pain of decommissioning, fish stocks had never been better.

Something the rest of the crew had been saying, too: it's never been easier to catch fish. But *Adorne* is long in the tooth now, and absorbing as much money in maintenance as Dave would have to pay out in interest. She's a good sea boat – Dave laughed about how sick I'd have been in the pair-boat *Audacious* – and someone will buy her. For what she's worth Dave reckoned you'd have to be a poor fisherman not to make it work. But even so, it won't be easy.

'The young guys want new. They want better. I started in an old wooden boat my first time as the skipper. To get a boat like this would've been a dream. That's what used to happen when the older guys built a new boat. The mate would automatically come along in here and it was passed along the lines. If the mate wanted it the office backed him and he got the boat.'

I could see how that would lead to proliferation in the fleet. Now perhaps the opposite is the problem. No one is coming into the industry. The two youngsters on Dave's boat – Frankie and Johnny – were from the Philippines and I'd noticed quite a few lads from the Philippines or south Asia around the docks at Peterhead. Dave was looking for an engineer and couldn't find one. Clearly there were jobs, but the rest of the crew had remarked that most fishermen had gone ashore now or moved off into the oil industry. I asked Dave why it was so tricky getting younger Scots into fishing. Was it the money?

'The money is not good enough. That is one problem. But it's the bad press too, I'd say. The industry has been driven down and down. TV chefs, the media. But yes, the money needs to be better.'

As I tried to understand what kind of future there might be for British high-seas fishing, I found we'd circulate round certain topics, coming in each time from a new angle, but back to the same old problems, again and again: quotas, discarding fish, the media, politics. It seemed to reflect the unfathomable architecture of all these things, because each problem seemed contingent on the one before and each shaped the one after, round and round in a cat's cradle of cause and effect. The problem of money in this particular conversation circled back to the aftermath of the decommissioning process and a rotten core of quota ownership.

To go fishing you need quotas, because without them you can't land or sell what you catch. The quotas are based in part on the historical record of an individual skipper or boat or even national fleet – in that sense they are something of a right. The Spanish fleet, for example, has a much larger quota for hake than the Scottish, because traditionally it is a fish they have caught more of. But as much as they are a right for a given skipper, or national fleet to catch certain fish, quotas double as a conservation measure, an apportionment of a finite resource. Dave has a larger quota for haddock than cod, for example, because of the attempt to revive cod stocks. But because quotas are also a licence to market something of value, it is a tradable commodity, a currency almost.

The problem for Dave and every other skipper, is that when the fleet was decommissioned – from the days when it was too large and too many boats were chasing a fast-diminishing stock – a lot of the quotas found their way into the hands of a coterie of banks and corporations or were kept by ex-skippers who managed to sell their boats but retain their quotas: the infamous 'slipper skippers'. And these institutions now lease their quotas to real skippers, much as a large landowner might lease acres to a farmer.

'Pisses me right off,' says Dave. Dave lost his quotas in the decommissioning process – they went to the bank – and now he doesn't own enough to make his operation viable. He has to hire them to get a licence to land fish, but he also has to hire them – and this I will emphasise – *to make sure he doesn't top out on one species before he has caught his quota of another.*

He is over a barrel, forced to hire quotas without much hope of making money on the deal. Dave hires cod at £1,350 to £1,500 a ton, but as often as not he'll only get £1.50 a kilo at the market. Dave really only makes money on the cod quota he owns, but he's paying money to land cod, so that he can keep on catching other species like haddock. As it stands, the money out of each week at sea is only a fraction of what it could be if the quotas weren't wrapped up in the hands of people and institutions who aren't fishing themselves.

'You're still having to pay the costs of the ship, and pay a crew. But there's nothing left to pay them. These are the things, I'd say, why you cannot get youngsters back.'

PURSES OF SILVER

I spent my days like this, chatting with Dave about the unfathomable mess of our fishing regulations, or occasionally in the galley, in lulls between the bouts of smoking, or when the crew were busy gutting fish. But the galley's heat, the stink of cigarettes and deep-frying, made it a tough place to spend time. I tried my bunk, but how long can you spend in a wooden coffin below the waterline, next to the pounding din of the engine and propeller? The galley, my bunk, the small bench in Dave's wheelhouse: there was nowhere else to go. So, I circulated between the three, lingering in each until I had either bored Dave with my company or bored myself with the unchanging view of the bunk ceiling or started to feel ill in the greasy sweatbox of the galley.

Relief came every three or four hours, night and day, in the form of a new haul. I would grab my camera and lose myself in photographing the crew at work.

From my bunk I would feel the boat dive, suddenly offbeat to the rhythm of the sea. A moment later another deep nod into the swell. A grinding of gears. Chains clanking across the deck. The boat dipping again as the winches began their work, cranking into the resistance of the net. Then raised voices. Instructions shouted over the mechanical din. The engine slowing to a heartbeat chug. Soon we'd be bobbing about like corks on the sea as the winch wound in the fishy treasure of our nets.

These really were purses of silver. Underwater the net is shaped like a vast, pointed parachute, tethered by bridles at its four corners. The bridles hang off trawl doors, one each side and these spread the net open. But as it is drawn in, the net collapses and appears at the surface as a long, trailing cylinder of yellow mesh and glistening fish, the water all about sparkling with scales and coated in a thin rainbow-film of fish oil. Thousands of gulls appear, as if from nowhere, swooping and pecking at the smaller fish which have drifted belly up through the mesh. Soon the sea is flecked with gulls and fish, like white and silver leaves on a rolling river. As the net is hauled in, the fish inside it roll deeper and deeper towards the 'cod end', until it hangs beside the boat, a meshed purse bursting at its seams and spilling over with money.

Even the etymology of this pendulous sack of fish is circular: cod derives from Middle English *codde* (meaning bag, purse or pouch), and is similar to the Dutch *kodde* (scrotum), Danish *kodde* (testicle) and Icelandic *koddi* (pillow). But no one quite knows what is named after what. Is the cod called the cod because it is caught in a net shaped like a purse, or because it has a sack-like appearance, or because it is fecund like a testicle? Or is the cod end called the cod end because of the fish caught in it?

However it was named, these Norwegian grounds were worth the journey because our cod ends were full ... of haddock.

'There's just a helluva lot of cod about in the North Sea,' Dave said. 'And this week is all about avoiding them. Good for us, because we have lots of haddocks to catch.'

The boats took huge hauls on Sunday. The first went to *Audacious*. So many fish that the final two lifts of the cod end were hoisted on to our boat so that the crews could share the job of cleaning and sorting them all. Everyone was happy, in spite of the work. Big hauls were good news, because they meant more money in the kitty and that we'd be home sooner. But they also meant no sleep.

The rhythm of the working day was remorseless. When Jakey complained about the first run from port and how it would be the longest they'd rest all week, he was not exaggerating. But for the subsequent twelve-hour sail to Norwegian waters, from the moment the first net is dropped the crews are working cycles of three-hour shifts. The first boat drops its net and the trawl last three hours. Time enough then, right at the beginning of things, for both crews to get something to eat and an hour or two in the bunk. But once that first net comes up, one or other or both crews are gutting fish, more or less non-stop for the rest of the voyage. If things pan out evenly the crew which has just trawled gets time at the gutting table, while the other crew grab a couple of hours' rest. But a big haul takes the duration of the next trawl to process, sometimes longer. If one or other boat hauls in a really big load, so big they must share it with the other trawler, then the work is almost never-ending. The crews are either dropping or hauling nets, or gutting and processing and stacking fish in the icehouse. When one job stops, the other begins.

The dangling sack of fish hangs for a moment in mid-air while Frankie wrestles free the knot that ties the cod end. It gives suddenly, the sack bursts open and the fish rumble like thunder into the metal chute below. Frankie reties the knot. Checks it once. Twice. A fumbled tie would lose the boat hundreds of pounds' worth of fish. Happy, he steps back. Michael levers the crane and drops the net back into the sea. The rope attached to the cod end pulls tight and the chain moves up the cylinder of fish, lifts again, cinches it and hauls the next dripping sack-load over the gunwale. Frankie slips the knot and another ton of fish thunders onboard: scoop after scoop, until the chute is bulging over with the slowly expiring bounty of the sea.

If the closest you've got to cod or haddock is the fillet wrapped in paper at your local chippy, there's little to prepare you for the mesmerising volume of a haul, or the grim, air-gulping death masks of those fish, their eyes agog, their bodies squeezed inside the mesh like half-finished toothpaste tubes. The haddock with their black eyes and clownish red lipstick – each and every one the perfect size for a fish supper – shine like white bars from amongst the spotted, lumpen slabs of cod. No matter how hard Dave was trying to avoid them, each haul brought more cod: vast green things the likes of which I thought had been consigned to history and old photographs from Grimsby. Given that only a few years ago the North Sea's stock of mature cod was thought close to a no-return threshold, these carcasses might at least indicate that our runaround week was working: the decommissioning, the imperfection of quotas, the monitoring of vessels, albeit inadequate and inconsistent, these things were all helping bring a fish back from the brink. Maybe. I mentioned the story of the Grand Banks to Dave, how there had been no fishing there for decades and yet still the cod had not returned.

'I'm certain the same will happen to Norway because they're taking far too many cod. Their total catch – North Sea and Barents – is about half a million tons. Our total catch for the UK is about 12,000 tons! That's the difference! So, they have to get rid of it all somewhere and the UK becomes one of the big dumping grounds for it.'

It isn't always a level playing field out here on the North Sea. This huge Norwegian cod harvest is – most of it – frozen at sea and yet it hammers down the price of the UK's fresh cod, making life so precarious for Dave and those crews that bring wet, fresh fish to the market. British chippies have come to rely on these frozen fillets, not least because a big problem over the years of decommissioning was the reliability of supply of a fresh alternative. Our reduced national fleet has lost market to the dull reliability of frozen fillets, most from non-EU suppliers. I had often wondered about this, how as the British fleet went through the pain of decommissioning the price of cod in the chippy remained more or less the same. It turns out that while our fleet is no longer raping the sea, we – the consumers – still are. At least when we are not particular about where our chip-shop fillets come from.

'The chippy goes to his laptop and sees: "Frozen at sea, size-three haddocks, such and such a kilo and delivered." If you talk to retailers or fish and chip restaurants, most of their trouble is "who can supply it?" And that's the problem we have. Because in bad weather or under certain circumstances a boat doesnae go out. Even some of our local fish and chip shops use frozen fish. Round Peterhead! Yellow tinge. You know it right away.'

Once the chute is full to the brim – and it was, with more to spare, several times over on Sunday – the remaining fish go to the other boat. Then, filleting knives tucked into their caps, the guys move quickly from the deck to the gutting room. One or two stay behind tidying up, but before long the nets are rolled and they are all – Michael, Jakey, Jake, Richard, Frankie and Johnny – lined up behind the conveyor, swaying backwards and forwards with the rhythm of the sea, heads down as they gut and sort the fish. Arrayed in front of them, the far side of the conveyor, a row of metal bins, one for each species: cod, haddock, saithe, whiting, ling, plaice. Along the conveyor are the expired or still-expiring bodies of thousands and thousands of fish.

The guys work with ferocious speed and precision, rummaging through the pile – if there's a pattern it's biggest first – hooking thumb into gill, their sharp stubby knives quickly slitting the fish open anus to gullet. The guts spill on to the conveyor in marbled, glinting heaps, one on top of the other, until the last man – always Jakey – pulls the few remaining fish out from under a pile of innards. Primary colours – a blue blur of rubber gloves, the shiny yellow of oilskins and the splattered crimson of blood and guts and gills – contrast with the pewter white and silver grey of the fish. The smell is intense, but not bad. It is the smell of the ocean, but condensed and stirred in with diesel fumes and cigarettes and fish shit. It is cloying, cold, oily.

Soon the deck streams with crimson, fishy water, ankle deep as it swills back and forth. The bins fill and once in a while Jakey steps out from behind the conveyor, goes round to the far side and releases a wave of fish and water through a metal hatch. They wash down the slide and are lifted from this cleansing river by a belted paddle, up and over and down another chute into the fish hold below. It takes a long time to clear the catch. From where I'm standing to take my photographs I can see the layer-cake of fish through the metal slats of the chute, the fish piled six feet high. As the belt jerks forward, slices of this cake are pulled from its underside and a shiny carpet of fish appears: haddock, the odd ling or plaice, whiting. And those vast cod, some with haddocks sunk head-first inside their gaping, python jaws.

Both crews were hard at it all through Sunday. Hauling fish, gutting fish. No one ate until late in the evening.

JONAH

After a few days at sea I felt well enough to offer a turn at the gutting table. The one thing I could do, I thought, was gut fish. But the offer was declined – for fear I'd stab myself, probably – and I don't suppose I really minded. Five minutes of that and I'd almost certainly have been sick again. I made some of the crew coffee instead and later I even felt well enough to brave the galley at suppertime. Richard had knocked up 'mince and tatties'. I spooned myself a healthy plateful.

'That's more fucking like it, Charlie,' said Jake, in approval. 'Get some fucking food inside yer. Get some colour in yer cheeks.'

'This is great,' I said, scoffing it like John Hurt in *Alien* just before the monster bursts through his ribcage.

'Tell us about this book of yours,' said Jakey. 'Why are you here?'

I told them how a few years ago I'd made a film in Japan about fish and fishing and Japanese culture and how I'd thought at the time there were parallels back home. Maybe not the lobster-vending machines so much, but the way fish and fishing were tied up with our history. Only here it is different, I said, because in Japan those ties are still very much alive, whereas here I feel they're fading.

'You're dead right they are,' said Jakey.

I worried that I'd put my foot in it, but of course these guys would be more aware of that decline than anyone. It was, after all, what we spoke about throughout the week.

There was no football match on that evening, just some programme about farming which no one was watching. Michael was sitting on the bench to my right, his back to the wall, an iPad in his lap. Richard finished clearing pans and sat down to join us at the table.

'So you're writing about cod and haddock?'

'Yeah. I'm writing about fish which are a major part of our history. Cod is one, of course. Cod and the sea in general.'

'What else?' asked Jake.

'Well, then I'm heading inland. To write about carp.'

'Carp!?'

'Of course! All those medieval fish ponds and monks and bloody huge fish in lost lakes. And nowadays, every other magazine in Smiths is about carp. Half the country observes Sunday worship at the side of a carp pond.'

'Fuck knows why. What else?'

'Eels too. I'm writing about eels. Go back to the Domesday Book and it's all eels. All the mills and manors are valued in terms of eels. They were like wriggly money.'

'Ha. Cod is money. Is that it?'

'Er ... no. There's salmon too, of course. My fish.'

'Oh no!' Jakey hung his head in his hands. Michael looked up suddenly.

'What?' I asked.

Jakey just shook his head.

'What? What did I say?'

'Nothing,' said Jakey. 'Nothing.'

Michael laughed up the last draw on his cigarette. 'Nothing,' he said, as if he didn't believe the 'nothing', not for a minute.

'You said the red fish, is all,' said Jakey.

'Here we go,' said Michael.

'What? Salmon?'

'Dennae say it again! For fuck's sake!'

'Okay. Sorry. But you did ask me what fish I was writing about. I mean it was kind of obvious one of them would be a fucking sa—' I caught sight of Richard shaking his head and stopped myself. 'A "red fish",' I said.

'He's very superstitious,' said Jake.

If I'd briefly passed some kind of test with the crew, I had now failed it again. Monday brought up two more good hauls, but on the second of these the net broke. Jakey wagged his finger at me and said, 'You broke it.' He had half a smile about his face, like he knew he shouldn't be saying such a thing, that it was ridiculous. But I could tell that he was dead serious. I felt like the man who shot the albatross. And I was pissed off that anyone would take that kind of mumbo-jumbo seriously and at my expense. Especially after I'd bought the yellow wellies.

The rest of the crew went downstairs to gut the haul – they'll be at it for hours, said Dave – and Jakey was left on deck repairing the net. Thinking I ought to get out of his way I followed the others down to take pictures in the gutting room. I went into the galley to catch up on my notes. I made a cup of tea and dawdled long enough to think Jakey might have finished. But when I came back up Jakey was still at it, knife tucked inside his TaylorMade golf cap, cigarette drooping from his lips, the ash just about to fall. He looked up and shook his finger at me again.

I backed away in to the wheelhouse and asked Dave how it was going. Dave was quiet.

'Sorry?' he asked, after a moment.

'Any progress ... on the net?'

'No. It's slow.' Dave nodded in the direction of Jakey. 'He's not a happy chappy anyway.'

'He's blaming me.'

Dave said nothing. Was Dave blaming me too?

'He is very superstitious,' Dave said after a moment.

'I'm guessing that. It's lucky I ditched the green coat and wellies.'

'He wouldn't be bothered by green,' said Dave. 'It's just that one word he doesn't like. In fact there's another one, but I'll tell you about that some other time.'

Dave was chatting to DG on the other boat. In between the 'fucks' and the mostly indecipherable remainder I picked out they were talking about the weather. The wind was due to pick up on Tuesday, which would be bad for the fishing. The fish tend to lift off the seabed in bad weather and that makes it harder to catch them. Dave showed me the map, scrolling through the days ahead. As he did so the wind crotchets changed from a benign green with one little tag to a more menacing red with several, showing that the weather was due to take another dive.

'Not so good for you,' said Dave. 'You've got maybe twenty-four hours to get everything you need, your notes, your photos.'

I must have gone pale.

'Ach. It'll maybe be okay again by the time we're heading in.'

I stepped outside and took a few pictures of Jakey snipping at the ropes, folding, unravelling, retying. He was very patient and obviously good at what he was doing.

'So, have you done this before, Jakey?' I asked.

'Aye.'

'So, you've broken nets when I wasn't on the boat?'

He came brandishing the knife at me, half a smile on his face.

'It's his fault,' he said to Dave. 'He said the S word over supper.'

'Don't give me that shit,' I said. 'I bought a blue coat just for you and now I find there are secret words I must never say ... only I don't know what fucking words they are!'

'Just dennae say the fuckin' S word,' said Jakey, heading back to his nets.

'You mentioned the red fish,' said Dave, laughing. 'Bad news. He's banned pork too. The Filipinos brought a head back, ears, snout, the lot. Jakey saw it in the oven. Threw a fit. Threw it overboard and banned it there and then.'

Only I didn't quite hear it all as clearly as that. And so I asked, dumbly walking into the trap: 'You mean they had a pig on board?'

'Ach shit!' said Dave. 'You said it now!'

'Bollocks! This is like a game of Animal Minefield. Jakey's banned pork?! So how come we're eating bacon every morning?' I said leaning out the door so Jakey could hear me.

Jakey had fixed the net by the time it was *Adorne*'s turn to trawl. But then a hawser snagged at the stern as we paid out the net. By the time anyone noticed it was too late. The hawser had pulled tight almost to breaking point over the gunwale, and was ripping out to sea in a shower of sparks. Within seconds it had worn a deep groove in the metal, which only trapped it further. Jakey, cursing and stamping his feet, took a hammer to the metal clasp and smashed it open and sent the hawser snapping violently back in line with the crane, while the net spun itself into a tangle behind us. I came back inside the wheelhouse to hear Jakey saying that it was all my fault for saying 'bad words'.

Lurking just under the surface of this sophisticated twenty-first-century fishing operation was a living voodoo, a sense that out here on the capricious sea you made your luck, or broke it, by respecting or transgressing taboos. Dave was only joking. So – perhaps – was Jakey. Even so, I was starting to feel the power of it all.

Then, in fixing the first break, we created a second. Dave had to run the hawser further back into the hub, exposing older, rustier metal. As the line paid out once more, so did an old weak spot. I watched it fizz past me down the deck, the smooth silver of the hawser momentarily morphed into a rusted, splayed frazzle. The frayed wire shot over the crane like an old witch's broom and flew out into the deep, the effervescent fizz of the running cable suddenly a sickening series of hollow clangs followed by a deep splash.

'Ach! Fuck it!' Dave fumed silently at the window; paced the cabin. 'Fuck it!' He flicked a switch. He went back to the window, looked out and sighed. Finally he called DG on the two-way radio and said he'd lost 'the whole fucking rope', that it was going to take a while.

There was a big part of me that wanted to disappear below deck and get away from this cursed luck. But a bigger part of me didn't want to dignify, or make real, the superstition by giving in to it. So I stayed.

The crew moved in wordless synchronicity about the deck. They had to splice a new rope together, and recover their broken rope from the bottom of the sea. Dave paced up and down. Every so often the volcanic frustration spilled over and he went to the window to shout another set of instructions. But the job took forever. Frankie and Johnny were under the window hammering away at a reluctant metal peg in a link when Dave – all out of patience – threw on his jacket and burst out of the door. He startled Johnny who missed his aim and caught Jake a striking blow on the hand. Jake stood up, biting his lip and shaking his hand. The peg would not give. I was about to suggest they try hot water when Jakey appeared with an angle grinder and set about the hawser like Vulcan in a golfing cap.

I tried several times to work out how all the cables and chains worked, the precise alignment of what linked with what as the winches flew and sections of chain, then rope, then chain flashed back and forth through pulleys, on and off winches. It was impossible. Ignorant of what the hell was going on whenever the nets were sent out or taken in, I tucked myself into corners and just watched. The crew moved from one post to the next, signalling instructions, when to start or stop on a winch, or pulley.

Jake spotted me and took a moment out of this silent, dangerous ballet to lean in at the door of the wheelhouse and say: 'You're a Jonah, Charlie.'

'Not you too,' I said.

'Hey,' he said, checking I'd heard. 'You're a fuckin' Jonah.'

Dave laughed after him. 'They want to keel-haul you, Charlie. For saying bad words.'

NO COMPRENDE! NO COMPRENDE!

'We'll make a trawlerman of you yet, Charlie,' Dave said as he came into the galley on Tuesday morning to find me tucking into a full fry-up. The Jonah curse had been lifted. On calmer seas and away from the rocky ground which had taken such a toll on the nets, both trawlers took good hauls.

It was Dave who bore the weight of the whole voyage – the crew's wages, the diesel, the ice, the bought-in quotas – and sometimes you could see it. All these things needed to be paid for no matter what. But the good hauls on Monday took us past break-even and into profit. So long as a big landing by a Norwegian boat did not yet undo our week. Dave checked the latest prices at market.

'Reckon we'll do okay,' he said. 'Should be back in by Thursday.'

Whenever I went up to the wheelhouse Dave was at the helm. I don't know how he sustained those hours in his captain's chair, surrounded by screens to which he paid constant attention. He looked dog-tired sometimes, just Dave and the sea and those beeping screens. He told me about the things he saw up here when he was on his own: the Northern Lights, meteor showers, whales and bluefin tuna. He kept thinking he should get a camera. All he had was his phone.

DG must have been keeping the same watch on *Audacious*. Every so often he'd radio in and begin an expletive-filled soliloquy about ropes or net pressure or trawling speed. DG going on and on, Dave replying in short, quiet and – to me – indecipherable Scots.

Jakey appeared at the window to give Dave the latest tally, reciting the boxes of fish now packed in the hold. Dave took notes and filled in his papers. He notified the authorities, as he was obliged to.

'Papers, papers, papers,' he said, bunching the stuff into two fists and making to throw it all over the floor. 'When I first started skippering there was nothing. The paperwork I came away to sea with was nothing. And now there's bags of it. It's never-ending. I could spend two or three hours a day on paperwork if I wanted to.'

It didn't take much to get Dave on to the disparity in monitoring out here in the contested – and shared – North Sea.

'Our own administration patrols us heavily. That's the frustrating thing for us fishermen: we know what our guys are landing and discarding. But we haven't a clue what they're doing.' Dave meant the Norwegians, the Spanish. 'Our guys don't board those boats. The crews are alongside but they cannot get aboard: "*No comprende! No comprende!*" They get aboard us no problem!'

I asked about the cameras above the fish-gutting conveyors, yet another form of monitoring. Dave had agreed to them in exchange for more days at sea. They recorded all the fish that went down the belt and this could be tallied up with Dave's declared catch. It was a trial for the new discard bans, the latest in a long list of innovations that have changed fishing from the bad old days of unfettered exploitation.

'You've got tow. Mesh size. Bigger mesh on the cod end. Real-Time Closures. Just now if this boat catches more than forty cod per hour, then theoretically they'll close this area. There's Spawning Stock Closures. Marine Conservation Zones. All these things have helped the cod, I'd say,' Dave explained. 'We've still got a long way to go, but the stocks are recovering. That's the main thing for us, for future generations. For everyone really. For the good of the industry. The long-term good. Even when I'm gone there'll be something left for someone else to come along.'

I might have assumed in the context of Dave's obvious support for anything that might save stocks, even from his acknowledgement of how the pain of decommissioning had also helped, that Dave would support the discard ban too.

As an angler who vexes himself stupid about whether or not to kill a single salmon when I catch one – I'll take one every so often, but only if I know I'll eat it that day and that the river can afford the loss – the idea of throwing back dead or dying, but edible fish had always bothered me. I knew that trawlermen did it, but not why; I had probably ascribed it to greed: throw back the cheap ones, fill the hold with the expensive ones. Then I read Charles Clover's book and found that the practice had as much, if not more, to do with the muddled Common Fisheries Policy. But either way, when Hugh Fearnley-Whittingstall took up Clover's cudgel and started to make TV programmes highlighting the scandal of 'discard', I supported 'Hugh's Fish Fight'. After all, the trawlermen seemed as angry about it as Hugh. I remember the films. Tubs of fat cod and hake which the skipper and crew emptied one by one overboard.

'The trouble is they never thought it through,' said Dave. 'There was this one commissioner, a bit of a madam and she just decided that she was going to eradicate discard throughout Europe. Because of the Fearnley-Whittingstall film. That's where it all kicked off. The guys took him out, thought they were doing the right thing showing him discarded fish. Then everything blew out of proportion. "It's time to stop the waste," everyone cried. But the government knows it can't work unless we get a huge increase in our quotas for fish like hake and saithe.'

This wasn't the first time Dave had linked two ideas that to me didn't seem connected. Why wouldn't the ban work unless fishermen could catch *even more* fish? Surely a discard ban was about preserving stocks, not exploiting them further? I said I thought that Hugh had been trying to do the right thing and create a market for the fish that were otherwise thrown back.

'But Hugh didn't know the complexities. Didn't look into why we were having to dump this or that fish.'

I couldn't see them either. Not yet.

Not until we'd gone round and round and round – probably to the point where Dave thought I was an idiot – did the light bulb finally come on. The 'complexities' – contradictions in fact – come out of the quota system and its multiple, semi-contradictory roles. Quotas as conservation measures. Quotas as licences to land and sell fish. Quotas as tradable commodities. Which is it?

Scottish trawlers, for example, don't discard hake because there isn't a market, or even because hake are cheap at market, they discard hake because *they aren't allowed to land and sell more than 350 tons of them*. They aren't allowed to because historically, culturally the hake fishery 'belongs' to the Spanish fleet, and that is reflected in today's quotas.

The quota in this sense is like an historically determined market stall. The North Sea marketplace is divvied up like this into zones and species, fleets and allowances. The hake quota determines who can exploit the stock and to what extent. But what exactly is the quota really managing? The stock or the market? Does it prevent non-Spanish boats from catching hake, for example? Not really. It might stop them from *targeting* hake. But a Scottish trawler trying to catch its fair share of haddock, say, will inevitably catch hake. Especially now the sea is getting warmer and those 'Spanish' hake all swim in Scottish waters. If they catch hake they are not allowed to land and sell, what do they do with it? They throw it away. Dead. This is the waste Hugh Fearnley-Whittingstall and the general public object to.

Looked at this way, Europe's Common Fisheries Policy uses quotas as stock management tools in the same way you'd use a hammer to repair a watch. The UK fleet may land (note the word 'land', not 'catch') 350 tons of hake a year. After that they must stop fishing altogether, lest they 'catch' any more. But so long as they don't 'land' more than 350 tons, they can 'catch' as many as they like. Whether the fish is alive or dead is lost in the distinctions.

In objecting to discards we were really objecting to the quota system, but the intricacies of the quota system don't make such good telly. The discard ban is a classic case of curing the symptom not the disease.

'As far as I can see quota and no-discard are mutually exclusive and we've half-fixed half the problem. Surely you need a different system?' I said.

'You will nae solve it,' said Dave cautioning me against even trying to do what many had failed to. 'It is impossible. Even though I'm trying to catch haddocks you'll see for yourself you're going to get cod, hake, whiting. It's a mixture. And that's the problem with the northern half of the North Sea. There are so many species interacting in the same area. That's the problem we have.'

Surely, though, the impossibility lay in building one flawed measure onto another? What if Dave had a clean sheet? What if he could wipe away forty years of Common Fisheries Policy and start again? It seemed obvious out there, living through Dave's trials and tribulations, that in contested or common waters, where different skippers and different nations are each competing to scratch a living (or make a fortune), soon enough everyone is racing everyone else to catch the last fish in the sea. The problem with a sea no one owns is how easily the link between husbandry and exploitation is broken. If one man forbears, the next won't. And so the history of the North Sea fishery, and of British waters since we gave them up to the EU, is of inadequate, after-the-fact husbandry and catch-limit measures that ultimately have more to do with licences to trade than with the conservation of fish. Hugh was right to hate discard, but banning it might not solve the problem of waste and it might not help conservation. According to Dave there was a big chance that the discard bans simply would not work.

A day later Dave's point was made when we set the nets near the Piper Alpha oilfields on the way home and three hours later pulled up the biggest haul of the week: four bagfuls dropped on to *Audacious* and four more to us. But Dave had been looking for haddock and pulled up hake. He reckoned a ton of it in one go, a not inconsiderable part of the entire UK quota ... in three hours' fishing. It had been a 'let's see what's there' trawl, a curious dip after haddock. Dave often found haddocks there at this time of year, but since he couldn't afford to catch any more hake, he'd go looking somewhere else when he started back out the following week.

'It's all different now. Once I'd go out looking for fish and having found them catch as many as possible. Now, I spend most of my time trying to avoid fish. I'm a fisherman who avoids catching fish!'

THE RHYTHM OF THE SEA

With the pressure off for the last two days Dave went below for longer breaks while Jake and Richard took turns in the wheelhouse. The sea was as rough as, if not worse than, the menacing rollercoaster that had done for me earlier in the week, and while I didn't exactly feel well, I almost enjoyed the chance to defy the waves. I took photographs through the wheelhouse windows – grey sky, green water, waves breaking across the deck – and chatted to Jake about his daughter's cake shop, or Richard about how he moved to Blackpool 'by mistake' and commutes from there to Peterhead. Up here he lives on the boat. 'This is my home,' he said, just as Frankie and Johnny had described it. Jake spoke quietly and only occasionally in between long draws on his ever-present cigarette. I joshed him about how he was supposed to have given up after his stroke.

'You'll die of something,' he said.

When Dave came back up he told me about how another boat had taken 'a lump of water', fishing not far from us. 'Can you imagine where you're sleeping half full of the sea?' he chuckled.

I could, but I didn't want to. So, instead I tried one last time to get Dave to nail down a better way of managing this North Sea fishery. Dave kept saying that it all came down to politics. Wasn't politics the problem? Politics *and* fishermen, Dave suggested. 'The trouble with fishermen is that whatever you come up with they will always find a way around it.'

But isn't that because it's always a competition to grab the fish before the next guy does? Surely you need a system where the fishermen don't want to cheat. And where there is better incentive to leave fish in the sea so there's something there the next year and the year after. What if the fishermen could either own or at least control their own fisheries?

'Regional management, you mean?' said Dave brightly. 'We'd love that. To manage our own fish stocks. That would be ideal for us. The thing with Europe is we've just given and given.'

I wasn't thinking of regional management within the EU so much as the almost-impossible-to-think-of chance of reclaiming a UK 200-mile zone. This was a month or so before the prime minister David Cameron unexpectedly announced the referendum on Europe, and a full year ahead of the vote. 'That'll never happen,' he said, when I raised the possibility that one day we might leave the EU.

Now, at least with regard to fishing, Britain has the chance to start again, to build a fishery that works for fish and fishermen, even if history has shown that is easier said than done. The Canadians got it more wrong than right when they declared an exclusion zone and finished the job the rest of the world had started on the Grand Banks. The Icelanders, who now run one of the world's most sustainable, conservation-minded fisheries, also got it wrong for a while. Having expelled the foreign fleets, Iceland made a good fist of overfishing their new exclusion zone all on their own. But as a measure of how a single nation with exclusive control can and will act sooner and with more resolve than a catfight of nations squabbling over who gets what, the Icelanders got themselves together way more effectively than the EEC/EU has ever managed. With fish stocks plummeting (in Iceland fishermen are recruited to assess stocks, which does help them accept the findings) and the lesson of the Grand Banks only a short stretch of ocean away, the politicians, scientists and fishermen of Iceland put their heads together and collectively agreed to tighten their belts until things got better. They reduced their fleet, their fishing effort and the overall cod quota, and they got rid of discard – by reforming the way that quota was administered – all in time to save their sea fisheries. Now Iceland's sustainable annual take of cod and haddock dwarfs Europe's unsustainable scraping of the barrel.

I'd spent the week stuck in a mind-maze with walls made of nets and glittering fish and reams and reams of fishery legislation going back decades.

'So, let's simplify this,' I said, marshalling my forces. 'If the quota and the discard ban don't work together, and if neither works on its own ... what if you got rid of species quotas, because quotas lead to discard, and just had limited days at sea to manage the effort and no discard so you have to be selective?'

'That's it!' said Dave. 'The only way I see you could do it is global tonnage. Get all your species together and say that the Dawn Fishing Company, for example, lands 1,000 tons of fish. You've got 1,000 tons and once you've caught it, end of story.'

'It would be up to you what you catch, but there'd be no discard at sea? Everything comes back?'

'That's the only way. They'd still have to limit your days, because a lot of our guys would fish 360 if they could get away with it. So, if you can get it structured right, give guys the right incentive to change their ways of fishing, incentive to be more selective, conservation-minded.'

I felt like we'd just stumbled into bright light on the road to Damascus.

'Couldn't that work? Global tonnage. Limited days at sea. And no discard, because that will encourage skippers to use larger mesh and things like that because they don't want their holds full of stuff they can't sell. Then reward the fishermen with extra days in return for their success at being selective. Put the onus on fishermen to be ingenious about what they catch and what they don't.'

I was almost excited. A week in the maze and finally at its centre something so simple. And so exactly like Graham's and Russell's 1945 proposals.

In 1883 Thomas Henry Huxley in his famously un-prescient eulogy on the apparently infinite bounty of the sea compared its productivity with farmland. One acre of 'good fishing grounds' in the North Sea, he claimed, will yield in a week what it would take a year to produce on farmland. It was a tellingly skewed analysis from an otherwise remarkable man, because to a large extent that 'infinite bounty' mindset has shaped our management of common fisheries like the North Sea from that day to this. Intellectually we now know that the sea is not inexhaustible, but our fisheries policies still have at their heart that warped assumption, or at least a wilful blindness to the opposite truth. It was telling also that Huxley's analogy between farmland and seabed highlighted, probably without him intending it to, one real difference between farmland and this wild resource, the sea: husbandry.

Huxley was wrong to compare the two in the way he did, not only because he was looking the wrong way down the telescope at that single acre – it was much less a magic apple tree than a barrel of apples – but also because a farmer sows his corn and feeds his cattle. Since there is no way fishermen can sow cod or haddock any more than they can feed them, husbandry must take a different form: namely forbearance informed by a deep knowledge and love of the resource. That comes from knowing what you leave behind will be there tomorrow. That it won't be grabbed by someone else. This is something the EU fisheries policy consistently fails to deliver because in the Common Fisheries Policy 'forbearance' is really just market apportionment in disguise. Most of all because no one owns anything. If a fisherman wants to fish tomorrow, next year, in ten years, if he wants his children to fish too, the forbearance comes naturally. It does not need to be imposed. The corruption of forbearance increases in exact step with the degrees of removal you go from ownership. Common ownership might work at a local level, or even national. But by the time it is dissipated across a continent, isn't Michael Graham's 'moderation' a long-vanished dream? Isn't imposed moderation a political and a legal nightmare?

We pulled the hake-filled nets at Piper Alpha at teatime on Thursday afternoon and rounded the Peterhead breakwater at about three o'clock on Friday morning. I'd been at sea for a week, the longest and yet also perhaps the most intense week of my life. As *Adorne* slid off the ocean swell and settled into the soft bosom of the harbour I vowed never to complain about anything ever again. Through the sea-soaked windows of the wheelhouse the dockside lights blazed like a bombed town aflame, the most welcoming apocalypse I've ever seen.

The lads were busy in the fish market by the time I went downstairs to get my things – I zipped up my bag listening to the same distant shouts I'd heard a week ago, the fish porters giving each other hell, and to the beautiful, empty silence in between. The Dolphin Café was closed but I wasn't hungry anyway. I was planning to stop at a pub on the way home and fish the evening rise of trout on the River Eden. I'd have fish and chips there. And two pints of beer. And I'd fall asleep in a room that stayed still and had no engine in it.

I went to find Dave. He was busy dragging crates across the floor of the fish market, exactly as I had found him seven days earlier. He had fish on his hands again but we shook anyway.

'Mind how you go,' said Dave as I stepped through the plastic curtains into the summer dawn.

Then I stopped on the road south out of Peterhead to get some fuel and a coffee. Armed with both I'd be in Cumbria by noon – fishing again, but in a trout stream this time, with stones under my feet. As the pump meter ticked and I gazed dreamily over the car roof across the road to the glinting waters of Peterhead bay I noticed how everything was still – the car, the ground, the petrol station – except me. I was rocking from side to side. And eight hours later, as I cast my line towards a rising fish on the River Eden near Kirkby Stephen, I was still swaying to the rhythm of the sea.

2. SOUTH

BIRTH OF A CREED

14 September is not the anniversary of the day Richard Walker shattered the long-held angling record for a British common carp: he hauled that legendary fish to the bank of a small pond in Herefordshire the day before, back in 1952. My plans to catch a carp on Walker's record-breaking anniversary had come unstuck before we'd even started.

I have to admit that until I phoned Chris Yates – legendary carp guru and the man who in his turn shattered Walker's record – to ask if I could join him for a day trying to catch a carp, 13 September had not been *that* significant to me. I knew – vaguely – about Walker's fish. Of course I did. Pretty much anyone who fishes with a rod and line will know something of the story. How, on that auspicious day in 1952, Richard Walker caught a fish so large that he redefined freshwater angling in Britain, how he called the fish Ravioli – the bait he caught it on. How Ravioli was given to London Zoo, where she was rechristened Clarissa, and swam out her days until in 1971, by then something of a shadow of her corpulent teenage prime, she died aged thirty-eight.

That's all fishing folklore and if you're a fisherman you'll probably know of it. But if you're a *carp* fisherman the story is more than knowledge. It's gospel. Didn't the late Bernard Venables – himself an angler of almost druidic status – call his essay on Walker and those early carp pioneers 'Birth of a Creed'? There were twelve of them, after all. When I asked Chris if he'd try to unveil to me this mysterious world of the impassioned carp angler, of course he hit on the idea of taking me fishing on that date: 13 September, Walker and Clarissa's conjugal anniversary.

'I'll even let you fish for an hour with Walker's rod,' said Chris. 'And that rod never fails. There's something magic about that rod.'

The date hadn't meant much to me. Now it did.

It was August. I agreed to ring again in early September. But Chris is always hard to track down. His daughter answered when I called, and she said he was fishing. Other times the phone just rang. I pictured it under a hat and an old oilskin coat, ringing away to an empty room while Chris meditated by a stream somewhere.

Had I fished with Chris before? It felt as if I had. Virginia Woolf said of another great fishing author, J. W. Hills, that his best writing feels as if it happened to you. Chris's writing is like that. It's easy to be confused. I have friends who fish with Chris. I fish with them too. Sometimes we fish the same water: if Chris is after perch, say, and I am after grayling or trout, Ronnie might tell me how he was here with Chris last week. And a week later he might tell Chris how he was here with Charlie just a few days before. Now that I came to think it through, I don't think *I* had actually ever fished with *him*, the two of us together by the same piece of water, at the same time. I was looking forward to it. 13 September drew closer.

I finally got hold of Chris just a few days before. He was hesitant.

'The 13th? It's a Sunday isn't it? Is it a Sunday?'

I checked my diary. It was a Sunday.

'Ah.' There was a pause. Chris explained that he had now promised another friend he'd fish with *him* on the 13th. Besides, Sunday was not a day he liked to go to the carp pool.

'There might be other people there,' he said. 'The lake is very sensitive to disturbance. One fish and that's it really.'

Of the two problems, Sunday at the lake was the bigger. His friend wouldn't mind, Chris reflected. Leave it with me, he said uncertainly.

Knowing how much Chris loves his perch I waited a day or two then emailed him a picture of our mutual pal Ronnie cradling one we'd caught fishing together earlier that year on a river Chris knew. It had been a gloomy day and the perch's butter belly and orange fins shone out of the photograph like wet paint. I said how much I was looking forward to our day after fatter, less stripy fish. Chris was wavering and this was bait. He replied, unusual in itself, and quickly, which is even more unusual.

'I got the perch pic!' he wrote. 'Lovely! As I said on the phone, Sunday is not a good day for the carp pool, but Monday is! So, I'll see you for elevenses at my place and then down to the secret water for a sofa-sized fish.'

I'd hooked him! Though not on the 13th. I wasn't yet a disciple of the carp brotherhood, however, and I wasn't about to let a super-stition bother me. Chris was undaunted and I was in the hands of a master. Best of all was that phrase 'sofa-sized fish'. Gosh.

Quite apart from how his words whetted my appetite, the description was a good one. There really is something upholstered about the look of a large carp: there's this tail at one end and head at the other – with beady brass buttons for eyes – and between there's a gentlemen's-club chesterfield that's gone at the edges and lost its shape. Some, the very biggest, are not *that* much smaller than a chesterfield. Clarissa's record-breaking weight of forty-four pounds is now a long-surpassed milestone in the inexorable expansion of the carp's girth. Clarissa was only an armchair. Chris destroyed that record with a monster of over fifty pounds in the early 1980s. But the record now is a full three-seater, closing in on seventy pounds. Five stone of fish in one body! They *can* get bigger still.

Strange then that for six of the seven centuries that have passed since carp were first brought to the British Isles, it was a fish of much more modest proportions. The ballooning of its midriff is a relatively recent phenomenon, as is its elevation from a creature only a few eccentric anglers bothered with to a behemoth hundreds of thousands of anglers are obsessed with. Yet when Walker caught his record fish the Carp Catchers' Club, as I mentioned, had only twelve members. Does this narrative ... er ... remind you of anything?

Carp have always had a religious air about them. I grew up with the story that carp were first brought to England from Europe by monks who reared them in stew-ponds and ate them on fast days because, like unborn rabbits, they didn't count as meat (unborn rabbits really didn't count as meat!). Attached to this was the story of how carp were brought to Europe along the Silk Road from China by Jewish traders who, excluded by anti-Semitic laws from practising conventional agriculture, were expert fish-farmers. Carp. Monks. China. It's a version of how the carp got here that has been repeated again and again until somehow it has stuck. There are bits of truth in there, but really it's a history muddied, rather as carp muddy the ponds they swim in, by the confusing taxonomy of fish.

There *is* a species of carp from Asia, the Amur carp (*Cyprinus carpio haematopterus*). But our common carp, the one that now swims in British waters (*Cyprinus carpio carpio*), came from the Danube. The two species are related, but they're not the same. We know this from their DNA and because vast quantities of the bones of the common carp (not the Amur) have been dug up at Mesolithic excavations near Vlasa: these fish were nibbled to their skeletons by appreciative diners long before the Silk Road existed and long before Jews or monks began to specialise in farming and cooking fish. It's probable that carp were traded up and down the Silk Road, that Danube carp were taken to Asia and vice versa: after all, carp are

hardy enough to have withstood this kind of piecemeal intercontin-
ental travel, back and forth until somehow the distinct origins of
the two species blurred into one not quite accurate story. But the
true ancestors of the blimpish fish I would soon be trying to catch
on a day out with Chris, were European.

The earliest reference to that carp, at least to something like it, is
thought to be Aristotle's anatomising of something he called *kyprianos*
– a fish which spawned several times a year in shallow water, had a
soft palate but was hard and fat all over and because it liked to swim
near the surface was easily paralysed by a clap of thunder. This all
sounds like it could be a carp. But then again a carp does not have
four gills, it doesn't guard its eggs, nor are they the size of millet seeds.
So it's hard to say. Pliny's *cyprinus* was a sea fish, this time rendered
sleepy by thunder and Oppian's *kyprianos* was a fish of the gently
sloping seashore. So already things are getting muddled. These look
most of all like factoids ripped from Aristotle and used to describe
different fish, rather than direct observations of a Danubian carp.

Much more convincing is Aelian's second-century description of
a black fish caught under ice in the Danube, or four centuries later
when Cassiodorus, sixth-century statesman and minister to the court
of Theoderic the Great, listed '*Carpam Danubius*' among the exotic
fishes to be served by the king at a feast for visiting ambassadors.
Here we have something that certainly was a carp, referred to by its
common name.

It took another 1,000 years for the two words, the everyday *carpus*
and the classical *cyprinus*, to become intertwined. In 1597 the Czech
churchman Jan Dubravius published *De Piscinis et Piscium* and with
it 'hissed from the stage' the barbaric word *carpus* to replace it with
cyprinus: basically because that word was Greek and in his mind
much better. We have Dubravius's linguistic snobbery to thank for
the fact that carp have been called *cyprinus* ever since, at least when
scientists are talking about them. More than that, because carp are

cyprinus, so the genera of carp and other fish like them became cyprinids: now over 3,000 species have that family name and yet there is a half-chance that not one of them is the thunderstruck fish Aristotle was talking about.

Regardless of its name, barbaric or Delphic, the common carp is an easy fish to identify from its bones and all the archaeological remains of carp which pre-date Cassiodorus's reference are from the middle and lower Danube alone. The Romans ate carp all right, but mostly at the very eastern edge of their empire, where they threw the skeletons out of the window for us to find.

It's the bones in the ground that tell us how the carp spread: slowly at first, one fish pond at a time through the centuries of the first millennium, north and west into the heart of the continent. Carp remains which date from later than Cassiodorus's menu suggest that between the sixth and eleventh centuries the fish were spread north and west – not by swimming, but because men were transporting and eating them – along the Danube catchment. Eventually they were taken over the watershed and into the catchments of the rivers Rhine and Elba and from this point the carp's conquest of vast new territories was probably inevitable.

Through most of that time the history consists of bones and little else: there are no written records – only the briefest mention in the eleventh century when William of Hirsau, an abbot of the Black Forest who grew up on the Danube, expanded the sign language of monks – who did not speak at table – to include 'the fish that is popularly called carp'. Mostly the carp is conspicuous by its absence. Neither its skeleton nor words to describe it exist much in this western part of Europe before the year 1200. Then suddenly the carp appears repeatedly: in fisheries legislation, in encyclopaedias, in records of pond-stocking and its bones in archaeological sites in a widening spread through the Rhine heartland, and south into the Seine basin and Burgundy.

It was only a short journey from here to England but the earliest reference to the fish in Britain appears on the shopping list for the enthronement of the Archbishop of Canterbury in 1248, when a hundred carp were ordered, along with a hundred pike, 400 tench and 600 eels. These carp seem to have been imported exotics, like Cassiodorus's fish of 600 years earlier, because but for this isolated mention carp dip again beneath the surface and then reappear only about once a century: in 1346 when eight pike and eight carp were ordered for the kitchen of Edward III and then in 1429 at the coronation feast for Henry VI. One suspects these fish were also imported, because not until the 1460s is there a certain reference to the living fish swimming in an English pond, when the Duke of Norfolk stocked his six ponds with carp and gifted fish to several of his neighbours. This must have spread the arriviste fish around East Anglia. But not so far afield that in 1496 Dame Juliana Berners, author of the first English-language book on fishing – *The Treatyse of Fysshynge With an Angle* – could say that she knew much about them: she knew little of carp, she wrote, 'as there be so few in England'.

If in 1496 there were a 'so few', there must have been some. The carp had arrived. Within fifty years there were many. By the 1530s we had carp in Norfolk, Suffolk, Hampshire, London, Surrey, Worcestershire and Gloucestershire. Prior More of Worcester kept them. In 1530 the prior of Llanthony Secunda sent a gift of carp to the king. If it was meant to placate him, it didn't. Starting in 1536 Henry VIII sacked the monasteries anyway, and though monks are popularly credited with their introduction, the historical window in which monks might peacefully have kept carp seems to have been a narrow one, after all. In 1537 a Mr Thomas Wriothesley set about plans to stock the 'former' monastic ponds of Titchfield with carp. In 1538 it was recorded that the monks of Charterhouse *had* kept carp: at the closure of the monastery the sackers sent the stock of Catholic fish to the king's pond at Foyerwell.

The same year, in what could have made for an episode of Tudor *Crimewatch*, King Henry – perhaps with a taste for them now – ordered carp from Thomas Gyffard, who duly drew his ponds and stored the fish in the unfortunately named 'Theves Pond' overnight. From a pond with that name of course they were stolen … by Thomas's brother Raffe, who was traced by his cart to his home in Steeple Claydon, where nets and various instruments of Raffe's nefarious trade were found. Raffe told those who had pursued him that he would fish those ponds 'before his brother's face'.

Meanwhile over in Mangotsfield another feud, this one involving sixty people, ended with a broken dam, fish all over the floor and carp to the value of £20 tucked under so many armpits as the sodden thieves made their escape.

All this gifting, plundering of sacked monasteries and thievery suggests a fish of some value. So, what was it about carp?

THE RIVER DECAYETH

There's a spot near the approach to Heathrow where the River Colne slides under the motorway. I cross it a few times a year. There's something about the juxtaposition there of the quiet, imprisoned river and the motorway, the scrapyard and the planes droning overhead. I rub out the pylons and poster-boards and imagine the pastoral landscape that came before: smoke furls up from a homestead, sheep graze on riverside pastures, a mill wheel catches the sunlight. And beyond is a deep, immense and silent forest. The dusky, eutrophic waters of the River Colne seep feebly under this five-lane car park, and it's difficult, impossible even, to appreciate how far removed even that imagined pastoral idyll is from the undeveloped wilderness that must have existed before it.

In the 300 or 400 years that preceded the carp's arrival in England the British population grew at a rate not matched until the nineteenth century. Political stability under Norman rule, the social stability of feudalism, church reforms, the growth of trade and the weakening bonds of serfdom: all these things combined with a warming climate (between 950 and 1250 global temperatures climbed considerably) and improving agricultural productivity (three-field crop rotation, the heavy plough, the watermill) to make the sparsely populated country conquered by the Normans a far busier place by the middle of the fourteenth century: 1.5 million people became 5 million. Subsistence farming became surplus farming. Surplus created trade. Trade created markets, towns and cities.

Sadly, economic expansion always leads to, maybe it even depends on, environmental destruction. The great clearances of the high medieval period cut swathes of pasture into those primeval forests. Pristine river catchments were destabilised. The ground was ploughed and began to erode, washing soil downhill into streams which increasingly were impounded by mills. All that grain had to be processed somehow: there were about 200 watermills in King Alfred's England. By the time the Domesday Book was compiled in 1085 there were 5,624 – a thirtyfold increase in two centuries, and that was just the beginning. There's no Domesday-type index for the thirteenth or fourteenth centuries in England, but records from mainland Europe suggest that the *greatest* expansion of water-mills occurred between 1150 and 1250. If a river was impounded with one mill, soon it was impounded by several, so that eventually a once free-flowing stream was turned into a series of slow-flowing ponds, warming under that unusually hot sun, filling with soil washed from the now bare hills.

The mills created barriers, too. Migratory salmon, sea trout, sturgeon and eels had to contend with a steeplechase of obstructions, as well as cordons of vile water washing into river estuaries from cities like Norwich and London. With all that food production, for all those people, inevitably there was a growing pile of excrement too. It had to go somewhere and it usually went into rivers. By the fourteenth century many English towns and cities had been compelled to ban the dumping of 'muck and other vile filth' in their rivers and streams. But people piled the stuff outside their front doors anyway and most of the time rain did the rest.

It wasn't just human excrement either. Butchers were a particular nuisance: their offal-dumping habits induced all sorts of civic decrees (most of which were ignored) in an attempt to limit the nuisance. In 1532, chronically troubled by the blocked and filthy Wensum, the authorities in Norwich instigated a river-management plan: an annual scouring of the stream requiring many men with spades and barrows to take the muck away. Trades deemed particularly responsible for the nuisance – bakers, dyers, launderers, parchment-makers, tanners, saddlers, brewers – were charged for the work. Twenty years later the city assembly complained that the river still 'decayeth and fylethe moore and moore'.

It's no big surprise that this all started to impact on the fish people ate and where they took them from. The medieval chronicler Aelfric inadvertently recorded the change when he interviewed a local fisherman at the turn of the first millennium. 'What fish do you catch?' Aelfric asked. 'Eels and pike and trout,' the fisherman replied, adding that he fished from a boat by throwing his net over the stream, or casting a baited hook, or by setting wicker baskets. This medieval fisher must have thrown his net over pools I know well, for Aelfric lived at Cerne Abbey in Dorset when he wrote his *Colloquy on the Occupations*, a Latin primer written for noviciate monks. A small chalk-stream rises in the grounds of that abbey, but if this fisherman caught pike as well as the trout that abound in the little River Cerne, then he fished downstream, beyond Dorchester on the main River Frome. 'Do you fish in the sea?' Aelfric asked. 'Sometimes,' said the fisherman. And what fish did the fisherman catch there? Herring, salmon, sturgeon, lobster, crab. And where did he sell them alongside his staple catch of trout, pike and eels? In the city, where city-folk bought them. Then the fisherman added, tellingly: 'I cannot catch them as quickly as I can sell them.'

Scientists call it the 'Fish Event Horizon'. In a Catholic Europe fish were an important part of the medieval diet. But until the eleventh century people ate mostly freshwater species like trout and pike and migratory fish like salmon, sturgeon, eels and lamprey, almost certainly all caught in local rivers and lakes – fish that were an abundant natural resource, or an annual bounty from the sea. A marked step change occurs around the turn of the millennium, just when Aelfric's fisherman was complaining about how he couldn't keep up with demand. The bones of cod, which were hardly eaten before the tenth century, show up with increasing frequency, along with saithe and hake and haddock. Herring too. Meanwhile those freshwater fish that made up almost all of the catch in the ninth century have diminished to less than half by the eleventh.

This change coincides with the early phases of that creeping environmental destruction: the world getting warmer, this warmth combining with technical know-how to drive agricultural productivity, population growth, land clearance, urbanisation and industry. Through the twelfth and thirteenth centuries there was a surge in legislation to deal with the pressures our rivers and fish were under: statutes and complaints relating to the passage of salmon, or to overfishing, or competition for a shrinking resource. The average size of fish went down: sturgeon (found in food remains) seem to have become progressively smaller between the tenth and twelfth centuries, and to have diminished as a proportion of the catch, too. The fish-bone remains, which indicate a major shift towards sea fish, also indicate a shift away from the environmentally sensitive freshwater species like trout, salmon and sturgeon towards fish that tolerate warmer, more enriched or even polluted waters: bream, tench, eels. The entropic forces of environmental degradation were moving only one way. Sure enough, by the thirteenth century the endangered English sturgeon was legally reserved for the king alone. And by the fourteenth century there is a recipe showing how to make fake sturgeon from veal. The actual fish has all but gone. A type of death knell that feels very modern was already tolling 1,000 years ago.

The carp enters stage right at the exact time these changes were happening, very likely *because* these changes were happening. Carp evolved in a more extreme climate than Britain's, and tolerate, or even thrive in, the increasingly impounded, warming and turbid waters of medieval England. Conditions that might be lethal to the likes of pike and chub, let alone salmon or trout, are the carp's easy habitat. They're foragers, too, and will eat more or less anything from weeds to plankton to worms, and are particularly fond of snouting out the bloodworm larvae of midges and mosquitoes which thrive in the muddy beds of such places. Like pigs they grow quickly eating what others won't, and like pigs they get big. Very big.

All this meant that while the carp happily adapted to and thrived in the degrading waterways of western Europe, it was also – and much more significantly – the perfect fish for rearing in ponds to be harvested as food. The fish pond – the other part of this sacred union – was where this Danubian immigrant found its home and made its place in British history.

VIVARIUM AND SERVATORIUM

To understand the origins of the fish pond we must understand that a fish pond is not quite the same thing as a pond with fish in it. From their beginnings formal fish ponds were sophisticated and laborious constructions involving dam walls, hatchways and spillways, and the diversion of rivers and streams. And although they were built ostensibly to rear fish for food, they were also a kind of status symbol, especially in their earliest incarnations.

In Britain these date from the first or second century AD, and the idea of them – along with their social cachet – came over with the Romans from Italy where a type of ornamental fish-farming was practised, especially along the coast. As the Roman scholar Marcus Varro pointed out, these conspicuously ornate pools – decorated with rocks and amphorae – had less to do with the easy supply of fresh fish for the table than with showing off. Their appeal was aesthetic not economic: 'for in the first place they are built at great cost, in the second they are stocked at great cost and in the third place they are kept up at great cost'.

The fish ponds at Shakenoak – a Roman farm and villa near Witney, Oxfordshire – appear to be an inland version of this Roman innovation: the three ponds are of a scale that would hardly have been commercial and the family seem to have lived in luxury. But perhaps social cachet proved a more worthwhile currency on the Amalfi coast than in our mist-draped landscape. The Shakenoak ponds were in use for only a few hundred years, whilst elsewhere the small number of ponds that date from these early centuries of the first millennium seem to have faded away when the Romans did. Which only goes to underline that beyond the iconography of status there was little real need for fish ponds in the relatively unspoilt and sparsely populated landscape of the early Middle Ages, when wild fish were abundant. Especially so in temperate Britain, surrounded by sea, veined by rivers, washed by endless rain. There would have been little need to use fish ponds for actual *food*. At least … not until the fish ran out.

In 1066 William landed and the English landscape was parcelled out, 'enfeoffed', as feudal baronies to those who'd helped in the fight. Suddenly the commoner ate fish only with the permission of his baron. As for the commoner, so for the monk: his holy days and fast days amounted to almost half the year. No one ate more fish than a medieval monk. But there's plenty of evidence to suggest how parsimoniously the new Norman overlords granted fishing rights even to the holy houses: the de Warennes, who had fought alongside William and were well rewarded with tracts of English countryside for their troubles, specified in their grant of fishing rights to the Chartulary of St Pancras of Lewes that the fresh fish taken from their waters were 'for the great feasts and for great guests' only. This distinction was echoed all over the country. Day to day, monks made do with salted sea fish, unless it was a very special occasion – unless, in fact, the occasion conferred holiness and grace upon the baronial giver.

This runs against the popular idea that monks were the pioneers of the English fish pond. In fact the Norman aristocracy were. Monastic ponds came later. The construction of formal fish ponds began in earnest under Norman rule and almost all were attached to important manorial houses or castles: for this wave of ruling-class invader the ponds were also about status. Only this time there was an increasingly keen environmental and demographic edge to the cachet.

In an unrefrigerated and horse-drawn Britain even an abundance of wild fish did not guarantee a fish would be fresh at the kitchen door – especially if that kitchen was some distance from a river or the sea, if the fisherman had bad luck, as they do from time to time, or if the salmon or the eels weren't running. To serve fish fresh – not salted or smoked – either you kept live fish, or you went to some trouble – and risked failure – to get very recently dead ones. Fish for everyday eating and everyday people, therefore, were almost always salted or cured in some way. Fresh fish were for special occasions and special guests. Thus freshness had rarity and social value of itself. But the status conferred on host and guest by serving fresh fish would only have become more pronounced as wild fisheries creaked under the twin pressures of environmental degradation and overfishing. And now that the Normans had locked down all the fishing rights, class was even more defined by what you could eat. William Wykeham, Bishop of Winchester, fed his household smoked and salted salmon. Only when King Richard came to stay did he take fish from the episcopal ponds.

This medieval fish-culture depended on two types of pond: the vivarium and the servatorium. The vivarium was the larger of the two. It was the stock pond, as the name implies, where the fish were grown to harvestable size. The larger the pond, the more productive it was. So almost exclusively vivariums were built by raising a dam across the valley floor to impound a stream. The stream filled the valley to the height of the dam wall and this gave the pond a meandering, almost natural appearance as the water followed the contours of the valley sides above the dam.

The servatorium, on the other hand, was built closer to the house as a kind of living larder, stocked with fish soon destined for the pot. Proximity to the manor would have helped keep the stock safe from thieves – herons, otters or people – but no doubt it was also easier for the chef to nip out and choose a fish for dinner if the pond was nearby. The role of the servatorium dictated its different designs. Set into the ground, or built with a bank all round, unlike the flooded-valley vivarium, the servatorium was much smaller too, square or rectangular, and shallow at one end, deeper at the other: so that the fish could easily be chased into a net.

To sort and harvest the fish, it was necessary to drain the vivarium pond from time to time through a wooden sluice set in the dam wall. The smaller fish and brood-stock were sorted from those which had reached an edible size, some were transferred to the servatorium and then the main pond was refilled. Where manors or monasteries operated several ponds, the drain-down and harvesting was done one pond at a time on something like a five-year cycle. Having been drained, ponds were left fallow over the winter before they were refilled and the cycle could begin again.

I've seen something like this kind of operation at work in the hills above Ojiya city in Japan. Here the fish were not being selected for food. In fact they were being taken from their summer lodgings to more pampered, heated pools for the winter: they were koi carp and each fish was worth a fortune. We drained the lake until the koi were swimming – quite non-plussed – in an orgiastic, gently writhing mass in muddy water at the foot of the lake alongside the dam wall. Then we encircled them with a net and drew it tighter and tighter until each fish could be backed gently into a clear, heavy-duty bag and hefted upwards into an aerated tank on the back of a truck. So, a few details would be different: the plastic bags, the truck. But swap those for baskets of wet straw and a cart and I imagine you have something very close to how this medieval fish-sorting operation worked.

Not every kind of fish could survive this level of handling, the muddy water at the base of the drained pond, the low oxygen levels, being carted about in wet straw: bream, pike and perch were the most adaptable and popular. Sometimes roach and tench too. Of these, pike make superb eating and perch are the finest freshwater fish of all. But bream were the mainstay, probably because of all the native species they could best survive and thrive in these ghetto conditions.

CERTAIN EXPERIMENTS CONCERNING FISH AND FRUIT

Which brings us back to the carp. What did carp offer that bream didn't? The same thing they now offer those who chase them obsessively with rod and line: growth rate and size. Carp grow much more quickly than bream, they get bigger, can tolerate even higher stocking densities and lower oxygen levels.

The problem was always one of productivity: before carp were introduced even the large ponds produced modest numbers of fish, at least compared to how much the medieval monks and pious citizens actually ate. The five-year harvesting cycle mentioned in medieval texts is how long it took to grow a bream to edible size. If a typical one-acre pond held a standing crop of 200 lb of bream, it would yield only 40 lb a year if fished on a five-year cycle. With 175 'fish days' in the medieval year (days when the church forbade meat) a monk could munch his way through a two-acre pond's worth of bream every year. Abbeys such as Eynsham with thirty brethren and three acres of water, would only ever have been able to grow bream for those very special occasions.

Carp, however, could be grown to harvestable size in a third of the time. In other words, carp trebled productivity. Carp were the loaves and fishes miracle fish of the fifteenth century. To top it all they were better to eat.

By the time this miracle arrived in England, fish ponds had lost something of their status among the highest aristocracy. The gradual decline of 'demesne' farming – where the baron farmed his own lands in a feudal system – meant that increasingly after the year 1300 farmland and fish ponds were leased to the lesser gentry, even to some of the country's wealthier peasants. This took the shine off a fresh bream or pike. No longer were they quite such a sign of high breeding.

For a while at least, the carp was a novelty. A fish fit only for a king, or those not far beneath a king. Early records describe a fish reserved for the most important feasts, celebrations and coronations. And when the living fish finally swam in English waters, it was in fish ponds belonging to the Duke of Norfolk, and soon after this in ponds belonging to the likes of Lady Waldgrave and others of the duke's aristocratic friends and neighbours. Correspondence amongst the glitterati of the day described a fish the gift of which must have been comparable with a box of truffles, or the best caviar. Thomas Cromwell, Lord Privy Seal, King Henry VIII and Sir Brian Tuke were all happy recipients of carpy largesse amongst the upper classes.

A rung or two lower down the social order, parvenu like Chaucer's Franklin, who had 'many a bream and pike' in his stew-ponds, were not slow in stocking a few of these parvenu carp too. And while the royal or more ancient orders of aristocracy did not appear to bother much with the vulgar business of trading the fish grown in their ponds, those on the move were not so shy about making a bit of money. Ambitious Thomas Wriothesley, for example, took on the former monastic ponds of Titchfield with at least half an eye on the profit it might bring him and his partners in the enterprise: the bailey of Gernsey supplying 500 carps, Mr Huttuft providing the freight, Mr Mylls the tubs and Mr Wells the conveyance of the carps, all so that Wriothesley might 'in three or four years' time sell £20 to £30 of them every year'. The fast-growing immigrant offered those who cared to notice the opportunity to turn a social statement into a business.

Within a hundred years carp had completely overtaken the affections of English pond-keepers. The Earl of Rutland had them – bought from Paul Robinson, a Lincolnshire carp-trader who charged twelve pence for ten-inch fish and two shillings for eighteen-inch fish. Thomas Marchant made a living – working in Sussex alone – netting and selling carp from one estate to the next. The post-Reformation monasteries stocked carp. There were carp at Cornbury Park in Oxfordshire, at the Archbishop of Canterbury's ponds at Harrow in Middlesex, at Frensham Ponds near Farnham; descendants of Thomas Wriothesley's carp still swim in the ponds at Titchfield. Lord Wharton's ponds at Upper Winchendon in Buckinghamshire contained many hundreds of great carp. Carp were more or less everywhere, documented in innumerable estate records, in agricultural and husbandry treatises too.

John Taverner's surreally titled 1600 publication *Certain Experiments Concerning Fish and Fruit* made no secret of his favouritism: a bream will be very long in growing, he wrote, 'as commonly five or six years before he be a foot long'. The tench will grow and prosper well, but nothing like as well as a carp. He had seen carp, he wrote fondly, thirty-three inches between the eye and the fork of the tail, but never a tench above twenty-two. Moreover the carp will abide 'the most hardness in carriage' and will survive five or six hours wrapped only in wet hay.

The hardy carp was also well adapted to Taverner's moral, utilitarian tone. For Taverner was careful to draw a distinction between the 'necessary, and profitable' ponds he advocated, and the 'vain and ostentatious' sea ponds of the 'prodigal' Romans, who had misspent their resources where fish could just as well be taken from the sea itself. No, Taverner would rather have ponds built far inland where it was difficult to find fish which are 'fresh, good and sweet'. Taverner clearly felt the need to advocate: if only fish were eaten on the days by law ordained for that purpose, it would be to the incredible benefit of the realm, for fresh fish is very wholesome for a man's body. Nowadays, he rued, those who should eat fish would rather spend their money on rabbits and cockerels and the like.

He was right. The British were eating fewer fish in general and fewer freshwater fish in particular. His gentle complaint reflects a changing palate and changing fashion. The carp came in on a wave, and rode out its dying crest – even if it was a slow wave to break: over a century later the lawyer and biographer Roger North was still extolling the virtues of owning a fish pond with which you may 'enlarge the expense of your house, and gratify your family and friends that visit you, with a dish as acceptable as any you can purchase for money; or you may oblige your friends and neighbours, by making presents of them, which from a country-man to the king is well taken.'

Despite Taverner's desire to improve the realm through eating carp, and North's endorsement of a fish pond's social benefits, we were perhaps too much an island, and too little of our island was ever far enough from the sea. Over the Channel in the heart of continental Europe carp-rearing took on a wholly more professional dimension, the like of which was never really seen in England. Here fish-rearing never quite lost its dilettante Roman beginnings. And as fashions changed, as cod, haddock and herring eased carp, bream and pike off the national plate, this gentle English idleness found itself a new outlet in the best waste of time ever invented: fishing. Even Taverner's puritan tome contains a nod in the direction of the expectations of the indolent angler: 'It may here be expected that I should set down the baits to be used for all kinds of pond fish,' he wrote. 'But I have not had such exact knowledge to prescribe unto the diligent practitioner any better than he can find out himself.' To think that some people might even angle for the fish in his beloved ponds!

A VERY SUBTIL FISH

If Taverner was reluctant to say what bait might trick a carp, it was because few knew. Dame Juliana Berners had little to say about them in 1496 except that 'they are an evil fish to take'. The first, but certainly not the last indication that the carp is very crafty and tricky to catch. A hundred years later Leonard Mascall of Plumstead didn't know a lot more. 'He is a strange fish in the water and very strange to bite,' he wrote, echoing Dame Juliana. 'No weak harness will hold him,' he added. As to what you might catch it on, here was the first hint that the carp owned an appetite to make quack chefs of anyone who might chase it: 'the red worme and Menowe be good baits for him in all times of the year, and in June with caddys or water-worme: in July and in August with the Maggot or gentyll, and with the coal worme, also with paste made with hony and wheate flower, but in

Automne with the red worme is best and also the grasshopper with his legs cut off, which he will take in the morning, or the whites of hard eggs steeped in tart ale, or the white snail.'

Sixty years or so later Izaak Walton published *The Compleat Angler*, a book which has gone through 300 subsequent editions and sold more copies in English than anything else except the Bible and the complete works of Shakespeare. The carp, he wrote, was the 'Queen of Rivers, a stately, a good and a very subtil fish'. By which he meant to say the same as Juliana and Leonard – the carp is terribly difficult to catch. Meandering through a speculative natural history of this fish that 'hath not long been in England', Walton ruminated on its breeding habits – like wild rabbits and some ducks; its size – like the crocodile and the elephant; and its longevity – a carp will live for ten years, or thirty, or perhaps as long as a century. While much more could be said of the carp, Walton was keen to get back to the business end of his treatise: how to catch them. And this is what he had to say: 'My first direction is, that if you will fish for a carp, you must put on a very large measure of patience.' He had known anglers fish for days on end without ever getting a bite. If you must fish for a carp, he continued, try them early or late, and know that you cannot be either too early or too late. Which advice, taken to its logical extreme, really meant there was no good time at all.

As for baits, Walton drew from and expanded on Mascall's maggoty alchemy. Bluish marsh or meadow worms and green gentles can work, he wrote. As do pastes, made with honey or sugar. Or the flesh of a rabbit or cat, cut small, mixed with bean flour and honey and ground in a mortar. It might be a good idea to mix the gentles with honey, he added. And maybe put them on a hook with a little sliver of scarlet soaked in oil of Peter. As for ground-baits, the stuff you throw in to get the carp on the feed, try grain mixed with cow dung, chicken guts and any other garbage you can find. God knows what Izaak's kitchen was like the day he set off carping. And that was pretty much all he had to say about this subtle fish. My next discourse, he wrote, shall be on bream, 'which shall not prove so tedious'.

Sifting through the carpy cogitations of angling authors over the centuries, one gets the idea that with each publication very little knowledge is added while much is copied: in 1787 Thomas Best wrote more or less the same things as Izaak Walton had in 1653. The queen of fish, lives longer than any other, patience is necessary, can't be up too early or too late, seldom refuse redworm in April, the caddis in May, ground-bait of garbage and chicken guts. Blah blah. Best had discovered nothing new whatsoever, except ... 'nothing exceeds a green pea, parboiled'. Thomas Salter had nothing much to add in 1815. The carp is very shy in biting at a bait, he cautioned, echoing the common lament, particularly the large ones, which seem to grow more cunning as they get bigger. They feed in the warmest months when ... you guessed it ... redworms make the best bait. Bread dipped in honey is good too. Sweetened ground-bait helps. Most of all, wrote Salter, keep low and well back from the edge of the water. Go at it very quietly. And watch your float, because the smartest carp will strip it clean without you even knowing they are there. At least with these last snippets of field craft, you feel that Salter had actually angled for, hooked and maybe caught a carp.

Now it was my turn.

KERDUFF

It had rained all night. I could smell autumn in the air. An earthy smell that always makes me feel sad. Perhaps because summer is passing, or perhaps because it's the same damp smell of the Sussex countryside in September and reminds me of dusky autumnal car rides back to school. I was driving now, over the ridge of chalk in

Wiltshire that separates the Ebble Valley from Cranborne Chase. The road was wet and covered with the year's first leaf-fall. I remembered: that's where I first fished for carp – in Sussex, in a pond called Stinkers. It was rumoured to hold a few good ones, along with wellington boots and underpants and cigarette butts. I don't think I ever saw the carp. I certainly never caught one. I used to fish the place with a pal called Nick, with whom I also shared a school room and a love of moody bands like The Cure, Joy Division and Echo and the Bunnymen. Stinkers was just a good place to escape to. A smelly hole in the hill that even the keenest of the smoker-hunter teachers couldn't be bothered to explore.

Then one Sunday after Mass, Nick and I took the bus to Mayfield. His mum taught at the girls' school there. We knew a few of the girls. I fancied one of them more than was good for me, given all that mournful music. I think we hung around the school until the nuns got wise and then Nick suggested we get a fishing rod from his house and try the local pond. We had a bottle of cider, a portable cassette player and someone or other's new album. I remember climbing a stile, setting off across a cow meadow heading for a circle of beech trees nestled in the hollow below, when some old boy called us back and asked to see our permits. We didn't have any, of course, but Nick said his was at the bottom of his tackle box and slumped his shoulders like it was the hardest thing in the world to put his kit down and get it out. 'Go on then,' the man said. 'Thanks, mate,' said Nick.

This pond, whoever it belonged to, was not like Stinkers. The water was clear and covered with lily pads. There were fish in it. 'What are they?' I asked. I never really expected our day to be troubled by real fish. 'Carp,' said Nick. 'Crucian carp.'

It is important to say here that crucian carp are not the same fish at all. They are indigenous, quite rare and not very big. 'All you do is float bread to them. Chuck it to a patch in the lilies and wait.'

So I did. I threaded my hook with a crust of Mother's Pride and dropped it on the water, sat down and waited for a bite.

Chris's house takes some finding. He had warned me, but I hadn't been listening that carefully. I'd been there once before and thought I'd remember. You can't see it from the road, he said. It's lost behind a hedge and an apple tree. But it's the second house on the right after you pass the speed-limit sign. And that last bit was all I'd noted down, scribbled across the 14th in my diary. Only the sign was ambiguous. The village had two. Suddenly I doubted that he had meant on the right. Perhaps he said the left. And what colour was his car? Was it red? I drove to the centre of the village. Perhaps his instructions assumed I'd be coming from the north. As in Norfolk. I turned round, drove back out and started again. But I had to do it twice before I took his directions as literally as I should have in the first place. The *first* house on the right was a modern brick box. Beside it was a concrete ramp and top left a blue Japanese car, not a red French one. There was no sign whatsoever of an actual house. Could he have meant here? The wild hedge to the side of the ramp was unbroken. No gate. No gap. But over the top I could make out the primary dots of a few apples. Maybe it was here. I parked and took a look. Halfway along there was a gap in the hedge after all, a tiggy-winkle gap of the sort nervous deer might use. And beyond it a barely discernible path threaded through rampant vegetation to the ambiguous front door of a cottage that was hardly there. Chris *is* a carp, I thought. As secretive as his secret carp.

A string of Buddhist prayer flags was suspended between a branch of the apple tree and the door. The garden beyond melted into an autumnal haze, the air heavy and gauze-like. A deep, deep silence. Only pigeons cooing in the wood behind the house. One half of the porch door had not been opened in years. Several days' worth of mail lay on a damp and dusty doormat. Ivy fingered through gaps in the timber. This must be the place, I thought. But I hardly recognised it. When had I last been here? Ten years? Fifteen? I knocked tentatively, not quite expecting an answer.

There was a noise inside. The door opened and Chris – an older, greyer Chris, but just as tall and imposing – stooped into the doorway and smiled and warmly shook my hand.

'Come in. Come in,' he said. He checked his watch. 'Plenty of time for tea. The goblins won't get us if we get there after midday.'

I followed Chris through to the kitchen, looking about at the cosy interior, the landing nets and coats, the piano, the lived-in sofas, the drainer piled high with crockery and the sink full of pans. On top of that pile was a sieve half full of tea leaves. Chris tipped his teapot into the sink, and knocked the dregs of the leaves into the sieve. He found two mugs and stood them by the kettle in readiness. Chris likes his tea. So do I. I knew I was going to get a good cup.

While the kettle boiled we went through to his study and I recognised the room we sat in years before, the lines of books, the desk, the reels and creels here and there, a few fishing rods in the corner, papers all over the floor, another piano. I spotted a painting. I'd already spotted several. Chris has an eye for art. But this one was fabulous. A small abstract half hidden behind a side-light and a vase of dried flowers.

'I love that painting,' I said. 'It's like a Sussex lake, and the carp ponds you describe so well. You know, it could almost be by Ivon ...'

'It is,' said Chris. 'And you noticed it before. Last time you were here.'

The kettle boiled and clicked off and we headed back to the kitchen. Chris filled the pot.

'They're a special recipe,' he said, gesturing to a neat pile of sandwiches wrapped in greaseproof paper on the bread-board. 'My fishing sandwiches. I'm not going to tell you what's in them, but they're perfect for a long day on the water. You're going to have to guess. One of those and you won't need anything else. But just in case, I have fruit cake too.'

Chris poured milk into each mug, then a torrent of steaming tea. We walked back to the front room and I slumped into an ancient and much-patched sofa that seemed to engulf me whole, so that it was an effort to sit back up again and take one of the Scottish oatcakes when Chris opened the packet and tipped them on to a plate.

'These are great with tea,' he said. 'Go on. They're open now. We'll have to finish them. They'll go stale otherwise.'

We began to talk … about carp, first of all about crucian carp which have become Chris's obsession lately. The little fish I'd encountered in that pond in Mayfield.

'Crucians are the true indigenous carp aren't they?' I asked, trying to clear up a point I was still confused about. '*They're* what you carp anglers call "wildies"?'

'Yes,' said Chris. 'Well, no. No! The *wildies* are the monastery fish, the ones that traditionally came over with the monks. They're sort of long and lean. They come from the Danube and the Rhine, Galicia, that kind of area. They were taken down the Silk Road because they travelled well and thrived in China. Then they came back again. That's how the story emerged that they had come from the Far East. They're what we call wildies, the medieval carp, because the bigger fish, you know the really big carp that everyone gets so obsessed about now, they didn't start to appear until the end of the nineteenth century, the beginning of the twentieth. In the middle of the eighteenth century the French had started selectively breeding common carp, you see, getting the biggest of a batch, the biggest male crossed with the biggest female and they kept on doing that until suddenly they were getting super-carp, fish weighing forty or fifty pounds. And from *that* stock, which were a completely different shape, deeper and fatter and broader, we got our bigger carp. They're called king carp. A few were imported to England, but not many at first.'

'So how did that happen?'

'It was all down to an amazing man called Donald Leney. He started importing king carp and in the 1930s he put carp into Redmire, a pond in Herefordshire, where they grew up to become the monsters of folklore. One was the fish Dick Walker caught, Clarissa, and one was the Bishop, the fish I caught.'

Chris handed me another oatcake. 'Three more each,' he said. 'Then we'll go.'

I wanted to know about how he'd first fished for carp, how he fell in love with them.

'I was five years old,' said Chris. 'There was a village pond that contained these mythical fish which I'd heard about but never seen. It wasn't much of a place. Small. About a quarter of an acre. I was walking around it one day with my father and suddenly these things appeared. It was like stumbling on a pit of dragons. I was completely terrified and yet fascinated too. Then, about two years later there was this old boy fishing there, sitting on a creel and puffing a pipe. He had something in his keep-net. I asked Dad if he'd ask if I could see it. The old boy didn't say a word. He just lifted the net. I asked, what is it, what is it? And he said "Carp." That's all he said. That was a wildie. Long and lean and bright gold. I was completely smitten. I fished there for about five years before I caught one!

'Then I found out about this other pond. I'd go down in the evening on my bicycle, telling Mum not to wait up. I'd sneak in through a gap in the wall and be out all night. Next morning I might make up something about getting up early and Mum never knew. These were all places to discover and poach. But then I heard about a local man who sometimes fished at Redmire. He was part of the syndicate there.

Tom. Tom lived just down the road from me, so one day after I'd been fishing I decided to go and knock on his door. I was soaked, because I'd had a good day and had to go in twice to get my fish and he looked at me and said, "You've been fishing!" I said I'd come to tell him about a big carp I'd caught and he invited me in and laid out newspaper on his sofa for me to sit on. I told him about my secret lake and my secret way in. I took him there and later he took me to his other special place called Longfield at Wraysbury. He had a thirty-pounder that night, the biggest carp he'd ever caught and he declared that I was good luck. And that's how I met Tom. And that's how, eventually, I got to fish Redmire.

'Talk about full circle,' said Chris handing me the final oatcake. 'Tom took that fish home – because there were plans at the time to fill in the lake – and put it into his local pond, which was crazy because the pond was only a few feet deep. Within a few weeks word got out about this monster. Some keepers from Chessington Zoo came and netted it out and they sold it to London Zoo, because Clarissa had died. You know, Walker's record fish from Redmire? I remember going to see Clarissa and being mesmerised by this vast fish. Tom's fish replaced Clarissa and she's still there. Still alive.'

'Still at London Zoo?'

'I think so,' said Chris.

'So how old would that fish be?'

'They live a very long time. Fifty, sixty, seventy years. As long as people. The fish I caught at Redmire was fifty years old.'

'So, tell me about Redmire. It's legendary. I've never seen it and in my mind I have a mix of all the ponds you've ever written about.'

'Here, I've got a picture of it somewhere.'

Chris rustled through a pile of papers on the table beside him and pulled out a black-and-white photograph of a small lake nestled in the hollow of a hill, built up behind a dam wall and surrounded by trees: basically it was a medieval vivarium with a 1960s car beside it.

'It was just a farm pond really. Before the carp it was just eels and gudgeons. Some trout that didn't do well. The record before Redmire was a fish of twenty-six pounds, caught on light tackle from a big reservoir. People basically thought there was no point fishing for carp in overgrown lakes, because you had to use light gear or you didn't hook them and if you did use light gear they'd smash you. Redmire changed all that.

'In that first year I fished with a friend called Rod. He was one of the best anglers I knew. A scaffolder from Grimsby, and good at football too. Semi-professional. He had never caught a twenty-pounder. I had caught only one. We met at the dam. It was like we were members of the village cricket club and here we were at Lord's about to get our heads bowled off. And while we were talking this fish came up and rolled. I still remember Rod's face: he was just incredulous, like we've got *this place* to *ourselves* for a *week*!? I caught a sixteen-pounder that time and the next we both had twenties. And then on our next trip I could feel something in the air. I said, "Tomorrow morning I'm going to catch something vast. I can feel it."

'In the morning there was rain. And a rainbow. Rod brought me a cup of tea. My baits were out and I was using sweetcorn. No one else used sweetcorn. And that was the key to it all, I think. I had sweetcorn because I had it with scrambled egg every morning. I'd saved a handful. So, on this morning bubbles started to appear in the middle of the central channel. Rod spotted them. When you see those bubbles it means the carp are truffling on bloodworm and disturbing the silt. It's a wonderful giveaway. I immediately recast and placed the rod on its stick. I had the pick-up open and a little fold of silver paper on the line. Rod hurried across to the island and cast to the same patch of bubbles. I remember he was rubbing his hands, saying "I think it is going to be an historic morning," and I said back, "It *is* going to be an historic morning."

'And then my line started to move. The silver paper lifted very slowly. And then stopped. Normally the line keeps going. It's one of my favourite sounds in the world, fishing line sliding through silver foil. But it stopped. So I pulled it back down again. I thought perhaps the line had drifted. Then it slid back up again. Just a short pull. But the line remained tight. And then it started to run ... *tsssss* ... through the foil. So I clicked the arm on the reel. It was a Mitchell 300 of course.' Chris stopped himself. Clicked his fingers. 'No! It was an Ambidex. An old Ambidex. And then I tightened the line. And then it was just ... *gnuuuuh*. You know? It went into the weeds and just stayed there, and that was it, until slowly, slowly it came to the surface with the weed wrapped all around it. And there was just this enormous *kerduff*. There was this island of weed and this huge tail. Anyway, it was forty-three pounds. It was the second biggest from Redmire at the time.'

I must have been pulled upright by the gravity of Chris's story, thinking I was hearing the tale of *the* record fish. I slumped back.

'Second biggest? So that wasn't your record?'

'No,' said Chris, enjoying the fact that he had *lots* of big-carp stories. 'In fact she weighed forty-three and thirteen ounces. The record then was forty-four. Walker's record. And when we weighed mine it was forty-four and two ounces. But the wind was up. We'd hung the scales in a tree and they were bouncing around, the needle quivering just above forty-four, forty-four dead, just below, then back up again. So, we decided to try again later. We put the fish in a sack. I think it had lost some weight by the time we tried again. We had to wait for Jack Hilton – who ran the syndicate – to drive all the way over from Hitchin, in his Jag, to witness it. Because he couldn't believe this complete amateur with his sweetcorn and his split-cane fishing rods had a caught a bigger fish than anything he had managed. I mean, he was a very good angler and I was just a noddy really.

'So, I fished Redmire for just a couple of years and then I had ...'
Chris paused. 'Well ... I had a very bad experience. An experience of
the heart. A girl, who I really loved, who I'd been seeing for eight
years. She wanted to get married. I wouldn't marry her. Marriage is
not for me. I knew that. Because I'm away such a lot, fishing. I'm out
all summer. But, she was *always* there when I came home again. She
was a Londoner too. A Chelsea girl. Then one day I came home and
she wasn't there. I'd always presumed. You can't take people for granted.
Especially when you leave them for several months of the year. I was
just in a terrible state. It was my own fault, but it blew me sideways.
I must have given up fishing for ... something like three weeks. I left
Redmire because it was Redmire that had done it.

'But then I got invited back. It was kind of nice, in the end, that
I nearly did it and then finally I broke the record with something
much bigger. A fifty-one-and-a-half-pound mirror carp. Incredibly
it was a fish I'd caught before. I'd caught it in '73, the last fish before
my girlfriend left me. It was thirty-eight pounds then. Often seen
but never caught. I caught it twice. I hadn't really set out to catch
a record. I was just there in this extraordinary place. All those huge
fish in this tiny pool.'

Chris checked his watch.

'Heavens,' he said. 'We've got to go! Or we'll never get fishing
ourselves.'

My tea was stone cold. All the oatcakes were gone and the day
was going too. I was ready for a sofa-sized fish.

CHRIS'S PERFECT POOL

Squeezing through the narrow front door we hefted Chris's arsenal
of rods and nets, Kelly Kettles and sandwich tins, bait boxes, camping
stools, boots and coats along the narrow path and through the hedge
to the cars.

'Think we'll go in mine,' said Chris. 'It knows its way there.'

We set off, classical music on low, the car smelling faintly of bait, and Chris telling me another story. We passed the tiny village pond, a puddle beside the bus stop and telephone box – Chris said he'd put carp in there once, and they got big too, double figures, until one summer it dried out – and out along the hedge-lined roads. Thinking about those bus-stop carp, I asked how long he'd lived here.

'Thirty years,' he said. 'And I'd live here for the walking, never mind the fishing. Especially around mid-summer. I wait until the sun goes down and take off. I walk all night along the paths and lanes that criss-cross the downs. There aren't any roads. You don't see any cars. And I walk to earn my sunrise. I always go when the stars are out. There's a hill, an iron-age fort, this amazing headland and if you get it right the sun comes up over a sea of mist. It's just fabulous.'

We came over the top of the hill like a tiny boat riding an enormous, swelling ocean. The undulating horizon of green fell away and ahead was a limitless view across the Nadder Valley to a distant shoreline of hills. The scarp of chalk downland peeled away east and west, bluffs like knuckles resting on a patchwork green tablecloth, the fields of wheat and barley on the flat land below. Chris paused to describe the carp fishing within our sight.

'The best crucian-carp lake in the country is down that valley there. Our secret spot is over there, where those pines are. Fonthill is beyond those distant trees. These are all ponds built where the chalk meets greensand. Along that dark ridge of trees and wrinkled ground.'

The first book I read by Chris was called *The Secret Carp* and the first story in it was called 'The Perfect Pool' in which he described riding his motorbike one moonlit, misty night through sunken Sussex lanes, getting utterly lost trying to find a pub. In the hollow of a wood he came across the scent of a lake, the smell of ancient water, weaving through the other smells of wild garlic and elder, like 'woodsmoke through a barn of apples'. He stopped his bike, propped it by a fence post and stumbled through brambles and undergrowth until he could see a pool nestling in the valley below, hemmed in by willows. He resolved to go back, not least because as he turned to go he heard the crash of a massive carp splashing in the shallows. But he never could find the place on a map and it was some years before he tried again. Even then there was no sign of the lake. Daylight revealed that all he had seen was mist lying at the foot of the valley, dense on the ground over a sunken marsh where an ancient lake used to be. And the sound of the jumping fish: a ghost carp, thought Chris, or more likely a badger. Of course that story set the scene because the rest of the book was about a real, perfect pool and the spectral carp which haunted it. But it also set in my mind an image so vivid I almost feel they are my own memories. The fact that Chris's phantom pool vanished by day hardly matters. It was still real to me and it was that perfect pool I felt we were on the way to now. A familiar journey along a strange road, to a place I'd never seen before but already knew.

Somewhere along a leafy road, where the rain still dripped from a cavern of trees and lorries hissed along sopping tarmac, we turned through a neo-Gothic gateway on to the rutted tracks of an estate road. Chris didn't like the look of the ruts, the churned ground. 'Looks like something's going on,' he said. A little further we passed an unmanned digger and a pile of aggregate. But beyond that the track was reassuringly overgrown. It was okay. They were fixing the track near the gate, but nothing had been along here in days. We slithered along the wet lane, passing enormous, ancient oaks with ragged sails of moss hanging off them until we reached a clearing at the edge of the wood. A thin path cut from the lane through bracken and brambles to a narrow gate. Beyond was a wide-open meadow curving across the face of the hillside. A line of trees filled the cleft of the valley. On the hill opposite, a grand, stone house loomed over ridges of meadow and a cockscomb of trees.

'You just wouldn't know,' said Chris, 'there's a string of lakes in those trees. Six in a line along a little stream. And you won't see them till you're standing beside them. It might be windy up here,' he said, 'but down the bottom, there won't be a breath of it.'

He was right. The lake was flat calm, though the tops of the trees shivered and bent in the wind and leaves came spiralling down on to the water. We stood in the corner by the gate.

'This used to be great, but that fallen oak means this is now a dangerous place to fish. Not physically, but because anything you hook will get you into that tree and break you.'

The tree was fifty yards away. I tried to imagine a freshwater fish that couldn't be stopped in fifty yards of open water. Chris sensed my doubt.

'That's the incredible thing about carp,' he said. 'They're so quick. The line hisses sometimes. They live this life of ease. They just float around. They sunbathe. You'll see them all docked in a bay, under the lily pads, like big ships. Sometimes they'll hoist a sail. I think they signal. The dorsal will come up and ease back down. And then they'll just slowly armada across the lake. But then you hook one! And it's like dynamite. You cannot stop them getting into the willows. These aren't even huge fish. And the tree might be fifty yards away – like that one – and the reel is just fizzing. And then they get there and it's a tug of war, the fish thumping, and thumping. Where does that strength come from? Why do they need all that power? The trick,' he said as we started walking, 'is that when they reach the tree you've got to let them go. If the line is tight you'll lose them.'

And I had just started to tell him a story of my own when there was a fizzing splash in the water under the bushes beside the path. My heart skipped a beat, but it was just a shoal of small perch. They came back after a minute and Chris threw a few maggots for them. When he opened the bait tin I knew what had caused the strange smell in the car.

We passed on round the lake heading for a particular spot, pausing at Chris's regular swims along the way. Every so often a gust of wind sidestepped the cordon of trees and pawed the water in snaking shivers. Chris was worried that we weren't seeing any fish, but the day felt autumnal to me, not summery at all. And then we saw one. A dark shape sliding under the surface like the shadow of a cloud.

'I remember a day just like this,' said Chris as we watched it swim away, as if that was the point of our mission. 'And I hadn't seen a thing till I came round this corner here. Then this shape came out from under the alders, and went down into the weed. I hadn't set anything up yet, so I pulled out the pin and quickly ran the line through the rings. I always have a hook tied on because I can't be arsed to tackle up. I rarely have the time. Three grains of corn. Just dropped it in front of the fish. It was raining. Light rain. Just like this. And I saw this welling on the surface. The float twitched and then moved. The line tightened and there was a tremendous splash and I was just soaked. It hit a weed bed. But it came out. And twenty minutes later I had it. A fantastic common. And in this light, with the September sun. They're just incandescent.'

With that we were off again, jousting our cane lances through the undergrowth, over stiles and slippery footbridges to the next spot and another story. Perhaps about bait this time, sweetcorn versus maggots, how Chris uses whatever everyone else isn't using, or his bait tin which he was given when he was fourteen. 'Go on. Smell it,' he said, inhaling the air of it like he was smelling a rose. 'It's a lovely smell. Maggots and curry powder.'

A kingfisher streaked past just as we reached the head of the lake. We set our stuff down and quiet as a bomb-disposal team crept to the edge of the water. Dammit! A whorl of mud. Another affronted shadow gliding away under the surface. A moment later there was the most enormous splash.

'They do that to clear their tanks,' said Chris. 'It's a sign they're feeding. That was a small one. Twenty pounds at the most,' he said smiling as the ripple fanned out across the lake.

I wondered if it was time to rig up, but Chris was into another story.

'I heard one jump at Redmire once,' he said. 'It was a moonlit night. The fish must have been a hundred yards away, but there was this enormous *kverrschhhhh* and then a pause ... and then a *badduphhh*. And it was like a cow had lost its footing and fallen in off the far bank. I knew what was coming. I waited. It was a few minutes, then the reflection of the moon started to wobble and then another pause and the ripple arrived and slammed into the dam wall and lapped and lapped at my feet. The size of it!'

And still we did not put our bait into the water. By now I was wrestling with both an impatient urge to grab a rod and start fishing and a certainty that fish can sense impatience and don't like it. So, feeling a teeny bit urgent I was also trying to go with the flow of things. Then again, I was also beginning to suspect that Chris has caught so many carp he really isn't bothered any more and also that carp anglers so rarely catch carp perhaps because they so rarely cast.

'I tell you what,' said Chris. 'We've set up camp. Let's tiptoe round the top and have a look up there.'

Off we went, slithering along another path, with just the bait tin this time. We crossed the brook at the head of the lake, where a frothy, tea-stained torrent trickled under rhododendrons and tree roots to spill out across a delta of sandy mud.

'Winter or summer, there's always the same flow. Maybe there's a bit more voice to it today.'

We were whispering, though I don't know why. Neither of us had seen anything. Chris threw some bait in.

'Look. Look!' he exclaimed with boyish excitement. 'Bubbles! That's where I threw the bait. Look at that.' I could see the bubbles.

I just couldn't see our fishing rods. Another storm-cloud puffed away across the lake. Three carp and counting. None cast to.

'I tell you what,' said Chris ... and here I have to admit, I really did expect a call to arms, 'we'll make some tea. Eat our sandwiches. And we'll give it all time to stew up here.' And heading back over the stream, Chris remembered yet another story: something about Diana Rigg this time and another very big carp.

Our camp was a furrow in the ground, like an old track across a ford, that led to a clearing in the willows and a patch of open water. Chris slid the rods out of their ancient canvas and leather holdalls. Every stick and twig of Chris's tackle is vintage, while his rods have names and recorded histories, each carp a chalk on the fuselage. I would be using 'Pope Joan Carp', built by Edward Barder in 1996. Chris joined the sections together, gave it a wiggle and handed it over.

'That's yours', he said. 'I was using Pope Joan on opening day this year. I caught a twenty-one-pounder with it. So it's got good luck that rod. I'll be using the Walker rod.'

Not *the* Walker rod, but another. Chris has a share in *the* Walker rod, the rod that caught Clarissa, whose two owners call it Excalibur. The one Chris was using today was built by Richard Walker for Horace Smith, president of the Leighton Buzzard Angling Club. It sat in a garage for twenty-five years. Then Chris heard about it and restored it. Walker's rods are legendary, and valuable. Someone offered Chris £4,000 for this one. But he turned them down. 'All that history,' he said ruefully. 'Besides, this rod,' peering down the shaft like it was a rifle, 'is actually a nicer fishing rod than Excalibur. And I'm sorry you have Pope Joan. But it is a fabulous rod too and this one ... I just can't let anyone use this.'

Never mind what rod I had, I felt an urgent desire to cast with it. I think Chris could tell. He passed me his box of curried maggots with instructions to thread on a bunch of them, one after another. Soon my hook looked like a hideous lock of Medusa's hair. The perfect look, apparently, so I flicked the writhing Medusa ball towards the edge of the willow tree where we had seen the whorl of mud earlier. The float cocked and bobbed.

'Do you realise,' I said to Chris, 'that's my first cast ever after common carp?'

'It's a good one.'

Chris lit the Kelly Kettle and told me about the time he lit the kettle and caught a twenty-four-pounder. Smoke drifted blue and gauzy across the water. Further out I saw shadows drifting under the reflections of the trees and bubbles pop lazily to the surface here and there. Another tank-clearing crash. Chris handed me a sandwich and looked at me expectantly. I took a bite.

'Peanut butter?'

'Yes.'

'And ... celery?'

'Yes! Two of those and you'll run a mile.'

I turned to see how the kettle was doing, thinking that I could more or less murder a cup of tea. Suddenly Chris stood and pointed.

'You've got a bite. You've got a bite!'

I couldn't believe it. Sandwich wedged in my face I leapt forward and hefted the rod into a strike. But the float sailed lazily out of the water and plopped a ball of soggy maggots at my feet.

'Never mind,' said Chris. 'Orange pekoe?'

I cast again. Chris handed me a cup and flicked his bait out to join mine. Chris on his stool, me on a mossy log, we ate our sandwiches, sipped our tea, watched our floats. Pope Joan and the Leighton Buzzard special were cocked at the horizon like vintage weaponry. A crackle of burning sticks from the dying Kelly furnace. Clouds of white smoke drifting out across the water. We sat in silence. Waiting. Sipping. Chewing. Once in a while the sky brightened, or the clouds and light aligned just so, taking the glare off the surface until we could see those dark shapes drifting here and there. Then fizzing fartlets of bubbles would appear in a busy ring or line and a moment later the water nearby would cloud. The carp were feeding. Just not near us. This is what Chris loves about carp fishing, he claimed. The contrast between these long, quiet periods of nothing and the sudden, insane violence of the take. There's actually so much going on, even when there's nothing happening, he said. And then very suddenly it's all happening to you.

Only it wasn't. I thought of Walton, and my great measure of patience. The far bank looked busier, I thought. After an hour we took our rods and tried there instead.

Bit by bit the afternoon sun cut in at a shallower angle, then finally it dipped under a low cloud. Almost exactly as the last ray vanished the wind picked up and a cool gust sent another confetti storm of yellowing leaves spiralling on to the surface of the lake. Every so often one or other of the two floats would dip and dance. But we'd worked out by now these were just tiny perch menacing our maggots.

'There was a moment back then when I really thought it was cooking up,' said Chris, with a sense of retrospection I didn't like.

He was right, though. The lake had livened for a tantalisingly brief snippet of time and now it was quieter, even if I couldn't quite say how. The odd bubble, but not so many. The dark shapes gone and the last one I saw heading somewhere else. No tank-clearing splashes. A spell had fallen on the place, but not in a good way. Chris kept up the stories. But increasingly it felt like these tales would be the only carp I'd catch.

Then the water swirled nearby. A line of bubbles. Were they approaching my float? No sooner had I wondered than it dipped, really convincingly this time, nothing like the timid taps of the perch. I struck hard and a perch came sailing out of the lake and over my head. Dammit. I stood to rescue the stricken fish and a hefty bow-wave burst away from exactly the same spot my float had been. Dammit squared! This bloody perch must have beaten the carp to my bait by a matter of seconds. I briefly wondered about feeding the saboteur to the foxes. But I like perch. It swam off unharmed.

By now the birds were singing out the onset of evening. The air had thickened and cooled. I sneezed. Twice. Chris commented on how nice it is to watch a float and suddenly his dipped too. 'Look! Look!' he said in a hoarse whisper. 'It's going. And I don't think that's a perch either. It has a sort of creepy look. When it goes again I'll ...' It did and he did. Chris struck and another small perch sailed into the undergrowth. A crow cawed from the trees overhead, laughing at us, I felt.

'It's colder,' Chris shivered. 'The air has lost that lovely softness. We should have come round here to start. And you know, I think the smoke might have put them down. But never mind. It's time for tea now. We'll light the kettle again and then, maybe, things will happen in the other direction.'

I don't think either of us believed it. As we trudged back we revisited the sightings and near misses of the day in a somewhat post-mortem state of mind. That fish came close. I thought that other one was going to take. And so on.

Nope. The day had faded and I was sure we weren't going to catch anything, here or back at camp or anywhere else for that matter. Except at the inlet where that enormous shoal of tiny perch still shimmered in the coppery autumnal flow. Chris couldn't help casting at them and before long it was as if this is what we came for: six-inch fish on twelve-foot rods. Never mind. Chris handed me the Walker wand. Have a go, he urged. And so I did. And ten seconds later I had a perch in my hand. Chris clapped in appreciation. 'A fish on the Walker! I told you it never fails!'

THERE'S SOMETHING ABOUT MARY, CLARISSA, THE BISHOP AND TWO-TONE

Still no closer to a large carp, let alone a sofa-sized one, I decided to go and see Clarissa's replacement at the zoo. I was in London a few days later on a sweltering, late September day, so hot that I crossed to the shaded side of the street on the hill between Camden Town Tube and Regent's Park. At the gate I tried to remember the last time I'd visited London Zoo. Maybe it was a school trip or someone's birthday. Suddenly I was in a duffle coat chasing pigeons across the grass. Early 1970s. Clarissa was already dead and according to Chris her Longfield successor must have been at the zoo a few years. But I couldn't remember any of the animals, let alone a carp. Just the pigeons. I wondered what the admission price was then. Forty-odd years later I had a tenner ready but needed a credit card. This was an expensive way to see a carp, I thought. Then a young woman with a camera asked if I'd like my photo taken in front of a jungle backdrop. I said no thanks and then kind of regretted it, but was too embarrassed to go back.

I guessed Madame Longfield would be in the aquarium and wondered which way I should walk, only to find I was right there in front of the word AQUARIUM scored helpfully in Trajan font over the doorway of something that looked like a Mexican bus station. I pushed open the heavy door and walked into a cool and dark interior, mouldy and damp like a river. Under its surface were rows of bubbling TV screens all tuned to the same channel: flittering shoals of colourful fish. Odd, I thought, how they shoal according to species in tanks as busy as Oxford Street: how do they know? There were coral reefs, Amazonian swamps, the Mekong River, Mexican springs. But no monk's pool and no carp, anywhere. Ahead of me a young-love couple looked distractedly at the fish

and intently at each other, canoodling their way from one tank to
the next. There was no one else. I looked around for a member of
staff, someone who could tell me if there was a large common carp
lost somewhere amidst all these arapaima and pirapitinga and
tambaqui. I went out and found someone in a London Zoo shirt
who told me to knock at the door on the left just back inside. I
did. No one answered. I went back out and found the information
desk. But the lady had no idea. I said that I'd tried to look it up
online, but the website wasn't very helpful.

'Don't *you* have a list of species?' I asked.

'Somewhere,' she said. She reached under the desk and brought
out a clipboard with a printed list. She started flipping through the
pages. 'Carp, is it?'

'Common carp,' I said. '*Cyprinus carpio* is how it will be listed.'
She found it eventually.

'It's here,' she said, showing me. 'But the list doesn't say where.'

I went back inside and found an empty tank I'd missed first time
through. I stopped in front of it and sensed something. A fishy vibe
telling me this was where Clarissa had lived all those years ago. So,
I took a picture of the empty space and me reflected in the glass,
as a keepsake to make up for the missed jungle shot. Then, just as
I was about to go a young keeper came out of a door I hadn't even
noticed, a door buried in the blackness of the hall. I stopped him
and asked if there was a carp anywhere.

'There used to be,' he said. 'Years ago. She had a name.'

'Clarissa,' I said. 'But that was fifty years ago.'

'Yes,' he said, thinking. 'I don't know why I know that.'

'I've heard there's another. But it would be very big. I think you'd
know it.'

'No. There's no big carp in here. No small ones either. Not now.'
Then he remembered something. 'I think there are carp in the giraffe
moat,' he said. 'Try there. You might be in luck.'

The lady in the information hut had been replaced by someone who looked almost the same, so when I stopped and told her the carp were in the giraffe moat she looked at me in bewilderment.

'You're not who you were a minute ago,' I said, realising my mistake.

'Aren't I?' she said.

'Sorry. Do you know where the giraffe moat is?'

'Not really,' she said. 'But I can tell you where the giraffes are.'

I had to go under the road and past the hippos. But I had the map she'd given me the wrong way up, and went the wrong way round the loop past the hyenas, asleep under a tree, and the warthogs, who were hiding. The giraffes were out, however, pacing about on a dusty lawn in front of a brick building with twenty-feet-high doorways. One of the giraffes had splayed its front legs and was nibbling the grass. In front of it was a log and some rocks and then a sign that read 'Danger Deep Water' pinned to the concrete above a shallow, dusty trough lined with reeds. My search for the Longfield monster had ended. If she ever did live at London Zoo she wasn't here now and she wasn't in this puddle. She'd have struggled to wet her back in there, I thought, let alone turn around. I was about to turn around too and go ask for my ticket money back when I noticed a ripple on the water. A half-dozen coal-black fish morphed out of the leaf mould and paraded at the edge of the pool. There were carp in there after all. Small carp, but carp nonetheless. I took a photograph on my phone, with the knock-kneed giraffe behind and decided the zoo could keep my money.

When I got home I did what I should have done to start with and called the zoo to ask. But I couldn't get any further than the man who answered the phone, who told me to put my enquiry in an email. By now I was becoming quite obsessed with the fate of these leviathan fish. I wondered what had happened to Clarissa, too.

I sent the email but a moment later an auto-reply bounced back thanking for me for my question, saying that the zoo aims to respond to all enquiries within five days. That seemed like a long time to wait for an answer I felt sure would be disappointing, so I tried searching online instead. I typed 'what happened to Clarissa the carp?' and hit return. Top of the list was a recording of Dick Walker himself describing the epic night which ended so well but began badly when his Ford Anglia broke in half on the way to the pool. He sounded very matter-of-fact about the capture of Clarissa, taking pains to say it was just luck really, but the interview must have been recorded many years later because at the end Walker mentioned Chris's much bigger fish.

Then I found something written at the time by the author Denys Watkins-Pitchford – who went by the pen-name BB – describing the impenetrably dark night and how Walker's fish had taken the bait in the very early hours of dawn, how it very nearly got away when the torchlight drove the fish 'like a bullet through butter' into a thicket of brambles, and how Richard Walker, fearing no one would believe his fishy tale, put the vanquished monster into a sack and called the zoo. As soon as he heard of its improbable size Dr Harrison Matthews sent a van down. Back in those days the zoo clearly responded more quickly to carp queries. His keepers packed the giant fish into a wooden tub and by 2 a.m. the following morning she was recovering in her new home in London: she looks like a small pig, wrote Matthews fondly.

Further down I found a page with pictures of all the British carp records from Walker onwards. First there was a black-and-white Dick Walker in his jacket and cords, the number plate of the broken Ford Anglia just visible in the background and Clarissa resting her heavy belly on the grass in front of him. Then a much younger Chris – in retro colour this one – looking a bit Bob Dylan in his ancient Barbour, a beard and crumpled hat, barely managing to lift the vast coppery slab of the fifty-one-and-a-half-pound fish he called the Bishop off the wet sack he had kept her in. Then the fish which followed: by 1996 it was no longer fashionable to look at the camera for carp pictures, so the young Terry Hearn in his woolly hat and soaking jeans is looking at Mary – a 'total stunner' apparently – who weighed almost fifty-six pounds. Finally there's Austen Holness in a camouflaged suit and baseball cap, almost amazed by the presence in his outstretched arms of the unbelievably enormous Two-Tone, caught for the umpteenth and final time on 16 August 2008 when he weighed a whopping sixty-seven and a half pounds. Clarissa, the Bishop, Mary and Two-Tone. Four record fish in sixty years of obsessive angling and piggy Clarissa at the start of the craze.

I never heard back from London Zoo and guessed, in the end, that carp and enquiries about them no longer featured in their range of interests, which seem to be focussed solely on selling cuddly toys and portrait-in-the-jungle photos to tourists. In fact it didn't take long to discover Clarissa's whereabouts and that she is now also a cuddly toy of sorts, stuffed and kept in a tackle shop in Coventry. I found a few photos on a chat forum. The bald gentleman who was disappointed to find such a famous carp hidden in the corner behind a load of fishing rods, is just visible in the photographs he took, reflected in the glass of Clarissa's case. There was nothing about how she got there, however, and the author hadn't named the shop. I typed 'Clarissa Coventry' and came up with Cakes by Clarissa and Clarissa's Nails at Home, so I tried 'Clarissa carp Coventry' instead. Top of the list was the item I'd just read but underneath that I found a link to a better photograph of her on the website of W. H. Lane & Son, a tackle shop opened by Billy Lane in 1936 when Clarissa would have been tiny. I phoned them and spoke to Tom, Billy's grandson. He said his father Alan had bought the fish at auction in the 1980s but Tom didn't know who from or how she came to be in a glass case. Tom wondered if Richard Walker's widow would know more and said I'd be welcome to come and have a look if ever I wanted.

I thought I might take him up on the offer: it was starting to look like the only way to meet one of these secretive fish. Clarissa must have been the last record carp taken from the water. The record she broke belonged to Albert Buckley, who killed his twenty-six-pound fish in 1930 and put her in a case. But Chris put his fish back. And so did Terry Hearn, though when I looked up the fate of Mary I found out that she had died back in 2001 only a few days after being caught and had been 'buried at sea' in her home pool at Wraysbury. 'A very sad day indeed,' wrote Yoda, when he broke the news and thus the hearts of hundreds of carp anglers on another carp chat forum. The angler who last captured her was distraught. And so was everyone else: 'Rest in Peace Mary!'; 'My thoughts go out to all those directly affected. RIP'; 'We have all caught Mary in our dreams'; 'I never caught her or even saw her. Can someone explain why I feel so sad?'

I was beginning to feel sad myself, so I looked up Two-Tone instead. But Two-Tone had been discovered floating belly up on the surface of Conningbrook Lake on 14 August 2010. Chris Logsdon, who owned the fish, must have taken the news badly. Two-Tone was legendary and had attracted hundreds of hopeful anglers to the fishery. Also known as 'the marriage-wrecker', Two-Tone had yielded coquettishly to their offerings on average about twice a year. Thus he had broken the record about ten times and broken about half as many matrimonial unions. One of Two-Tone's mostly unrequited suitors had even recorded the obsessive relationship in a book. Lee Jackson, who worked in a tackle shop when he wasn't at the lake, described how he had spent 12,000 hours chasing Two-Tone, Sunday to Monday and Wednesday through Friday every week for six years, how his ex-wife thought he was crazy; he described the agony of hearing when Two-Tone was caught by someone else, and the tears he cried when Two-Tone was caught by his best friend! And he described the comedown anticlimax of everything else in life once he finally consummated the quest and caught Two-Tone at a (briefly) record-breaking sixty-one and a half pounds. But now Two-Tone was dead too. He had 'swum out of reach forever', Lee had mourned. 'I wish you well in that great lake in the sky.'

Only Two-Tone wasn't there yet, it seemed. Two-Tone was still in a chest freezer in Essex. The August 2010 report suggested that Two-Tone would soon be buried, that he was in the freezer only until the service, booked for 11 a.m. the following Sunday, when dozens of mourners turned up. One had baked a cake. But then I found another story published only a few months ago, which said that the body was still in the freezer because Chris Logsdon had been worried Two-Tone might have been dug up, stolen and sold on. He'd had a tip-off, apparently. So he'd offered it to the Natural History Museum, but the museum had agreed only to preserve it, not to put Two-Tone on display: a decision the angling community had found upsetting. So Two-Tone was still in the freezer and no one knew what to do with him. Some local wag had suggested a big fish-and-chips supper. I tried to call to find out, but got through to Chris in Hong Kong airport as he was about to board a plane. He promised to call me once he got home. But like the zoo, he didn't call back and though I tried again once or twice I didn't get hold of him again either. I wasn't having much luck with carp.

HOOKED?

I decided the only way I was going to get up close to the wet, leathery reality of a carp was to try again with a fishing rod. It was early August. The year had come full circle and I realised that the auspicious 13 September was only a month or so away. Once again Chris Yates was elusive. I wrote a hopeful email, explaining how my carp explorations needed a conclusion. The weeks ticked by until I remembered that Chris had written to me the previous year apologising for his tardy reply and explaining that he didn't often 'turn this engine on' in the summer, the engine being his vintage computer. So I tried a letter. I thought about using a raven. Meanwhile I started to make enquiries of my own. I live in East Anglia after all, the landing stage of those immigrant carp more than half a millenium ago. I hunted around online and found carp fisheries here and there, most of them recently excavated ponds or stocked gravel pits where I was sure the carp would be almost impossible and the tactics and kit needed to tempt them quite beyond me. I liked Chris's style, just a rod and a bait tin. I could relate to that. It wasn't unlike how I learnt to catch trout. But to stand any hope of success fishing like this I needed a forgotten lake where the carp weren't harassed every day. Such places are not advertised on the internet. They are locked away in private parkland and the chance to fish them tends only to follow years of careful diplomacy. I wasn't about to walk in on carp paradise, in other words.

I gave up on Google and dug out a map of Norfolk. I liked the idea of finding a carp in the remnants of a medieval fish pond but most of those I found reference to – at West Acre and Castle Acre, at Creake Abbey and Great Snoring – had been filled in long ago, and were now only imprints of ditch networks lost under nettles. The one or two that held water were either hidden away in the formal gardens of private houses or were miles away, and I had no idea if there were carp in them anyway. I would have better luck, I thought, hunting down an old estate lake of exactly the sort Chris had taken me to in Wiltshire. Many of these started life as some kind of medieval vivarium anyway, before they became grandified in later centuries by the likes of Humphry Repton or William Kent. No doubt most had been stocked with carp at some stage in their histories. A few are dotted around Norfolk. I asked Dickie, our local fishing-mad decorator, about the place his son Dan used to fish before he left for Australia. Dan had caught the carp bug for a while, and I remembered the stories of his obsessive pursuit of them. It was an estate lake all right, said Dickie, just down the road in what remained of the grounds of Heacham Hall. But the place had been sold since Dan went there. No one fished there now. Dickie gave me the number of the old caretaker, but when I called the line was dead. I drove down there and mooched about, but short of poaching I wasn't going to get anywhere.

So I kept looking. There were some ponds in Hunstanton Park. I wondered about those. The ponds must be old, I thought. The house certainly is. The moat around Oxburgh Hall? I saw a carp in there once. Or was it a pike? It was so long ago. Or the old pond at Baconsthorpe Castle? What about Bayfield? Holkham? Soon I was surrounded by maps and my notebook was filling with possibilities. I imagined those beady eyes and leathery flanks ghosting amongst water lilies. Any one of these places could hold carp, though I wasn't so sure about being allowed to fish any of them.

Finally, I remembered a lake near Downham Market that I had once stalked, unsuccessfully, for pike. It was an old estate lake in the grounds of a country park, and what's more I was very distantly related to its owner. I sent an email and later I called and left a message. I got hold of him eventually and mentioned in passing this tenuous link, as if it might help. I needn't have bothered. He said I was very welcome to try, though he had no idea if the lake held carp. He wasn't a fisherman, he confessed. All I had to do was post a note through the door along with a £5 note. That was the arrangement. The lake was there for all, though he couldn't think when a fisherman had last paid a visit.

I drove there that afternoon, stopping only at Budgens for sweetcorn. With neither the time nor inclination to mix green gentles with honey, or cow dung with chicken guts, I remembered that sweetcorn was one of Chris's favourite baits, not least because he could nibble it when hungry. Thus armed and with my pike-spinning gear adapted for the job at hand I drove through the gates and parked in a yard of old farm buildings, as instructed. There in front of me, tucked under the eaves of a brick storeroom, was a rain-buckled plywood box marked 'fishing'. I lifted its lid, disturbing a few spiders. Inside was the fishery record book, wrapped in a plastic bag. I signed in. The owner was right. No one had been here in months. A hand-painted sign pointed 'lake this way' along a track which snaked through undergrowth into a sunny meadow studded with ancient oaks and cedars, some weather-blasted and broken. Beyond was the lake, a clover-shaped imprint of sky rippled here and there by the afternoon's sultry breeze. It was perfect. I sensed downhill momentum towards an addiction I didn't need.

As I approached the water I noticed a slight ripple in the weeds further along the bank and only a few feet out. Seconds later a tremendous boil. There were fish here all right. Taking a loop away from the edge I rearranged my approach so that I could hold the place I'd seen the splash in line with the shadow of a tree-covered island: now I could see into the water clearly. A few sheep utterly absorbed in their grazing suddenly startled away from me. One ran close to the shore. The water boiled again. The wake of something moving under the surface arrowed across the water and settled. I could see its outline now. A long, lean outline and trefoil fins. A pike.

I walked on, heading instinctively for the dam wall where vast oaks loomed over the water in the shade of which I found a tumble-down boathouse, a jetty and a mossy, wooden diving board, like a deserted vignette from *The Go-Between*. I was already hot. The water was six feet deep and clear as glass and I thought how nice it would be to dive in. But I had carp to catch. By the outflow I saw bubbles fizzing up to the surface. Once. Twice. A carp snouting in the weeds, perhaps? It was enough of a hint to crack open the sweetcorn. I tossed a few pieces over the margin of loosestrife and nettles, hunkered down and waited. After a few moments I dared another peek. The sweetcorn lay unmolested, pinpricks of yellow studding the leaf mould and silt. This was as far as easy walking could take me. Beyond the outflow the track parted company with the shore, and from here on it was a thicket of brambles and willow. I had to press on. I might find a carp mooching about in any one of the bays and inlets along a shoreline that must have amounted to a mile in circumference.

It felt like five miles by the time I'd fought my way round the whole thing. Two hours later I arrived back at the boathouse bathed in sweat, lacerated with cuts and stings, wishing I'd brought food with me, something to drink at least. I'd seen a perch, about two dozen jack-pike and one large hen-pike cruising malevolently over the shallows. But I hadn't seen a carp, or even a sign of one. I sat down on the diving board, my boots touching the surface of the water, and consumed by hunger and thirst I ate the bait with which I had hoped to catch a carp.

I texted home with news of my withered state, wondering what I had been thinking of chasing these spectral fish on my own. But no sooner had I resolved to leave the matter to Chris, should he ever get my entreaties, than my wife Vicky replied asking if I'd called Jim. Duh! Jim is a deerstalker. He knows every estate in Norfolk. I called him from the car. There were carp, he said, at one of the estates he manages. At least there used to be. He'd put a few in the ponds in the woods, fifteen or twenty years ago. An otter had found some of them, but a few might be left behind. He'd be up there next Wednesday if I wanted to come over.

And there I was again, burning incense at the altar of carp.

It was overcast and sultry when I drove in through the arched gatehouse and along a tree-lined driveway. Both the weather and the approach seemed auspicious. Out of instinct more than any idea which way I should head I took a left fork after the trees and found myself on a bridge crossing a weed-covered bay on the edge of a lake. It wasn't the pond in the trees Jim had described, but a movement on the surface caught my attention. I stopped the car and got out. Swimming towards me, head on but spotlit by a high sun and towing an enormous shadow, was an equally enormous carp. The first rule of fishing is don't leave fish to find fish. I called Jim and described where I was standing. There's a Zeppelin here, I said.

'Crack on,' said Jim. 'You're on the house rod.'

I parked the car under a nearby tree. Too excited and flustered to bother with floats and split-shot I decided to go back to the basics I knew from long ago. I tied on a hook and wrapped a ball of white bread around it. That would do. With the rest of the loaf tucked into my waders I crawled to the edge of the lake on my hands and knees, baffling a few nervy sheep as I went by. The inlet was lined with reeds, but there was one small alder bush just about tall enough to hide me. I inched my way up behind it until I could see through the gaps in its leaves. The bulrushes along the far bank heaved and parted. A boil in the water. Seconds later the wake lapped against the reeds at my feet. Then all went quiet. I waited. A shimmy in the water, further away this time. Then nothing.

The minutes passed agonisingly. I rolled a few balls of bread and flicked them one by one into clearings in the weed. As the last one landed with a plop I noticed the head of a giant carp almost within touching distance, still as a statue. Any moment and this seismograph of a fish would pick up my heartbeat. It nudged forward, and then as if the weeds were some kind of restriction it heaved and surged into the clearing. A great dorsal fin broke the surface, and a back like brass armour-plating. Without pausing, the carp tipped on its snout and hoovered a ball of bread. Shaking with nerves I reached for the line, ready to flick my offering in ahead of it, but I turned for a second and when I looked up the carp had simply vanished. How could something so enormous disappear like that?

My only hope was that it was on some kind of circuit. I flicked my bait out over the weeds. It took a few casts, but eventually one landed just right, resting on the surface of the weed just the far side of the clearing where I'd last seen the corpulent fish. I don't know how long it took – ten, twenty minutes – until the carp morphed into visibility on the same languorous journey around its bay, ambling through the passageways of weed. I pulled the line and the bread plopped off the weed just as the carp edged into the nearside corner of the clearing. With a slow, fanning undulation of its tail the blimp idled forwards snouting through the clouding silt, like a hovercraft running over dusty ground. It paused some feet short of my bait. Had it sensed or smelled something? Danger, or a tasty morsel? The blimp sidled forwards again, paused, snouted. A puff of silt. And slowly, falteringly, my line began to move. Was it simply the fish brushing the line? I had no way of knowing. The carp moved forwards. My line moved too. Now it was all or nothing. I lifted the rod and the lake erupted as if a grenade had gone off. My reel fizzed angrily as the carp bolted headlong through the weeds. I'd hooked it. But until this moment I was so intent on getting the carp to take I'd ignored the vanishingly small chance of getting it in. Now we were connected I was trying hard to process the inevitable loss of this leviathan. I had ten-pound breaking strain line. The carp was double that weight, if not more. And now the line was threaded through a forest of undergrowth. But the carp had stopped at least. Fifty yards away the surface of the lake heaved as my carp ground its wheels for traction. It was stuck and so was I. We were at an impasse.

At that moment Jim turned up.

'Is it big?' Jim asked, straight to the heart of the matter.

'I'd call it big. I don't know how big, but it's over twenty.'

'Big enough.'

I asked how hard the bed was. As far as I could tell my only chance was to wade in after it. Jim thought for a moment. It's pretty solid, he said.

'I don't see there's any other option.'

'Is there anything I can do?'

'Er. Tow me out?'

Within two paces it was obvious that Jim's assessment was either out of date or plain made up. If the water was two feet deep the silt under it was four. I was close to my armpits and going under when I turned back to shore.

Having scrambled back through the reeds I assessed my options again.

'Either I strip off and swim, or I heave and see what happens.'

'Heave first?' suggested Jim.

'Good idea.'

I tightened the drag on my reel and pulled. My carp sensed the pressure and heaved back, lashing at the surface. The rod pulsed. I was still connected at least. I heaved again, winning a few feet of line from the jungle. It surged skywards dripping with weed like a washing line hanging with green rags.

'Progress,' said Jim.

The carp bucked. Another few feet of line ripped upwards and suddenly I was free of the weed. Now, if I could only persuade the carp to head back this way ... I set the drag, then slowly I pulled. The carp broke the surface, a broad leathery brown back, scales like chain mail.

'Fucking hell,' said Jim.

The slow heave was working. It took a few minutes but somehow I got the carp to the bank.

'What are you going to do now?'

I had no idea. It was just so bloody big.

'If I had a net it would help. But I thought I'd be catching little wildies, not this airship.'

I let the pressure off so the fish wouldn't bolt, and waded back into the gloop. My only chance was to get it close enough and put my arms around it. But the sudden presence of me in the water spooked the formerly compliant fish into another surge for freedom. Luckily the weed was on my side. Every way out was blocked. I lifted the rod and turned it again.

'If I touch it, it's landed,' I said in desperation. 'Without a net I'm more or less fucked.'

'Okay,' said Jim. 'I'll accept that.'

The carp cruised towards me, its bovine eyes rolling in their sockets as I reached forward and touched its clammy shoulders.

'There. That's it. My first carp.'

'Your first? Your first? I've never had a carp that big! You lucky bastard.'

Neither had I. Not quite. Still I desperately wanted to get it in. Properly. I needed to unhook the blimp for starters. But a grip-and-grin photograph would have been nice. A memento. I lifted the rod and tried to surf the carp towards me, holding the bulk of it over the weeds. But it was a heave too far. The rod bowed and bowed and suddenly snapped straight. One moment I was looking down the oval of my carp's bewhiskered mouth, the next I was grasping impotently after it.

My golden carp slipped under the water and away through the green weeds.

3. EAST

Nicky's Eel

It's hard to separate myth from memory with eels. Unlike trout and salmon, pike, grayling, bass, mullet and so many other fish, I've spent no time at all deliberately trying to catch eels and have few memories of them that are first-hand. And yet eels seem to have wriggled into my mind in all sorts of ways. They're like that, eels. If I open the damp and silty locker in my head where eels are stored I find a writhing mass of fact and folklore and fishy tales told round pub tables wet with beer and I can't really be sure what amongst all that happened to me, or how much I've grafted someone else's story on to a rain-washed teenage summer. So, I'm reaching back across four decades to County Kerry in the west of Ireland where I often spent July or August staying at my godmother's house with her two sons Simon and Nicky. Simon was my age, Nicky only two years younger. So we spent most of the time fishing together, though at first we hadn't a clue what we were doing and it took a long while for any of us to catch anything.

Our first fish was a flounder taken from the rocks where Lamb's Head butts against the southern end of Derrynane strand. I remember the rod top bouncing up and down, Simon flicking his ciggy across the rock pool and springing to his feet to winch in this living thing, a fish! An actual fish! We ate it with melted butter and I remember that it was soft, and tasted of the sea.

I would have sketched it before we ate it, and went to check just now, hoping to reanimate the memory. My sketchbooks from those years are in a plan-chest not far from my desk. At the bottom of the pile I found the right one, a black C. Roberson & Co. 'Bushey' for 'pen and pencil', its spine held together with masking tape. A few pages in there's a sketch called 'Jerr's house'. Jerr was the farmer who lived next door to my godmother, and his accent was so thick I couldn't understand a single word he said. When Jerr got ill he took a cow into his bedroom to keep himself warm.

On the next page there's 'Simon – fishing' ... just as I remembered the scene when we hooked the flounder: a cigarette in his mouth and a stack of Terry Hall hair. And then sure enough the 'Flounder, Derrynane', emerging from the past as amazingly as when we dragged it on to the sand all those summers ago.

I feel encouraged that my memories are reliable and flick on to see if I drew the eel. But no. There's 'Rocks and Sea' and more rocks and more sea, and then 'Trout from Sneem' all laid out on a plate and two more sketches called 'Trout from the lough over Eagle's Hill'. Then I flick back and find a 'Pollack from Reene 16th July' *before* the sketch of the flounder, meaning the flounder was not the first fish we caught, and that my memories must be in a muddle after all. I was so sure and have been for decades that the flounder was the first fish we'd caught, the start of things.

The eel, if it existed, was from a burn that flowed nearby to that 'lough over Eagle's Hill', which itself was a little corrie, perched halfway up the hillside. Sometimes we cycled there, but it was a long ride over the pass to Waterville and up the southern edge of Lough Currane. The first time we went Simon's dad drove us in his Citroën 2CV up the track that snakes over the hills above Caherdaniel. He dropped us at the top. The peat workings there smelled of wet pub fireplaces. It wasn't far across the bog to the precipice of rock we then shimmied down, but the descent was a bit too much like mountaineering to ever have been repeated.

Another time we were given a lift – in the 2CV again – and instead of climbing the hill we walked a short distance over wet ground to fish Lough Isknagahiny where we thought we might catch a sea trout. I had a Devon minnow and spent an hour or two hurling it across the water while Simon drowned a worm. After a while the sky went dark and it started to rain heavily and we moved around the lough and began to fish our way down the burn that flows from Isknagahiny into Lough Currane: the rain had lifted the water, and there was something about that frothy, beer-head flow that gave us hope of a bigger fish. I think we must have arranged to be collected where a small track crossed the burn, because now Nicky appears in the story and I'm wondering if he came back with his dad and was waiting there for us. At any rate I remember the red 2CV parked by the road like a red jelly-mould under the grey sky and Nicky hunched under stair-rod rain dangling a line into the pool under the bridge.

'I've got one,' he shouted.

His dad, who wasn't an angler, urged Nicky to 'wind it in'. But this fish wasn't about to be wound anywhere. Nicky heaved back. The rod hooped into a bow. The fish was heavier and more solid than anything we'd encountered. I thought for a moment that he was just stuck fast to a rock, but then whatever it was shifted under the dark water, scything stubbornly to and fro. A head appeared, black like the peat, a worm still hanging from the hook in the corner of its mouth and a long, snake-like body, fat as a forearm and writhing. From that point my memory seems to divide. I think up to now it must be about right, but in one version the next thing that happened is the line broke and the eel slumped back under the water, while in the other version we caught it.

After that I have only fragments. I remember that the eel was impossible to kill, that we tried to bash its head on a fence post, that it was still alive when we got it home, that we cut its head off, that it was still alive even then, that we looked up what to do in a book and then nailed it to a board to pull the skin off, and that the fillets kept wriggling long after they had been separated from the fish. Or at least I think I do. All of this could have happened to us, I just don't know if it really did. We may have fried the eel with potatoes and onions, or I may have read that in a book. The head-bashing and neck-chopping and the eel's stubborn immortality, no doubt this has all happened to any schoolboy who once caught an eel. It's been talked about and written about and has become a kind of collective mythology, a shared memory. But however that eel inveigled its way into my brain, it is still there under hammering rain and dark water and grey skies, it wriggles demonically and it will not die.

CLOUD OF UNKNOWING

If this is how I feel about the eel, and how I remember it, my feelings and memories don't quite fit with what I know about its currently precarious existence. Certainly this idea of their immortality or at least their resistance to death – which might well be the way of things when one angler vies with one eel, and which has no doubt been shaped by the eel's ability to survive out of water, to wriggle for miles across wet grass and live for decades in some land-locked village pond, and also by their one-time bewildering abundance – this is all turned on its head. Now the eel is a beleaguered fish on the edge of survival, whose numbers keep plummeting. It is not a demonic survivor after all.

I remember back in the 1990s a fishing friend of mine, exasperated by another foreboding headline about the status of the fragile Atlantic salmon, said: 'If only the bloody salmon could be more like the eel.' Now it turns out the eel is more like the salmon. It's disappearing just as quickly. According to the scientists the number of young eels reaching Europe has declined by 90% since the 1970s. That is one very big fall. As a result the European eel is now critically endangered, as classified by the International Union for the Conservation of Nature. And yet we're still only guessing at the reasons for this crash, in large part because the eel is such a mysterious beast.

I have to admit that despite the frustrating, maybe even disastrous implications of our ignorance, I feel there is also something wonderful in how this common creature continues to defy science. Even now, when particle physics has taken us to within a quark's breadth of understanding the origins of the universe, we still don't *quite* understand the origins of the eel. The bare bones of our knowledge have remained unchanged for centuries: the eel comes from the sea in springtime as a tiny larva, transparent and no bigger than the tag-end of a bootlace; it skulks its long life in mud, moves about only under the cover of night and then, after ten years, or twenty, or even longer, something triggers; the now fully grown eel turns silver and on the stormiest, darkest nights in autumn when rivers are running brown with rain, it swims as fast as it can back to the sea; and there it disappears ... apparently for ever.

The reproductive phase of its life, if not quite a complete mystery any more, is still mostly hidden deep within the weirdness of the Sargasso Sea: a spiralling and almost bottomless isle of sea within sea where strange forests of weed grow miles from land and, if you believe the legends, ghost ships drift in imprisoning gyres, crewed only by skeletons. The becalming vortex of ocean that is the Sargasso is also known as the Sea of Lost Ships or the Horse Latitudes (marooned mariners would put their horses overboard to conserve water) or the Doldrums. No wonder no one has seen eels spawning there. That we even know they do took some discovering.

Over the centuries the conundrum of the eel, this soot-backed, silt-wrapped, nocturne of a fish, where they come from or go to and how they reproduce, has inspired a host of crackpot theories and theorems: eels slide into the water from thatched roofing; they come from wet horsehair shed by stallions; they are born of little beetles. Aristotle thought they came 'from the entrails of the earth', Pliny that they reproduced by rubbing themselves on rocks. Izaak Walton suggested that eels come from the action of sunlight on dewdrops and that somehow the whole process was catalysed by barnacles and goslings. Even the great Carl Linnaeus was wide – very wide – of the mark when he suggested that eels were viviparous: that they gave birth to living eels. He was not the first: the thirteenth-century friar Albertus Magnus, and the seventeenth-century scholar Antonie van Leeuwenhoek both made the same mistake.

The problem was that for a long, long time even the eel's reproductive organs evaded observation: scientists were mistaking the bladder for its womb and the parasites in it for baby eels, all the while seeing the real ovaries as some kind of weird adipose tissue. Even after the ovaries had been correctly identified by Carlo Mondini in 1777, it was another century before the Polish naturalist Szymon Syrski defined and described the male eel's genitalia. Neither were in a state of readiness: the ovaries were apparently eggless and the testes so immature as to confound even the young Sigmund Freud whose first ever paper – as some kind of portentous metaphor for the rest of his life's work – was on the frustrating search for the eel's evasively shrivelled balls.

Then in 1897 we had a kind of breakthrough: Giovanni Grassi, a biologist from the University of Messina in Sicily, discovered at sea a male eel with ripening gonads, presumably on its way somewhere. Alleluia!

At the other edge of this shadow of ignorance were the strange creatures on their post-natal voyage … or perhaps drift would be a better word, because infant eels cannot really swim. For the first part of their life cycle, baby eels are completely at the mercy of ocean currents: they move like willow leaves in an autumn wind and in fact are shaped very much like willow leaves too, only with the microscopic face of something from your worst nightmares stuck to the front and a kind of frayed, knicker-elastic tail at the back. By the time they reach shore they have changed again ... and out at sea, well who's going to notice this transparent sea creature only a few centimetres long and as diaphanous as an insect wing? Larval eels went unrecorded for an awfully long time, until the naturalist William Morris found some in 1763 in the Irish Sea near Wales, though at the time Morris had no idea what they were.

It was a German naturalist Johann Kaup – strangely sympathetic in appearance, I feel – who properly described the odd-looking creature with its underworld eyes and lipless, fanged mouth. But Kaup mistook this transparent, leafy micro-monster for a distinct species of fish in its own right and named it *Leptocephalus brevirostris*, now commonly called 'thin-heads', which well describes their hammer-flattened appearance.

Grassi was not convinced. He and a fellow naturalist Salvatore Calandruccio, suspecting *Leptocephalus* as the larval stage of something else, counted its vertebrae and found a match in the eel, *Anguilla anguilla*. Then they watched one metamorphose in a fish tank from the leaf-like form into a transparent miniature eel – a change that naturally occurs somewhere between the continental shelf and the coast when the flattened leaf inflates and rounds to become a tiny, see-through bootlace with two dark eyes and a slightly less terrifying face. It is adapting from drift-mode to swim, if you could describe their snakeish locomotion as swimming. Finally Grassi and his colleague found one of these larvae at sea, in this same state of metamorphosis.

'Eels come from the Mediterranean!' they said, for that is where they had made the discovery. Grassi thought he'd cracked the code. But he hadn't. Not quite. Not at all, in fact.

In 1904 a Danish research scientist called Johannes Schmidt bumped into a *Leptocephalus* while looking for cod near the Faroes ... rather a long way from the 'home' Grassi had given them. How could a tiny, larval eel born in the Mediterranean, a fish that can hardly even swim, get itself to the middle of the North Atlantic near the Faroe Islands? The discovery painted a large enough question mark over Grassi's Mediterranean theory to encourage a search for other thin-heads, a search that became Schmidt's obsessive life's work. In fact Schmidt had been no more than a junior research assistant on that fateful voyage, but he was sharp enough to realise the importance of the discovery, that it meant Grassi was almost certainly wrong, and that the adrift *Leptocephalus* might hold a clue to one of nature's great mysteries.

He began to trawl the sea, heading south from Iceland, around Scotland and the Hebrides and down to the mouth of the English Channel, then west of Gibraltar and finally into the Med itself. All the *Leptocephalus* he found – and he didn't find many – were about the same length: two to three inches. Where were the small ones, he wondered? Schmidt, so it proved, was something of a cavalier scientist, but with a good instinct for the truth. Tom Fort, in his fabulous monograph on eels, describes how Schmidt based his restless searching and ultimately accurate conclusions on the scantest of evidence: for example a total of forty-five larvae in the critical Grassi-debunking stage of his self-termed 'solution to the eel-problem'. Fort also shows that it was in fact a Norwegian scientist, Dr Johan Hjort, on a Norwegian research ship commissioned to survey the North Atlantic, who took and noted the locations of enough thin-head eels to truly indicate a direction of travel. Hjort found thin-heads metamorphosing along the continental shelf, but he found other, as yet unchanged thin-heads south of the Azores. Crucially, they were much smaller. Some were only one and a half inches long. The eels, Hjort theorised were coming *towards* Europe from somewhere *out there* in the southern part of the North Atlantic. It was thanks to Hjort's discovery that Schmidt realised he had only to chase the paper trail of shrinking eels back to where they were at the smallest to find the place they – most likely – came from.

At first Schmidt had trouble finding a ship, so he recruited the help of Danish skippers crossing the Atlantic and asked them to dip trawl nets every so often. Though the findings were still scant they hinted at the same migration pattern as Hjort's samples had done. Then in 1913 Schmidt got hold of a research ship, the *Magrethe*, and he set a course south-west from the Azores. In total he trapped 714 thin-heads, and though they were smaller the further he travelled, and though he actually reached the central Sargasso, the eel larvae were never *quite* small enough to conclusively suggest a place of origin.

Instinctively Schmidt felt he'd found the right place, but that he'd been there at the wrong time, a few months after the eels had hatched. He had to wait seven agonising years to find out because in 1914 his ship ran aground, and with the outbreak of war, so did his research. It was 1920 before he tried again, this time aboard the research ship *Dana*. He made straight for the Sargasso – earlier in the year on this voyage – and on 8 June Schmidt found more than a thousand thin-heads less than half an inch long. A few days later he found them again in huge numbers. Now he was sure this was the right spot, even if the young eels were most likely weeks not hours beyond hatching.

Still unsatisfied, the following year he set sail even earlier and on 12 April 1921, a fraction west of the previous year's find, Schmidt came on prodigious numbers of tiny eel larvae, some less than a quarter of an inch long: a day or two at most, if not hours, beyond birth.

Schmidt had found the breeding grounds of the eel.

Almost a century later we still don't know a hell of a lot more than this. We can at least divide their life cycle into all its known stages:

the larval *Leptocephalus* which drifts on oceanic currents from the Sargasso Sea to Europe; the glass eel it morphs into at the continental shelf; the elver (or bootlace) that enters freshwater; the yellow (or green) eel that skulks its long life in estuaries, rivers and lakes all over Europe; and finally the silver eel on its mysterious spawning run. Their migration routes are unknown, no one has seen mature eels mating, nor has anyone ever seen them in the Sargasso Sea or arriving there, nor has anyone seen what happens to them after they have mated. And with so many gaps in our knowledge it is difficult to say precisely why eel numbers are crashing. But crashing they are: estimates vary but all are dire. According to our Environment Agency the number of young eels arriving at the coast of Europe is down by 95% since the 1970s. Other reports are even more worrying than this: according to a 2011 paper by Peter Henderson et al., since 1980 the population of eels in Bridgwater Bay has declined by 15% ... each year. Eel numbers there are now 1% of the 1980 population. According to the International Union for the Conservation of Nature the stock of silver eels is estimated to be about 50–60% down since 1970, the stock of yellow eels is lower than this, and the recruitment of elvers at our coasts is down by 90–95% throughout the North Atlantic, Baltic and Mediterranean. The North American first cousin of our eel is crashing too, as is the Japanese distant cousin.

There are a number of theories as to why, but papers are still coming thick and fast and no one really knows for sure. Is it lots of things, one on top of the next? Or is it one big thing?

It might be down to overfishing: vast numbers of elvers are netted every year in the Bay of Biscay by the French and Spanish – legally. The legally caught fish *should* be used to restock eel-less rivers. The black-market juvenile eels are packed off east to feed the ceaseless appetite of the Asian market for a delicacy called *unagi*. A kilogram of elvers is worth up to £600 when the runs are low and demand high, and more like £1,000 on the black market in Asia. The French 'legal' quota is about sixty tons. With 3,000 elvers to the kilogram this is, after all, an annual harvest of a dizzying 225 million so-called 'critically endangered' fish. And that's just the French legal catch.

It might be down to the barriers we have constructed blocking the migratory pathways of eels ascending river systems. The dams and tidal barriers, marinas, weirs and lock gates we build to control and orchestrate the flow of water in the highly managed and artificial waterways of Europe are so many hurdles, many of them insurmountable, for tiny eels. On their downstream spawning run barriers are less of an issue for mature eels, but they are still problematic, while turbines on hydro-schemes can make literal mincemeat of the migrating eel.

We've been catching eels and harnessing water like this for centuries, however. Consider that a large female eel can shed several million eggs, that the elver run on the Severn once darkened its waters, an apparently endless black rope threading its way upstream, and that this dark tide of elvers ran more or less every river, stream, ditch and dyke in our landscape, year after year. Eels are nothing if not fecund. While both the fishing and the barriers to migration must make things worse for a fish under pressure, surely something more sinister is at work?

Look at the charts and you'll see eel numbers really began to crash in the 1970s and have continued to fall ever since, while the biggest decline has been of the migrating infant. Perhaps we ought to be looking for something more pervasive and more obviously pinned to the second part of the twentieth century, for something like global warming, say, or climate change? It is not easy, though, to imagine how global warming might impact a fish whose range spans fifty degrees of latitude from North Africa to the tip of Norway and includes every conceivable type of habitat from estuaries to rivers, lakes, canals, farm ponds, old bomb-craters, ditches or even persistent puddles. A few degrees of temperature either way might subtly alter the limits of the range, but surely it is not going to make a huge difference to a creature as adaptable and widespread as the eel?

At sea, however, the story might be different. There the larval eel appears to feed on what the scientists rather poetically call marine snow. The abundance of marine snow is linked to the productivity of phytoplankton, which is in turn linked to sea temperature. A warming sea-surface yields less phytoplankton, less marine snow and perhaps fewer young eels.

Moreover, the willow-leaf *Leptocephalus* is one of the ocean's most feeble swimmers: it doesn't so much swim as drift on ocean currents. It must therefore be vulnerable to any changes that occur to these currents. Recently scientists have started to hypothesise – and find evidence for – all sorts of causal links between weather systems, ocean currents and eel recruitment. Changes in the North Atlantic Oscillation – a fluctuation in atmospheric pressure between the Icelandic low and the Azores high, which in turn impacts on wind and storm paths across the Atlantic – appear to correlate with numbers of returning infant eels. Changes in the way currents bifurcate close to the Sargasso Sea can create a shortcut or close one between the spawning grounds and that eel conveyor belt, the Gulf Stream, and these changes also appear to correlate with infant eel abundance at the continental shelf. Changes in the Gulf Stream itself may also have had an impact. The speed and power of the Gulf Stream must influence the duration of the eel's journey back to Europe. Recent evidence suggests the Gulf Stream is slowing. Imagine the Gulf Stream like a giant eel-hose spraying baby eels at the coastline of Europe. A change in the intensity – or direction – of the current could have a massive impact on the numbers of young eels that reach our coasts.

All this seems convincing. Yet a recent study of recruitment in the Sargasso Sea itself also turned up lower numbers of larvae than similar trawls conducted in 1983 and 1985, suggesting a problem, or perhaps *the* problem, lies at the recruitment phase. Of course there may be fewer larvae because fewer eels are spawning. Or because there is less marine snow. Or because all of the factors above have combined. Or because of something else entirely: polychlorinated biphenyls (PCBs), say.

PCBs are a man-made organic chemical resistant to heat and acid. They were once widely used in electrical equipment like TVs, regulators and capacitors, and in plasticisers, inks, adhesives, and flame retardants, until we discovered in the 1970s that these useful chemicals gave us cancer. PCBs were banned in America in 1979. In Europe it took a while longer. But all the time we had been making PCBs – for fifty or sixty years – waste from the manufacturing process was dumped in landfill sites and from these sites PCBs have leached into the air and into our waterways. Being resistant to heat and acid, PCBs are nothing if not persistent. When the initial research was done in the 1960s and 1970s, PCBs were found everywhere: in the atmosphere, in soil and water, and in humans and animals all over the world. PCBs were even found in the Arctic. And because PCBs attach to organic matter and micro-particles of soil, they had accumulated to very high densities in the sediment and silt on the beds of our waterways. Exactly where eels hang out.

PCBs also bio-accumulate: that means they build up in animals over time and are stored in fatty tissues. They also bio-magnify, which means the PCBs accumulate in greater concentrations in animals higher up the food chain. There are greater concentrations of PCBs in diatoms than in seawater, greater concentrations in shellfish and crustaceans than in diatoms, greater concentrations in fish than in crustaceans. And so on. Eels, being fatty, omnivorous predator-scavengers that live a very long time, pick up a mother lode of the stuff.

PCBs are problematic for most species of fish because as well as being carcinogenic, PCBs lower their reproductive success. Most fish spawn every year and thus annually offload some of their toxic PCB burden, but eels spawn only once at the end of their long lives and at the far end of a very long journey.

Which brings us back to that eelish cloud of unknowing. Because their whole reproductive cycle remains something of a mystery, we are still theorising. Nevertheless scientists now suspect, and tests of eels in captivity seem to have confirmed the scientists' suspicions, that it is the arduous nature of this long journey, during which the eel does not feed, that precipitates the cataclysmic impact of the PCBs. The reason why no sexually mature eel has ever been found in fresh water, the reason we have had so many mad theories about eels springing from mud, dewdrops or horsehair is because the eel needs to swim non-stop for thousands of miles in order to bring about the physical changes that precede reproduction. Unfortunately this marathon also remobilises the PCBs which have bio-accumulated and bio-magnified in the fat which the eel has built up over a long life in order to fuel that final journey. Thus the eel is made a victim of its own wonderful biology: the PCBs are transferred from body fat to eggs. As a result the baby eels die.

It may be that our eels have been caught in a perfect storm, with one massive problem – infertility caused by pollution – feeding into an escalating cyclone of cause and effect: capricious currents at a time of lower phytoplankton production in an adverse phase of the North Atlantic Oscillation as the Gulf Stream slows. Suddenly, overfishing and barriers to migration, which might not have had much of an impact on a healthy population of eels, become the two straws that broke this camel's back.

All of which sounds like the end of the world for eels; except that PCBs do break down over time, albeit slowly, and we have at least stopped making them. Recent silt deposits, which contain fewer PCBs, are now covering the older, more toxic layers. Arjan Palstra, the Dutch scientist who managed to get eels to spawn in captivity and thus showed how the PCBs transferred from the eel to the eggs, suggested in 2006 that perhaps only eels from Europe's least polluted rivers were still successfully breeding. But recent studies have indicated that PCB levels in eels are now falling, even in rivers like the Thames, whilst elver runs from 2012 onwards have seen something of a return to the good old days. Maybe we have been through the worst of it. Only time and the eel will tell.

FISH SILVER

Their stubborn mysteriousness notwithstanding, I wanted to experience eels less vicariously than through my half-baked memories and all these scientific papers I'd been consuming. I wanted to find an eel fisherman who could put me in touch with the wet, slimy reality of them. Like the creature they seek, however, these eel men are a vanishing breed and hard to find. I struggled even though I live in Norfolk, only a few miles from the Fens, the most eelish of places. The cathedral that looms like a sentinel over this flat, once miasmic landscape was built from eels: its stone was traded for vast numbers of this distinctly Fenland harvest. It is named after the eel, too: Ely means eel island. You have to imagine Ely as an island now, but the rise of land is obvious enough, while the waterlogged, willowy corners of the regimented fields and dykes that spread away on all sides are remnants of the flooded swamp that once lapped Ely's shoreline. These isles – Wisbech, Ramsey, Thorney, Spalding – were the first settlements on the Fens: isolated towns and villages on gentle rises of ground. Their one-time seclusion – which is still palpable – made the Fens a peculiarly English 'Holy Land' and on most isles you'll find a priory, abbey or some other kind of ancient religious house. To every one of these the eel would have been a source of sustenance and wealth.

These isles are surrounded not so much by marsh now as a patchwork sea of drying peat, cross-hatched with dykes and drains, studded with drunken telegraph poles, sagging chimney stacks and window-less pumping stations. The pumping stations are a palimpsest all on their own, in a landscape that is the ultimate palimpsest, like the successively abandoned cottages that surround them, or so many generations of farm tractor you see here and there slumping inside the soil they once tilled. Wind, steam, oil and now electricity have all been used to pump the Fens dry and keep them dry so that nowadays this corner of East Anglia adds up to half of England's grade-one arable land. Once, the Fens were the least arable place in an otherwise arable kingdom. They were a wild waterland, the accessible edges of which might have been good for the seasonal setting of livestock, but which were otherwise mostly good only for wild-fowling, for cutting reeds and for fishing. The *Liber Eliensis*, a twelfth-century chronicle, describes a Fenscape inhabited by 'innumerable eels, large water-wolves [pike], pickerel, perch, roach, burbots and lampreys'– fish in such quantities, echoes William of Malmesbury, 'as to cause astonishment in strangers, while the natives laugh at their surprise'.

There is hardly a document from the medieval Fens that does not make reference to the fish and fisheries there. The Domesday Book comes alive with the slithering industry of the place. King Edgar's 974 foundation charter of Ramsey Abbey is wet with the boot prints of its fishermen with their boats and nets, fisher-tenants who paid their rents in 'fish silver', namely eels. So ubiquitous were eels, and yet so valuable too, they were currency in the Fens, counted and traded by the tens of thousand or in 'sticks' of twenty-five. The fishery at Doddington returned 27,150 of them in dues, Littleport 17,000, Stuntney 24,000. In a roll call of Anglo-Saxon names that have vanished like the water they described, the *Chronicon Petroburgense* of 1020 portrays Witelsmere, where these men fished, as a vast anastomosed lake, full of bays and swamps: Wellepol and Trendmære Bec, Kyngesdelf and Thescuf, each lovingly measured and itemised in furlongs and fisheries. Witelsmere supported nine fisheries, and dozens of fishermen who will have dried their nets on its shoreline. Once in a while the fishermen themselves rise by name, all leather-skinned and muddy, from the dry pages of these ancient charters: Alfgar of Hilgay, or Hugh of Wiggenhall, or Thomas of Thetford who held Upware and Swavesmere and paid 3,036 sticks of eels in rent. Or the wonderfully named Henry the Fisherman, who with Martin of Swafham fished Midelstwere and Nakedwere and paid 14,500 eels on the first Sunday of Lent to do so. Across a thousand years their earthy doughtiness is still palpable. But Witelsmere is no more than an immense prairie of patchwork fields and ditches now, as are all these other meres, lodes and lakes. And its fishermen are gone. Almost.

In 2005 I read an obituary in the *Telegraph* of Ernie James who had died aged ninety-nine. Ernie was one of the last Fen Tigers, native Fenmen so called by the Dutch drainage engineers who'd come over with Cornelius Vermuyden in the seventeenth century to help complete the drainage of the Fens. Ernie's swamp-dwelling forebears had depended for their livelihoods on a wet landscape which these foreigners and their rich clients were syphoning away. So they resisted with guerrilla-style disruption of the drainage works and with occasionally violent attacks on the strangers. They lost in the end, the Tigers. By Ernie's time those who were left were a more peaceable bunch, even if the badge of the wetland predator had stuck. They continued to eke out a living from those corners of the Fens that were not quite tamed, and they adapted too, by working the fields their ancestors must have hated, by including ditch-cutting and harvesting in their rota of seasonal labours.

Ernie's daughter-in-law Audrey James had transcribed his memoirs into a book called *Memoirs of a Fen Tiger* and I bought a copy. I discovered that Ernie had lived just down the road from me in a spot where I love to go pike fishing at Welney, and I wondered if he had been the old man I met in a pub there on the banks of the River Bedford one cold day in the late 1990s. I had retreated into the bar for beer and peanuts and got talking to this ancient mariner who was sitting on a stool beside the piano. I remember he told me how to drain all of the 'snot' off a pike. Whether it was him or not, Ernie had lived in a cottage there on the bank between the Old Bedford and the Delph, though like the pub, Ferryman's Cottage is now gone. His father had given sixteen-year-old Ernie the running of the winter ferry and Ernie would take people across the washes when the main road was flooded. He left school and spent his whole life at Welney eking out a living and never travelling more than a few miles from the place. In addition to the ferry work he netted plovers, shot duck with punt guns, cut reeds and trapped eels. He had fished for eels, so the obituary told me, into his late nineties.

I wondered if there were any more like him and so I typed 'Fen Tiger eel fisherman' into Google. The first hit was a feature in the *Morning Star* where I read that there was only one left of this curious breed known as the Fen Tiger, that he was called Peter Carter, that he still made woven willow traps just like in the old days, that he was a fourth- or fifth-generation Fenman and that he could be found in his waterside shop where he also sold wicker baskets in the village of Outwell on the Cambridgeshire border. Here was a latter-day Ernie James and exactly who I wanted to meet and go eel-trapping with. He even looked the part in the photo, punting along the river in a scruffy leather hat, his face wild and sun-browned, the bows of his punt piled high with willow traps.

I read a few more stories. Here he was on a BBC audio slideshow, *The Eel-man of the Fens*. And again in the *Daily Mail*, 'Slipping Through Our Fingers', a story of how an eel tradition going back five centuries will soon die out. And again in the *Ely Standard*, 'Eels Could be Slipping Away', a story about falling eel numbers and the dying breed of Fenmen, of whom Peter Carter was the very last. The basic facts were always the same: Peter came from a family of traditional Fen-folk and had plied his trade on the Ouse and its tributaries all his life. He still made willow traps in the traditional way which he baited with roadkill. But whereas he might once have taken up to 150 pounds of eels in one night, now he was lucky to take a third of that in seven. Things had got so bad that he could make more money now selling his traps as trinkets than he could using them to trap eels. All of the stories emphasised that Peter was the last of his kind.

The more I read, the more disappointed I became. Not with the message so much, though of course that was disappointing, but with the nagging feeling that all this plaintive prose was more a kitsch nostalgia than anything real. There was something of the cormorant man about it all: the fisherman I met in Japan who had been retained by the town's tourism authority to continue catching *ayu* – a particular delicacy of a fish – in the traditional way with a flock of trained cormorants held on leashes. Cormorant man fished at night with flaming torches on the prow of his boat and flanked by flotillas of tourists. I got the feeling that Peter's story was repeated again and again in the media because in just the same way it appealed to a collective, wistful longing for that which has gone or is fading, a plaintive whimsy that puts no fishermen on the water or eels back in the rivers. In a way these stories were the opposite of what I was looking for. I hoped that when I met the real Peter Carter I'd get beyond the bygone press releases.

One of the website stories, the one about basket-weaving workshops, had an address and phone number. I called, but the phone rang without answer. I tried again and again over a week or so, but had no luck. So I drove over there and parked outside his shop in Outwell. It looked less occupied than in the Google Maps images, but there was a handwritten sign in the window announcing 'Eels

Now In' and another on the door that said the shop was open. I knocked, hopefully, but no one was in.

It was lunchtime. The people in the fish and chip bar round the corner knew who I meant but hadn't seen Peter in a while. So, I ate fish and chips on the jetty by the creek outside, flicked a few chips to the ducks and when I'd had enough lobbed a small tail of the cod into the creek wondering if it might sink to the bottom and feed one of Peter's eels. The shop was still lifeless when I went back, so I got in the car and drove home.

Off and on over the next few weeks I tried various ways to track down this enigmatic eel-man. I was given a new phone number at some stage and must have called it a dozen times without answer. Peter became more intriguing with every failed enquiry. For a man so prominent in the media he was very hard to find, and as with the eel, the fascination of him grew in proportion to his mystery. After a while I started to suspect he had simply disappeared just like his beloved eels, with the same bewildering lack of explanation.

I never did find Peter.

Instead I called another fishing pal, Chris, a bailiff with the Environment Agency. I told Chris about how I had failed to find Peter Carter. Chris wasn't convinced by the whole 'Last of the Eel Catchers' folklore that had accumulated around Peter. If I wanted to meet the real thing, Chris said, I should call John Spalton instead. *He* was a full-time eel fisherman. I wondered aloud why I'd never heard of him or read his name anywhere. Because, said Chris, as I just told you, John's the real thing. He doesn't want anyone to know what he's up to or where. He might not even speak to you.

I left a message. John called back a few days later and finally, after about four weeks of searching, I was in touch with a real, living eel man, a latter-day Fen Tiger. The eels were thin on the ground at present, said John. He'd be happy to take me out, though. Only because of Chris, mind. He didn't normally talk to anyone, but Chris had said I was okay, so I must be. Any day would suit. I could get a feel for it and then maybe we could meet again later in the year when the silver eels were running.

A FEN TIGGER

We met a few days later by the River Ouse somewhere south-west of Ely. It wasn't a dawn start, not even a particularly early one. John's wife had had a stroke a few years ago and his day only began after he had dropped her off at his daughter's house. John had given me careful directions, which was a good thing because he took some finding. I was threading my way deep into the Fens as I switched left, then right down increasingly narrow and corrugated roads through villages I'd never seen before, except that they looked like most Fen villages with their neat hedges, bungalows and lawns, their phone boxes wrapped in bindweed, their bowling-club lawns and disused Methodist chapels.

I stopped outside Today's Local in the nearby high street and bought a banana and apple, a Snickers bar and some water. Enough to keep me going through a hot day on the water. Then I remembered something about bananas, bad luck and boats and quickly ate the banana as I looked for the hidden turning John said would get me to where he launches his punt. I missed the turning, as he said I would, and turned round where he said I'd be able to turn round after I missed the turning. Another mile or two along buckled tarmac, hot air shimmering the vanishing point of the road into liquid. Then the track hump-backed a flood-bank and beyond was the River Ouse, meandering between willows, and there was John waiting by his white van, a black terrier at his feet. I wound down the window and waved as I pulled up. John walked over, a broad smile on his face and we shook hands through the window of my half-open door.

'So you found me all right?' he said, fiddling with a broken brace-strap on his waders. 'Bloody thing. These aren't old, you know. Bloody strap keeps coming undone.'

'Who's this?' I asked as the terrier pushed itself between John's legs and under the car door.

'That's Jack,' said John. 'He's getting on a bit now.'

I patted Jack's warm, dusty coat.

'Would you like a Coke?' asked John, handing me a tin. 'It'll be hot out there today.'

John's punt was ready in the water. It wasn't obvious where I should put myself between all the nets, the fuel tank and the buckets of this and that. Jack took his spot in the prow and curled himself up inside a hairy hollow in a pile of old coats. I sat in front of him as John pushed us out across the water and jumped in. He yanked the starter cord on the engine. Once. Twice. The boat rocked with each pull, sending our flotilla escort of water boatmen sculling back to the shelter of the willows. Then the engine coughed into life and a plume of blue smoke drifted across the water.

'It's nice and clear at least. But this isn't exactly how I'd pictured it,' I said, surveying the underwater jungle, the minnows flitting away from our shadow. 'In my imagination eels are all about stormy weather and muddy water.'

'Well, you don't exactly want it clear,' John said. 'The eels keep their heads down when it's clear like this. Plus there's three bloody seals in here and they don't help. But you know, I have to keep on fishing. In the autumn it's like how you picture it. New moon. Shit weather. Rivers running coloured. That's when it can be really good for silvers.'

We wouldn't be catching silvers today. In the summer it's yellow eels or green eels (the same thing, it just depends who's describing them): these are resident eels that haven't yet turned for migration.

To catch yellows you need the eels to be on the move, scavenging. They're fundamentally nocturnal and the darker the night, the murkier the water, the better the catch. John uses paired fyke nets which he anchors to the bed of the river with old disc-brakes. The fyke net works because it exploits how eels love to hug the bed of a river or nose along edges, exploring by touch and smell. Each trap is a series of funnel-shaped nets feeding one into the next and finally into a 'cod end'. Between the two is a wall of netting so that the mouths of the two funnels face each other. The foraging eel bumps into the wall of netting and instinctively follows it into either of the two traps. It's a one-way journey for fish, especially eels: the first funnel sits inside the second, so that once the eels have swum inside their instinct for feeling their way along the edges of the net will never guide them back to the exit. Some nets, for reasons John doesn't understand, are better fish-catchers than others. He thinks it's to do with the smell. But when the water is clear and the moon is out the eels see the nets all too easily and avoid them. John's nets had been in over the new moon, but even so he didn't fancy he'd get much. It was too hot, too clear.

'But you know ... if you come to every net expecting it to be empty, if there's something in it, that's a bonus isn't it?' John said cheerfully.

We puttered down the Ouse under a bright sun. It was a fine day to be afloat, if nothing else. After a few hundred yards we slowed into a nondescript bay in the willows. John picked up a grappling hook tied to a rope, lobbed it out and pulled it back in. On his third or fourth throw the hook snagged at something solid and soon the first net was rising to the surface like some archaeological treasure hoisted from the deep. It smelt of mud and dead fish but there was nothing in it. There was nothing in the next either. This was probably no worse than expected, but even so John was disappointed. Not least because I'm sure he wanted to show me a good haul.

'Thirty years ago that would have been full,' he said. 'Absolutely full. When they were a pound a pound, small-time eel fishermen with only twenty or thirty nets was earning a thousand quid a week. This was when the average wage in a factory was about 150 quid. That's why we were so secretive, you know.'

Secrecy is a habit not lost in spite of today's more scant returns. It explained why none of John's nets were marked.

'I dunno how I managed before I had this,' he said as he checked a small GPS plotter that hung in a waterproof bag round his neck. 'I'd mark that tree or that fence post and then just hold it all in me head. Trouble is, now I mark the new drops but never remember to delete the old ones, so even the GPS is a muddle. But I've no choice. Anyone who marks their nets with floats will find them gone the next week.'

John described his main rival – with some affection, I felt – as his 'opposition'. When I first met 'me opposition', he said, as if this meeting marked the beginning of a very long, but nevertheless quite formal grudge match which would run and run on the playing fields of the Fens. It was twenty years ago, before John fished for eels. He was shrimping and had taken his catch to sell to a guy named Oxo from Boston. Then this other man showed up – 'ever such a nice chap he was' – the same age as John. They chatted for a bit and when he'd gone John asked Oxo who the visitor was. Oxo said it was his best friend, Terry, and best friend or not Oxo wouldn't trust him as far as he could throw him. Later John would see Terry on the Fens, or at least someone he thought was Terry. He'd see the white Bedford van and know the driver was an eel man because he could hear the air compressor feeding oxygen to a fish tank in the back. John got the feeling Terry was spying on him. Eventually they ran into each other: Terry was waiting in a lay-by. John knocked on his window.

'That give him a fright,' said John. 'So I told him, "I know who you are," I said. "You're Oxo's mate and you're gonna nick me nets. But let me tell you, if I have to work for a fiver, I'll work for a fiver. You'll never get rid of me." You could have knocked him down,' said

John. 'He was fifty miles from home. He had no idea I knew who he was. Even so,' John said rounding off the story, 'two days later and all me nets were gone.'

As far as I could tell from John's numerous anecdotes about eel men nicking nets off each other, in the back of every eel-man's van are an assortment of nets only a few of which belong to that man, but the sum total of which amount to more or less the number he owns. John even had a story about how he'd bought nets that turned out to be his own in a no-questions cash-only exchange in a darkened car park. He couldn't believe it when he got them home. Well I never, he said.

I asked John if it wouldn't be better if everyone just left everyone else's gear alone.

'I suppose so,' said John. 'But it doesn't work like that.'

As each net came to the surface empty, John became more despondent.

'This is crap for a fortnight,' he said. 'I've not seen it this clear all year.'

The next haul did bring up an eel. A dead one. John dropped the net in disgust, gunned the engine again, in a hurry to find something. 'These nets normally fish their heads off, they really do.' He threw the dead eel in the bushes.

The next haul was even worse. There was a dead jack-pike in the cod end, but the fish had turned white and was quickly putrefying in the summer heat. The stench was awful, and then as if it couldn't have got worse John didn't so much pull the dead pike out as shake it out in his impatience to catch something he could sell. The fish disintegrated, flicking chunks of stinking flesh all over the place. Some of the pike landed on my trousers. A bit hit my forehead.

'Christ, what a terrible smell!'

'Is it?' asked John, genuinely curious. 'I can't smell it.'

'How can you not smell that? It's the most awful stink I've ever known.'

'That's nothing,' he said. 'Sometimes you'll get a net of dead eels. Don't know why. Most of the time they're fine. Sometimes they just die on you. Fifteen, twenty of them. They seem to rot instantly. You've never smelled anything so bad.'

We glided from one net to the next, a few hundred yards between them. Jack remained fast asleep in the prow, in spite of the fact that the punt had slowly started to fill with water and his bed of coats was shifting on the rising tide. 'Sometimes you have to check he's not dead,' said John.

I picked up the plastic milk carton I guessed was made for the job and started to bale.

'Good idea,' said John. 'We *are* sinking ... very slowly.'

I asked if he'd always lived in Norfolk. He said he was from Lincolnshire as if it was an important distinction. He was born in Boston. Not exactly far away and still the Fens, but John was not from a long line of eel men, nor even a long line of Fen Tigers (besides, wasn't this keen and friendly eel man more a Fen Tigger than Tiger?). John's father was a policeman and they moved all over the place when John was growing up. As a long-haired teenager without any real ambition to become a policeman, John passed the entrance tests and followed his dad, but hated every minute of the three years he served. He didn't like the bureaucracy nor the business of arresting people. He made only one arrest in his final eighteen months: an ice-cream man who had 'gone ballistic' when John had inadvertently melted all the man's ice cream by turning off his generator while investigating a car-tax fiddle. He hadn't done a lot wrong to be honest, said John ruefully.

When John's auntie died and left him £5,000 he couldn't get out fast enough. He jacked in the job and bought a shrimp boat. His father wouldn't talk to him, but John was happier catching shrimps. Now, decades later, he has no idea when he'll stop. If ever. It's not a job that's easy to retire from. Not when you can't wait to lift your nets every morning. Most of the time the money's not great. When John told Terry all those years ago that he'd work for a fiver, he had not realised how true that would be. He gets help from working-tax-credits, help with the rent. When the fishing's crap he earns about £150, £200 a week. When it's good he'll pull in £300–£400. Sometimes it's good, sometimes it's crap. Just at the moment it's more crap than good, said John. But he and his wife don't need a lot. They don't watch telly. They don't drink or smoke. They don't have a computer and don't need a fancy car. So long as he can pay the rent and go shopping.

We reached the final line of nets. This one will be okay, John thought aloud. They were set close to the lock gates and any eel mooching around this cul-de-sac would have to bump into John's nets. They took some finding. But finally the hook caught on something and John's face went stern with the strain of it. He was hoping – and so was I – that this weight was chiefly a writhing mass of eels. In fact it was weed. And mud. Somehow the dozen or so eels that did come spilling out on to the floor of the boat, along with two crayfish and a small roach which John flicked back in, underlined the paucity of our catch more eloquently than if there had been nothing. John picked an eel up using the net to hold it. I tried to get a good look but the eel writhed in John's hand and all I saw was a restless, slimy coiling movement, which made me shudder.

'I suppose the ceaseless wriggling only adds to the whole fear and loathing thing,' I said. 'Even if you wanted to find the eel beautiful, it's never still enough to tell.'

We turned and motored back up the river. The sun was bright. Too bright for eels. A few cows kicked up dust as they threaded down a well-worn path towards a gravel beach where they spooned pink tongues into the cool, green water. I asked John if he ever went on holiday. They'd gone three weeks ago, he told me, smiling. They had haddock and chips on Mablethorpe seafront. They walked along the beach. They came home. It's not that John's a recluse but since he's been eel fishing he finds that he just likes to be alone with his dog.

I laughed and wondered aloud if John wasn't becoming more and more like the eels he sought.

'It's weird,' he said. 'I leave the house every morning and I'm still looking for that golden eel. I've been catching eels for twenty-four years. But I still can't understand them. I can understand the shrimps. But eels, I just can't fathom them out. I thought there'd be loads of eels in that net by the lock gate. Where you think there's eels there's none and where you think it would be a waste of time there's tons of them. I used to fish a little drain at Guyhirn: you'll see it on the way home. When I first started I went to the lock-keeper there and asked if I could put my nets in and he said "Well, boy, I've lived here seventy-five years and I've never seen an eel." That little dyke, no wider than my boat, paid my rent for two years.'

We kept in touch over the late summer and winter. John was keen to know about my week on the cod trawler, and laughed himself sick when I mentioned the superstitions and my banishment as a Jonah. He also remembered a Scottish skipper he once worked with who could not abide the word 'pig'. He asked lots of questions about the boat, how they worked the trawls, the size of the crew. I got the impression that happily solitary though he was, he also missed the camaraderie of the sea. At each call he told me to try him again in a week or two. And I kept calling. I kept watching the weather. Bad storms blew through in the late autumn. The rivers rose and were full of colour. Still the silver eels never ran. It was spring before John felt he was catching enough to justify another trip. If it hadn't been for the mitten crabs, he said, he'd have never survived the winter. Luckily there were thousands of these nasty, invasive crustaceans, the price was good and the Asian appetite for them apparently insatiable. Then in late spring John started to get some good hauls of yellow eels and he suggested we meet by a little river he knew near King's Lynn.

It was a warm, May day. Blue skies. Catkins on the water. Mayfly fluttering skywards and the lazy-fly drone of a propeller plane far off across the Fens. John had his boat ready in the water again. Jack was ambling about the bank, circled busily by two new dogs, puppies almost, who came barrelling towards me, their tails wagging.

'That's Luna and that's Rosco,' said John. 'The names they came with.'

Luna came up for a pat. Rosco turned and barked at something across the water, his little body recoiling back in a series of jumps like he was a canon firing ordnance.

'He'll bark at anything. I never know what it is,' said John. 'He'll bark at shadows and fence posts and all sorts. But you know, without dogs I'd end up talking to myself, wouldn't I?'

I wondered how Jack had taken it.

'He's come alive! I thought he'd be dead by now, to be honest.' We paused to watch Jack who wandered off in no particular direction and then stopped as if he didn't know where he was or why he was there. 'He's still bodging about, I suppose. He drives me mad sometimes ... but it comes to us all, I guess.'

We lifted Jack into the boat and he snuggled down as before into his hollow. The puppies jumped in after. John needed a pee before he set off. This precipitated his big news, that he'd been bitten by a mosquito somewhere delicate.

'Everyone laughs when I tell them,' he said over his shoulder as he dropped his wader braces. 'I had to go to the doctor. She took one look and said, "Bloody hell! I better give you antibiotics." It's just going down now, but I have to drink loads and when I go for a wee it's like getting whacked on the end with a bunch of stinging nettles.'

'The hazards of the eel-man's life,' I said.

'There's loads of those bastard mossies down at Welney Washes. I didn't feel it at the time. Just the next day I thought, whatever is going on here? The pain! I can't describe it.'

'Well, some people pay for that kind of thing, John,' I said.

'Ha ha. Yes. Me mates at the Agency asked what I was complaining about when I said it had doubled in size! Anyway,' said John as he clambered in and pushed us away from the reeds, 'the stinging's gone now. And the swelling's gone down too.'

We moseyed downriver much as we had before on the Ouse, though this little brook was a tenth of the size. A breeze stirred the willows and the grass at the top of the bank, but we were tucked down in the hollow of the dyke where the air was still and warm. John used his GPS to find the nets, which he had set in pairs every few hundred yards. It was a different way of fishing to his mate, Gary, from Grimsby who strung all his nets together in a long line: six to eight pairs at a time. John can't see the sense of that because it's easier for someone to pinch them all. Only last week someone had taken a line of Gary's nets, cut the cod ends off them and left them in a pile. It's the pike anglers, John reckoned, who were too thick to realise Gary's not catching pike.

'They're fucking thick, those bastards,' he said.

The first net contained one eel.

'You're a jinx,' he said.

'Well, I haven't mentioned the red fish yet, nor the four-legged animal that bacon comes from.'

'No. Well don't mention them either. Just in case.'

Luckily, the next pair had a few more eels in it and the pair after that a few more again. Bit by bit the net sack on the flooded decking began to fill. John was relieved.

'That's got some weight to it,' he said with satisfaction as he lifted the accumulated weight of eels off the deck. They writhed themselves into a slimy knot, pushing shiny noses at the netting. The eels made this odd sucking noise, one or two at first, but eventually as the numbers built a background chorus of wet slurping kept us company as we trundled down the stream. This wasn't bad for a full-moon week, John reckoned. Especially as the temperature was all over the place. He could do with a few good hauls to make up for some lean months. Now we actually had some eels in the boat and the question wouldn't cut too keenly, I asked how he felt about eel numbers and his future. Was there a future?

The silvers just hadn't run last autumn, John said sombrely. Which is why we hadn't met up. He'd had one haul of about sixty pounds. After that his big nets by the lock gates – so big you could catch a bus in them – produced two or three eels. They just didn't want to run. He'd had ninety pounds of yellows the previous week when really he needs more than double that to get by. £160 for the week and he'd had to work his brains out for that. He keeps waiting for it to get better and numbers *are* rising in places. And sometimes there's just no rhyme or reason. You get to one net and there's loads and the next has none. Sometimes John thinks he was twenty years too late. Other times he thinks it might turn back around before he has to pack up and retire. The elver runs have been good lately and there's hardly anyone catching eels any more. When or if the numbers do come back, he might still have something to retire on because there's just less competition nowadays.

I asked who was left.

'When I first started there was the Rooks brothers. Terry Smith. There was Steve. There was Ian Simmons, the two boys from Peterborough. How many's that? Seven. There was ... wotsisname, that's eight. There was John Baxter lives over here, a right bloody animal. That's nine. Oh, Nick at Holbeach. Ten. There was another little old boy, so that's eleven. Six years ago there was eleven. Peter Carter. That's twelve. And another old boy from Attleborough. So, that's maybe thirteen of them. Now there's just me … and Terry really. The R brothers are about to be locked up. There's two on the Norfolk Broads who work at it for half the year. There's Steven when he thinks about it. And there's Gary from Grimsby. You should go out with him,' John urged me. 'You'd have a laugh with Gary and he's really catching them at the moment. When his nets come up I doubt you'd believe your eyes.'

John was obviously relieved to have shown me a few eels, however. He heaved the sack of them out of the punt and stood for a moment with the ball of eels hanging in his hand, a wild swamp-dwelling Perseus holding the head of Medusa.

'There's a bit of weight there, mate. Feel the weight of that. With a bit of luck there's about fifty pounds maybe. At least I've caught some for you. I was worried to death. Made me day. You think you're not earning anything, and suddenly you've got some money.'

A YELLOWBELLY

John called the following evening and asked if I was ready for a day out with Gary. Gary wasn't one for hanging around. When I called he asked what I was doing the next day. Not much was the real answer, since I just couldn't get down to writing anything.

'Are you an early riser?' Gary asked. 'How are you in the mornings?'

'Er, not great,' I said.

'Okay,' he said. 'I'll have a lie-in. Can you be here by … seven?'

'Seven?'

'Yeah. Late start.'

Not wanting to lose face or give Gary the idea that I wasn't routinely up and about by seven I said that was no problem at all. Gary gave me his address. I could almost have seen his house on a good day. Sometimes, when the light is right, the Lincolnshire coast looks as if it is on the other side of a wide lake. As the crow flies Grimsby wouldn't be such a tall order for a seven o'clock kick-off. Even for me. But I wasn't travelling by crow and Grimsby is bloody miles by road. I'd have to leave at four. Which meant not really bothering to go to bed because I'd get three hours' kip even if I managed to fall asleep, which I never do when I have to get up early. In the end I did nod off in the early hours and might have grabbed two hours before the alarm disturbed me into a grainy, amniotic dawn.

I got up quietly, patted my bleary but excited-to-see-me dog (she thinks a dawn start means a rare trip across the marsh after duck), defibrillated myself with an enamel-staining cuppa and set co-ordinates for Grimsby. Not a bad drive at dawn in early summer with the rising sun at my back lighting up the poplars and windmills like candles. Across the Fens west of King's Lynn and then north along empty, straight roads through the smaller of the two New Yorks and up into and over the Lincolnshire Wolds. I was there half-an-hour early, much to Gary's surprise. He pulled back the curtain, waved to show I was at the right house. I went round to the side door as Gary opened it and squeezed himself out. Behind him an Alsatian the size of a wolf snuffled and pined, keen to lick or bite me, I wasn't sure. Gary's firm handshake suggested a day-job lifting nets heavy with eels. He was thick-set and had a fisherman's weather-scorched face framed inside a neatly trimmed beard and cropped white hair. He'd been up for hours he said, in an accent that – to my blunt ear – had traces of Liverpool.

Before long we were on our way, in Gary's van. I put my tape recorder on the dashboard and settled myself in to another two hours on the road. We were heading to one of Gary's secret venues – they're all secret – inland and north, where he'd been getting good hauls lately. Once we'd negotiated Grimsby's early rush hour and a garage stop for fuel and coffee I asked Gary directly his take on eel numbers. John had been struggling, I said, when it sounded as if Gary hadn't been. This puzzled me, as every headline I ever read and all the science indicated that eel numbers were plummeting.

'No change.'

'Over your entire career catching eels?'

'No change whatsoever.' He was unwaveringly, surprisingly confident. 'Now, if you go back to your 1980s, in England, Scotland and Wales, there was 1,200 commercial eel fishermen. The average catch in them days was anywhere between forty-seven and fifty ton of yellow eels every year. That's not elvers. That's just yellow eels. Nowadays – we don't count Scotland and Wales now cos you're not allowed to fish there for eels any more – in England we have got 124 licensed eel fishermen. But out of that 124, *commercial* fishermen like John, myself, Terry and a few others, well, you can probably count them on one hand. There's lots of other people that's licensed to catch for the pot. Last year's catch was forty-six ton and you've only got fifty or so commercial anglers. So, you tell me that there's a decrease in the eels when you've got less anglers, less commercial people. Yeah? A lot less and you're still catching the same.'

Gary didn't have a lot of respect for the scientists who'd disagree with him, nor for whoever had been the architects of the real problem. Just like John, Gary was sure that the travails of the eel (such as he admitted to them) were caused by barriers to migration and especially by the transition from leaky, wooden sluice and lock gates to concrete and steel. He described a river he fished, a tributary of the Humber: 'A typical dirty, shitty eel man's river. You've got dead cows in it, you've got buses floating in it, cars upside down. There's a massive great big weir goes across it, a big concrete wall, probably 150 feet across and it's probably twelve feet high. The banks are thirty feet either side. It's tidal. Very, very tidal. It's got a nine-hour ebb and a three-hour flood, so that gives you a rough idea of what it's like. It's a shitty, shitty, nasty, nasty river. But I can put nets in there, leave them for four days and I'd get thirty-five, forty kilo of eels. Some days I'd get seventy. And my eels are from year-old yellows, to five-pound silvers. The other side of the weir – beautiful, greenish, deep river with canal boats on it and everything, yeah, and it goes for miles – I can put 1,000 nets in there, leave them a week and if I got one eel I'd be lucky. That concrete wall there is stopping every-thing going through.'

Our conversation meandered this way and that, taking in pike anglers who pinch or cut his nets, mitten crabs, daft Environment Agency policies – a frequent refrain – the European referendum (it was just days before and neither of us believed that the UK would actually vote to leave the EU), daft European laws, flooding, health and safety, trawlers, how carp taste like shit and how giant squid attack submarines. More or less every bridge we crossed precipitated a new story about the fecundity of eels in Gary's part of the world, and how the authorities refused to acknowledge it.

We crossed the Ancholme and Gary told me about a fisheries survey the Environment Agency had done with electric-shock equip-ment, something Gary says simply doesn't work on eels in deep water, which yielded a classification of no eels. Gary took a fisheries officer back to the same place and pulled out seventy kilos in his nets. We crossed the Trent and he told me that the Agency refused to believe enough elvers ran it to justify a fishery. So, Gary took the fisheries officer there and gave him a dip net. This man used to net elvers on the Severn, so he knew how to do it but even so when he pulled out sixteen kilos of elvers on his first night he could hardly believe his eyes. Neither revelation made any difference to the Agency's standpoint. So why, I wondered, are the authorities in this state of denial? Could it be because so much funding is attached to the idea of eels being endangered?

'You've hit the nail on the head, Charlie,' said Gary. 'Jobs for the boys. But it's not just "endangered". The panda is endangered and there's 300 of them left. The tiger is endangered and there's like 600 of them. The eel is "critically" endangered and yet there's billions and billions of them!'

Now I didn't know who or what to believe. I had some sympathy for Gary's frustrations. The Environment Agency is often paralysed by its own bureaucracy, haunted and hunted to a state of ineffectuality by the chronic conviction that it is being made redundant by successive cash-strapped governments. Which it is, to be fair. This drives practical men like Gary to distraction: he had no end of examples. But I also felt that the entire scientific community could not be so wholly wrong.

Gary paused at the top of a hill. 'Look at these trees,' he said. 'It's stunning, isn't it? Absolutely stunning.'

The lake below us was flat like glass, reflecting a hazy shroud of thin, grey cloud.

Down in the valley Gary parked just so. I took a stroll, easing off five hours of sitting in a car. We had plenty of time and Gary had to sort his stuff. Gary's fastidious tidiness, everything going into the boat in a set order, contrasted starkly with John's chaos. Gary's boat was clean. Not a scrap of weed or mud on it. His outboard too, which he hefted in and hooked up carefully. Then his nets all in a neat pile on the prow. He counted them out, hesitated over one or two, put them back in the van, then took them out again. His lunch and a thermos went into a bucket in the stern. Then he moved the van to a particular gap in the trees, apparently lining up the sliding door with the small indent in the bank where his boat sat. He got out to check and said it was no good. He moved the van again, no more than a few inches, but enough to make him happy.

Then I asked if I could hang my radio microphone around Gary's neck. He agreed, but with obvious reluctance. You won't notice it, I said. I will, said Gary, but go on anyway. He lowered his head and bracingly tolerated me hanging the receiver round his neck, and pinning the lapel mic to the inside of his coat.

'I can take it off if you don't like it.'

'I already know I don't like it,' he said.

We pushed off. The hull of the punt scratched across gravel and then eased into a silent drift. Gary cranked the outboard. It caught on the third pull, the revs climbing wildly for an instant. As smoke drifted over the water Gary eased open the throttle. 'We shall see,' he said, switching left and right between sunken trees. 'I've been made a liar before, but we shall see.'

Gary needn't have doubted himself. The first net came aboard absolutely rammed with eels, fat as cucumbers and twice as long. Red in the face with the effort of hauling them aboard, Gary said they were babies, that I hadn't seen anything yet. Eels and nets, eels and nets came splashing on to the floor of the punt, piling into a towering wet heap until the nets were spilling forwards and backwards, sliding into tangles in the footwells. And still Gary kept pulling and the nets and eels kept coming. Gary fussed and stressed as the heap became more unruly. It was the longest net, he explained and he couldn't place it all neatly where he normally does – in the stern – because I was sitting there snapping pictures. Then, once the wriggling, wet mountain of the thing was aboard, Gary couldn't get back over the pile to work the engine.

'You'll have to start her up, Charlie,' he said. I put my camera down and gingerly guided us back to shore where we tethered ourselves to a stanchion on a small jetty and began to sort the catch.

'They're all males,' he said, grabbing an eel out of the first net and tossing it back in. The liberated eel rifled across the silty bed of the lake. 'Always put the first one back. For luck.'

Gary worked quickly. One by one he untied the cod ends, slipped the open net inside the hooped mouth of a sack and shook out all the eels. Between nets he spun the hoop to close the sack and stop the eels wriggling back out again. Then he placed each empty net like a folded concertina on the deck of the prow, curling the connecting rope into a neat coil before starting on the next one. Watching him work I wondered if John only fished paired nets because he'd never have managed this level of shipshape and tidy. Meanwhile Gary apologised for all the water and weed, for flicking my camera with gobs of eel slime. I said not to mind and remarked how tidy the punt was compared to John's.

'John is a scruffy bastard,' he admitted. 'By now, if you were with John you'd be absolutely covered in shit.'

'I'd be covered in terriers,' I said. Gary laughed.

'That's just me though,' he said. 'Being brought up on ships. A scruffy ship is a dangerous ship. So, I always try to keep everything neat and tidy.'

Soon the eels were sucking like lambs on the teat. It struck me now – perhaps because of the sheer numbers and the fact that we were clearly going home with a ton of them, all destined for the smokehouse – as a rather plaintiff, endearing noise. I wanted to set them all free again. But Gary guarded me against assumptions. You just can't tell, he said, from one net what the others will be like. It depends on how the nets are lying and where the eels are moving on the bed of the lake. It's impossible to tell. He explained how the lake was basically a drowned river – as so many estate lakes are in lowland England – and that the eels still follow the old channel, like they don't know there's a lake above them.

'They follow the rivers all the time,' he said. 'Which is what I want you to do now.'

He asked me to start her up again. He liked being chauffeured, he said. I steered us away from the shore, feathering the throttle as I navigated the archipelagos of weed. Fifty yards out Gary told me to turn the boat, point her back to where we'd come from and then quickly spin the engine so that we reversed slowly up the lake, more or less following the line of the riverbed ten or twenty feet below us. The engine hammered and jumped in my hands as the pulses from the prop bounced off the hull. Through palls of smoke I lined up the steeple of a far church to a gap in the trees and tried to keep a steady course. Gary lobbed the first disc-brake weight over the edge and then fed his nets out one at a time.

'Lovely,' he said, at the end of the run as the last float bobbed over the side. 'Dead good job that. Couldn't have got that better. Right, we'll do the next set and then stop for a cup of tea. It's nice when I've got a skipper. Lovely! That's me first set. Then I've another there running across. Then one there.' He started to count, like he'd forgotten how many sets he had. 'Five. Okay. Follow the coot! It's gonna be all or nothing today. I can feel it!'

I followed the coot and cut a course up the lake between billows of filamentous weed rising like cumulus clouds from the dark bed of the lake. It was growing at such a rate that Gary felt the place would soon be covered, at least up here near the shallows. He wouldn't be able to set his nets here beyond one more haul.

'That'll do, knock her out of gear and then switch her off, mate. Thank you.'

We found the tailing rope of the next set and began to pull. It was heavier still. Now Gary started to haul the big female eels and so many he cautioned me to be careful when I moved: the punt was becoming top heavy and he didn't want to fall in.

'There … what did I tell you? See that?' He laughed like a pirate looting treasure as he hefted over the gunwales a net so heavy with eels that the punt dipped to the waterline.

'Now we're starting to get into them. You might get a bit wet. Are you ready? The next one should be even more rammed. I like the feel of this one. They keep me fit these bags! Ooh yes!' He grunted, triumphantly, huffing and puffing like he was weight-lifting.

And so it went on. Not every net nor every set was as full as these, but soon we'd filled one sack, then two, then three.

'It's nice this,' he said. 'When someone is on the engine. I could get used to this. Want a job?' He lit a cigarette, spat a bit of tobacco off his tongue. 'Left a bit. Through that gap. Watch that branch. Beautiful. I'll just let this lady go by, have a quick wee, unbag 'em, put a float on 'em, get 'em back in the water.'

An old man walked past with his dog. How are you, sir! Gary called out with bravado. He was friendly to anyone who passed. They talked about how late he was today, blaming me. They talked about the weed, the weather. A pretty, middle-aged lady came over. Hello, darling! Gary recognised her. People's gonna start talking! Especially when you start bringing cakes and coffee!

The man asked if Gary had caught much. Gary shrugged, ambivalently. He started on about his research and tagging and I wondered, briefly, what he was talking about. He pulled out a big silver eel and described how it was typical of the eels that can't get out, as if he was here to change that. Another lady strolled up and asked what on earth he was going to do with them all.

'I'm gonna chop off their heads and eat 'em,' Gary answered with a twinkle. It was more or less the truth presented as a joke. 'Nah. These will get released. All the silvers. Get counted and things like that.'

'I see,' said the lady, somewhat reassured. The old man smiled. I think he knew. Then the curious walkers drifted off. After they'd gone Gary whispered: 'You always tell 'em what they want to hear.'

We motored back out and dropped our three sacks into deeper water and marked them with a float. As the sacks of eels sank slowly through the depths, bubbles fizzing skywards, I wondered what the eels thought of all this, if eels think anything. They seemed so mutely resigned to the treatment. I asked Gary why he told the onlookers that he was surveying not fishing for eels. I was puzzled by the idea that anyone might object to artisanal fishing on this scale.

'It keeps the peace and it keeps people quiet,' said Gary. 'I don't like having grief. I've had all my days of grief. I'm sixty year old and I just want a nice happy peaceful life and what they want to hear, that's what I tell them. It's as simple as that.'

You could tell the type, he reckoned, the birdwatchers and the squirrel lovers and bunny cuddlers. Rather than confronting them with what they don't want to or might find difficult to hear, he does the opposite. If he told them he was a commercial eel fisherman, that all these eels were going to be smoked, well some people would be okay with it, Gary thought, but some wouldn't. The worst are anglers, he said. You'd think they'd get it, but they're the worst.

As if to underline his point we were waylaid by three curious carp anglers when we got back to the van. They'd followed us round the lake and were full of questions which Gary answered evasively. I think he suspected they had something to do with the nets he'd found sliced up a week before. I waited in the water with the sacks of eels, not wanting to give away the extent or nature of his venture. As I stood there furtively whistling at the sky, while my comrade-in-arms gave these three camouflaged nosy-parkers the runaround, I realised I had – albeit temporarily – become an eel man. Its innate secrecy had seeped into me.

'Right,' said Gary, sliding the panel door closed after they'd gone. 'I'm gonna finish me coffee. Have a pee. Pour another coffee. Have a fag, and that's us done.' Gary leant back against the van and smoked his cigarette. I sat on the step of the passenger door. The aerator bubbled noisily behind us, soaking a tankful of eels with oxygen. Reflected in the water, and towering above the smooth lake on the bank opposite was a stand of oak trees.

'Look at those trees!' said Gary. 'Ancient, ancient, early oaks. Imagine what they've seen! Kings and queens. Battles. Lovers. Some people think I'm mad for thinking about that kind of thing.'

*

On the way home I asked Gary about his background, how he'd got into eels and his life on the water. Something told me he wasn't from a long line of Fen Tigers either. In fact Gary was Irish and from a family of travellers. He was born in County Clare, but he came over when he was a baby and has lived in Lincolnshire ever since. You can't take away your past, he said, but he doubted any of his family were still on the road, so to speak. Even so, Gary is a country boy. He was never good at school, though he's by no means stupid, he said. His life was built around trees, the countryside and poaching. He would sneak out of his bedroom window all the time and before he could even write his name he could set a snare, catch a pheasant, skin a rabbit. He had a Woolworth's pocket knife, a methylated spirit stove, a pan and a duffel bag.

'So with a bag on my shoulder, with my little burner in it and my little pan I used to sing my name out at school register and then I used to just disappear. I'd go and catch eels on the rods, little flounders, trout. And that's how I was. I learnt how to tie flies, did a bit of fly fishing. I used to net jay birds, pull their necks and we'd take the wings off and get sixpence a pair.'

His mentor was Bob, an old countryman and father figure for Gary whose parents were often away. Bob didn't have any kids and nowadays people might think him a dirty old man hanging out with a ten-year-old kid in the woods. But he wasn't. Bob was just an honest, dishonest countryman: a poacher. Pheasants at the back door of the pub, rabbits to the butchers, sheep even. If it had an arse and you could eat it, it got shot or netted and sold. A Lincolnshire poacher. That's how it was then, said Gary.

It was Bob who showed Gary how to trap eels. Roadkill and a sack was all it took. A dead rabbit, or pigeon maybe. Throw the carcasses in a sack and fill it with straw. A hoop of strong willow or blackthorn to hold the net open and a brick to weigh it down. Then just chuck it in the river. Come back a few days later.

'And in them days,' said Gary, 'there were plenty of eels because we didn't have the obstructions on the rivers. I've seen him pull bloody ten, twenty, thirty eels out of a sack. I can still remember it now. I can still see it vividly.'

Bob was a 'bobber' too. He showed Gary how to bob for eels, how and when to get the worms, on a warm night after a storm, and how to thread the worms on to a piece of Worcester yarn. The eels bit the worms and got their teeth tangled in the wool. And so Bob and Gary would just sit there on the edge of the river bobbing the worm and pulling in eels, one after another.

'Basically I was taught how to bob and how to catch eels here in Lincolnshire. I'm a yellowbelly through and through'

'Yellowbelly?'

'John's a Fen boy, like I'm a yellowbelly. Lincolnshire. Lincolnshire yellowbelly. All John's class up that way, not so much Terry, but John and old Wally Mason and all the rest they're classed as your Fen Tigers. But I'm this side of the border. I couldn't – even though I've fished the Fens and I've lived in the Fens, you know – I couldn't class myself as a Fen Tiger. It wouldn't be right. I'd get my balls chopped off. I'm a Lincolnshire yellowbelly and that's it. But what Bob showed me more than anything is that eel men aren't made. They're born.'

Like John, Gary had started off trying for a conventional career. He had been a chef. But something in the water kept calling him. He'd passed his exams and had a job at a hotel, but he went fishing at the weekends and every night after tea, and eventually the fishing took over: long-lining for cod and whiting in the harbour, or running down the coast catching skate. Then in quiet periods he went to Spain as a deckhand in the Bay of Biscay. He hated the place and the boat he was in, which they called the Green Submarine because it spent more time under the water than on it. He hated the way they fished too, stacking every nook and cranny on the boat with black-market fish. The day after he left, that boat went down with all hands. Gary disliked trawling: it was dangerous and boring, and so eventually he went back to what he'd learned as a kid and to his beloved eels. Now he was sixty and he still loved every minute of it.

I mentioned how John didn't think he'd ever stop.

'Oh yeah,' said Gary. 'I'll do it till I can't physically do it any more. I hope I'm still going when I'm seventy, eighty. But the day will come when I can't lift the nets. I'll know when I'm there.'

Which brought us round to what had been troubling me throughout my time with John and Gary. Setting aside the differing lives and viewpoints of scientists and eel men, there is common ground between them: even Gary acknowledged the impact of barriers to migration. We are clearly approaching either a turning point or precipice with eels. I like to think we can keep away from the precipice. I certainly think that it's up to us. But the other part of that story are the men like John and Gary. They are dying out more certainly than the eels they hunt. Where are the next generations of Fen Tigers and Yellowbellies?

'That is the one thing I regret,' said Gary. 'Not having anyone to pass my skills on to. If I had a son he might have followed my footsteps. He might not have done, of course. Each to their own. But we're a dying breed and once we've gone that's it. That English tradition of eel fishing and bobbing, the whole country way of life just seems to be disappearing. And the Environment Agency is just playing along with that, reining back the licences. Derek Johnson died the other day. He had 200 licences. Barry, he had fifty. But if you asked now you'd not get a licence. I bet you 500, maybe 600 licences have gone out of the system in the last few years.'

Of all the problems that beset the eel, are fishermen like Gary and John really such a threat? Somehow the tradition of fishing is and should be bound up with the fortunes of the fish. Who's really going to care about the eel if there's no eel fishery or fishing? And will those who do care altruistically, so to speak, pick up the baton of day-to-day management and responsibility? The state can't afford to and the NGOs can't either. And yet conservationists and agencies throughout Europe have run away with the statistics and homed in on fishermen – with the blessing of the WWF, eel fishing has been banned in Norway, for example – an easier target than PCBs, barriers to migration or smugglers.

'It's crap,' said Gary, passionately. 'It's terrible. It's disgraceful. They think just one person pottering about is keeping a tradition going. It isn't! People don't realise. Soon there'll be nothing left. And it's not just eels. There's your trawlermen, the men that go potting and gill netting. I reckon in fifteen years there'll be no such thing as a fisherman. But fishing isn't the problem. The problem is the Agency shutting off rivers. The black market in elvers. There are something like 15,000 miles of river, dyke, drain and canal in the Anglian region alone. If you got every eel man in the country and tied all their nets together it wouldn't stretch three miles! Small-scale fishermen aren't the problem.'

We were back to the outskirts of Grimsby now. Gary pointed at a row of run-down houses and empty shops. They'd belonged to people in the fishing industry, he said. But it's all gone downhill over the last few decades.

'Since our fishing industry went, our fantastic fishing industry, all knackered up by Europe so everybody else could fish our waters except us, it's just gone downhill. The docks. The shops. It's a shithole, now. The whole east coast. You can see the decline,' said Gary. 'And it's disgraceful.'

I wondered if anyone in Grimsby would vote to remain part of the EU.

'I don't think they will. I honestly don't think they will,' he said.

*

We were back at Gary's by six, unloading his eels one dripping sack at a time from the van, down the garden path and into his shed where a water tank fizzed in the darkness. Gary switched on the light and scooped a net through the wriggling cauldron. It came up with so much weight in it that he could only just lever the net above the surface. This was his week's catch: today we'd added about 170 kilos. Come the weekend he would empty the van, put two or three tanks in the back and drive, as he does almost every week, to meet a Dutchman called Willem – John would be there too – who'd buy his eels for £4.50 a kilo. These being wild eels and worth a premium Willem would most likely export them to Holland or drive them in his smart delivery van to a few select restaurants in London. Some to Billingsgate. Some to Gloucester.

As for Gary he'd be out again by two in the morning.

'I'll be in bed by two,' I told him. 'Tea at seven. Up at eight. Desk by nine. If all goes well I might get more words down than you'll get eels. But I doubt it.'

And with that – and after a one-for-the-road cuppa sipped under the watchful guard of Gary's enormous Alsatian – I said goodbye and set a course for Norfolk, the long way round.

A GREEN TERRORIST

I wasn't sure who or what to believe, or if anyone knew the truth when it came to eels. Gary was making a good living off the back of their 'disappearance', if disappearing is what they are doing. It was hard to believe in a 90% decline with all those eel-stuffed nets we pulled aboard one after the other, and which by the sounds of it Gary pulls aboard his punt more or less every day. Even allowing for the fact that he knows where to look, you can't find something that isn't there.

It's also hard to believe those stories when the French still catch forty tons of elvers every year: millions, if not billions, of young eels. The scale of *that* catch did worry me, but like Gary, I was sceptical about the impact a few independent fishermen could have on a fish like the eel. It struck me as a real shame that the eel-crash headlines are creating innumerable jobs for eel scientists while the traditional craft of netting them is dwindling away to nothing.

I see this dialectic all the time in conservation, the push and pull between the wisdom of traditional countryside management and 'enlightened' conservation. The latter is slowly winning and often I am on that team: passionately so when it comes to opposing the dredging of rivers, for example. But as often I feel I'm straddling a divide, frustrated by the unnecessary polarity of the argument and the inexorable annexation of tradition by the academy and an urban elite ... at an as yet unknown cost. What happens, I wondered as I drove home, after the scientists have their funding cut? Who notices when an eel population crashes because of some engineering scheme or pollutant?

Hoping to find the overlap I felt must exist between the conservation and sustainable exploitation of the eel, I hunted the internet for someone I could talk to and eventually I bumped into Andrew Kerr, director of the Sustainable Eel Group. The name gave me hope, 'sustainable' implying usage and management. SEG had formed in 2009 and is dedicated to the restoration of 'healthy wild eel populations so that they may fulfil their role in the aquatic environment and support sustainable use for the benefit of communities, local economies and traditions'.

So far, so good. After a short rally of email ping-pong we scheduled a meeting at a suitably aquatic pub beside the Thames near Cookham – roughly halfway between King's Lynn and Gloucester, where he lived. It was a place I thought I knew well, but when I idly looked up Cookham and eels I was delighted and amazed to find a photograph of the nearby weir at Hedsor taken in 1875, half of which was made up of wicker eel-bucks – pointed baskets used to trap eels on their downstream migration – jutting above the waterline: an apposite reminder of the vanished fecundity of the Thames, but also of the fact that we had dammed our rivers long before the eel disappeared. I mentioned this to Andrew as we took our drinks to a window table overlooking the water.

'The thing is,' said Andrew, 'when we're talking about eels and numbers we just don't know, because they are so dispersed and they arrive over such a long period of time and they are so difficult to catch. We're ignorant. Take the River Severn, which is at the northern edge of the range: the last ten-year average is about four tons. That's caught! Not what's arrived. That's something like 13 to 15 million elvers. The lowest year – 2009 – the catch was something like a million and in the highest years of the last decade, 2013 and 2014, we had something like 40 to 50 million.'

The extreme variation notwithstanding, it is almost impossible to know, Andrew explained, the size of a given eel population or migration up or downstream even when you have catch statistics like this, going back years. The only legal way to fish for elvers in the UK is to stand on the side of the river and use a dip-net. But the size of any catch made this way is hopelessly linked to weather conditions. The elver migration needs lots of rain and warm weather. The migration must then coincide with big tides and a full moon. Thus, the fishing only works on a couple of nights in the year when conditions are right. On those occasions you can take a lot, but no one really knows what percentage of a run is represented by any given catch. Fishermen will tell you it's not many. Scientists will tell you it's a lot. Then we have the additional complication that once the eels have settled into their freshwater habitat it is also incredibly difficult to survey them.

If that's all true, I wondered, aren't these doom-laden headlines about crashing eel numbers based on some questionable correlations?

Don't the numbers just as much describe the weather or the fact that eels are very hard to find?

Andrew was not keen for me to jump to this conclusion. The trend is downwards, he said, so something must be going on. No one is denying the enormity of the crash.

'Well, Gary is,' I said.

'Okay. Gary is,' Andrew admitted. 'But no one else is denying a massive decline. It's one hundred down to ten, one hundred down to five. That sort of order. In the face of how difficult that decline is to quantify and monitor, scientists have elected to use the number of elvers arriving at the coast each year as a 'proxy' indicator to assess the total population of the European eel.'

I could see a problem with this right away: *we don't know* how many elvers arrive in any given year. Andrew had just told me that. We only know how many have been caught and that depends on a lot more than how many there are. Andrew then revealed that in 2013 and 2014 the elver run was so large that the French elver fishery reached its quota within twenty-four hours of opening. At that point fishing ceased while the elvers kept on running and running. Any correlation between the catch and the numbers must have broken down completely.

Andrew agreed there was much we didn't know. But he insisted on the 'indisputable' decline. Because of it, he said, the International Union for the Conservation of Nature has classified the eel as 'critically endangered'. And ICES EIFAC (International Council for the Exploration of the Sea – European Inland Fisheries Advisory Committee), a working group on eels consisting of scientists from across Europe, has advised that we should 'reduce *all* human impacts on eel mortality to *zero*'. Fishing is a human impact, Andrew agreed, but they also have hydro-power and barriers to migration in mind. Neither organisation is against fishing per se.

'But if they want to reduce anthropogenic impacts to zero, then surely they are against fishing? And that must be why our Environment Agency is phasing out licences.'

Andrew insisted that many scientists are totally unconvinced that a ban on fishing would have any impact or produce a recovery. They're angry, he said, that their precautionary advice has led to this one-dimensional thinking: 'stop fishing'. Particular culprits are the NGOs in northern Europe: WWF and Greenpeace. They have had quite an influence on Germany and Denmark and Sweden. Eel fishing is now banned in several European countries.

Pausing briefly to wonder how these places would ever now detect a recovery, I moved the conversation on to the causes of this decline and asked what can we do about it? I mentioned the various theories I'd read.

Andrew produced a map of Spain showing blue veins like the capillaries on leaves, fingering across the whole country. These blue lines marked the distribution of eels along Spanish waterways in the nineteenth century. On a second map – which marked the distribution of eels today – the blue capillaries have been reduced to a finger-width smudge around the Atlantic coastline. The interior of Spain, as far as the eel is concerned, had simply disappeared.

'This is all because of blocked rivers. You can write these maps over the whole of Europe. In the UK we dammed our rivers earlier than other countries, ever since the tenth century, and especially since the Industrial Revolution. But following the war, Portugal and Spain and all of North Africa along with Belgium and Holland, they've all done it. And while at first the dams were made with wood and the eels got through them, now we have cement and steel doors and only small numbers get through. We have engineered the eels out. So, when you ask what we can do – well, opening up our rivers again is something we can do. As I keep saying, it's tens of thousands of people taking tens of thousands of small actions over decades. It's cumulative. Hundreds of years of industrialisation and engineering. Now that we're trying to correct it we will not be able to do it in one budget cycle. It's going to take half a century of sustained management to make a difference.'

Andrew had a vision and a 'get on with it' attitude to conservation that is all too rare. I asked about his background, how he had 'got into eels'. It turned out he'd been in the army. But I knew that already if I thought about it. The way he dissected problems with an efficiency of attention, skimming over the intricacies perhaps, but focussed on forward movement, on making things happen. After he left the army Andrew worked in management consultancy, but then he got cancer. The doctors told him to change his life and his lifestyle, to do more gardening.

'So I was looking for a new challenge. I was already involved with some conservation charities and was aware of the eel issue, that it was an endangered fish on my patch. So I thought I'd see what I could do. I thought I'd shake some trees.'

I wondered if the doctors hadn't rather meant a gentler type of gardening. Andrew laughed. Now he is regarded as a 'green terrorist', he admitted. He's been fighting terrorism all his life he said, and now he's considered a terrorist himself. In fact he's still fighting it.

'Who thinks you're a green terrorist?' I asked. 'And how are you still fighting terrorism?' His answer took us to the murkier side of the eel's struggle, as if it could get much murkier.

Andrew has been crunching data these past few years, trying to get his head around what happens to the enormous numbers of eels caught by the French and Spanish. He has summarised hundreds of hours of detective work in a bar chart printed over a map of Europe. He took it out from his pile of papers, wiped the table between us clean and placed it front of me. One bar marked the declared legal catch of European glass eels in 2015/16: about 214 million elvers, or sixty-one tons. The second bar marked how many of these reached their legal destinations, as far as Andrew and his team could deduce, spread between farming and food and restocking: about 98 million, or twenty-eight tons. Between one and the other, therefore, 116 million elvers had disappeared.

'Where have they gone?' was the question innocently stamped across the diagram above an arrow that pointed east.

The problem these elvers face and the biggest threat by far to the European eel as a species and a part of our heritage, is that they are worth $1,500 per kilo on the black market in Asia. That's almost a dollar an elver. Strictly speaking most (60%) of the elvers caught in European elver fisheries should go to restocking rivers that have been made otherwise inaccessible. But with that kind of price on the black market, Andrew claimed, the French elvers mostly go east. The traffickers pack the eels in ice in styrofoam boxes. These are then packed in suitcases and sent on passenger jets to Asia. Andrew showed me photographs of the illegal cargo looking just like someone's holiday luggage.

There's a $50 million black market in eels, all of which are caught under 'legal' quota. But Andrew's data thus far describes only the eels 'missing' from the catches we know about. You can double that, he estimates, to account for the eels that are caught illegally. In Portugal eel fishing is banned and yet every year 30–50 million elvers are caught in Portuguese waters and sent to Asia.

I asked if this black market played any part in the British story. I'd read about past links between the IRA, eel money, drug money.

'It used to ... years ago. But we've really cracked down on it.'

Does that imply, I wondered, that the French and Spanish governments are complicit in the illegal trade, or are at least turning a blind eye to it?

'Yes, in a word,' said Andrew. But it plays a part in our fortunes because eels are an international fish. 'In Britain we are the leaders by miles in terms of eel conservation. In the next four years alone we'll be spending £100 million. Why should the money we're spending on unblocking migration pathways subsidise illegal trafficking operations in France, Spain and Portugal?'

I could see what he meant by shaking trees. I didn't suppose this work had made him popular in France.

'That's why they call *me* a green terrorist!' he said.

Andrew was my kind of conservationist. To him science was a tool to catalyse action, not a surrogate for it. I had the feeling that if Andrew kept on shaking those trees we might get somewhere. As if to prove my suspicion, a few months later I noticed a post on Twitter made by an outfit called 'repeuplementanguille' and a link to a publicity brochure boasting how France is the 'essential restocking actor' in European-wide moves to conserve the eel, how it supplies 60% of the eels used for the restocking programme set up by the member states of the EU. Had Andrew's identification of the shortfall prompted a round of PR spin, I wondered? The brochure protested mightily: 'Every year in accordance with EMP objectives ... under the authority of...restocking initiatives are happening within a scientific framework ... it is in such an open-minded and responsibility-sharing spirit', etc. etc. Taken at face value, the trumpeting was a good sign. Even so, I was uneasy.

The mechanised shifting of eels from one place to the next, however 'scientific' the 'framework', is something about which I am instinctively sceptical. Is there any evidence, I wondered, given how notoriously difficult eels are to track in the wild, that a restocked eel fares any better, circumnavigates mortality risks any more effectively, if we've scooped it up in a net and taken it somewhere it wasn't otherwise heading, in the back of a van? Might not this enforced and blindfolded migration discombobulate the eel's internal compass? And what of the way in which an eel's gender and the timing of its migration back to sea appear to be determined by its environment? A paper I read on this subject concluded 'Further research into the timing and mechanisms of sex determination in eels is required to effectively and efficiently manipulate sex for conservation.' A typical pitch for more work, I thought, and an unjustified insistence on the idea that through science we can improve on a natural system. It also showed that we don't know what impact we might be having.

Another paper from the USA, published in 2015, showed that elvers which had been caught, moved and restocked for conservation purposes, grew, sexualised and migrated to spawn at completely different rates and times from native eels in the same water. So much so that the stocked eels began their spawning runs when they were six years old, the same age as the native eels which were *arriving* in the lake the stocked eels were leaving. Eels move upstream over years, not days.

My guess is that if you move the eel about by artificial means, you probably muck everything up. The same kinds of antics played with salmon are now seen as a non-starter: moving strains of fish from one catchment to the next, artificial stocking. Salmon populations belong to specific rivers and are therefore specifically adapted to those rivers. It's different with the eel because they spawn en masse in a writhing, mid-Atlantic orgy according to no known order, something which is called panmixia. And yet, only a few years ago some scientists were theorising the opposite, that the eel did spawn in subgroups after all, defined by geographical origin and the timing of their arrival in the Sargasso Sea. Like the salmon. A glut of papers has recently 'disproved' this, but for a few years 'conservation stocking' was looking like a real Pandora's box.

The fact is we don't know. And with the endlessly mysterious eel we *really* don't know.

ODNEY WEIR

I had to pick up my son from Heathrow later that afternoon, but with an hour to spare I took a walk along the river to see if I could find the site of the Hedsor eel-bucks. The nineteenth-century picture I had with me showed eight drooping wicker baskets, white water below them and springtime leaves above shimmering and ghostly from the slow shutter speed of Henry Taunt's plate camera. Taunt was an early landscape photographer who specialised in views of the Thames. He used the wet collodion process and had a mobile studio set up in his punt. It must have been quite a palaver to sensitise the plate in his 'darkroom tent', capture the exposure, develop and fix the image, all whilst afloat. Afterwards he washed the plates in the river and dried them in the sun, all of which only adds to the peculiar presence of this picture, as if the moment had been bottled, somehow. That connection with the past was something I hoped to find now as I wandered down Odney Lane, over the footbridges and channels that lead to Sashes Island. I found Cookham Lock, crossed the meadow and stood more or less where Taunt must have anchored his punt.

The eel-bucks are gone now and so is the weir. Only a few stones remain below the surface, a (deliberate) hazard to boats no doubt, should any ignore the Private Navigation and Mooring sign at the foot of the island. It's a contentious bit of privacy, and has been for over two centuries. The eel-bucks play a part in the story.

The bend in the Thames here, where the main river thrusts against the chalky scarp of Cliveden Cliff, was a notorious hazard to barge traffic when the Thames was a major arterial route for grain, malt, timber, metals, stone and – believe it or not – cheese. You wouldn't think so to look at Turner's oil painting of the place: a few cows wallowing midstream, bargemen unloading at the river's edge and smoke curling up from a pub chimney, white against the towering scarp of trees beyond. It looks very peaceful. But those gravel shoals claimed barges every year. Heavily laden, they'd breach on the shallows in low water, turn sideways in the current and break in two. The Thames Commissioners implored Lord Boston, who owned the land either side, to allow a weir to be built. But Boston made a tidy sum from his wharves and towpath – both necessitated by the treacherous meander – and he wouldn't agree. After all, the barges which sank were those which had run the risk of avoiding his tow.

In 1829 the commissioners lost patience. They cut a channel through Sashes Island and installed a pound lock. Suddenly Boston's towpath was redundant. He sued and was awarded £1,000 and costs. But then the commissioners built a new weir at the head of the island – more or less exactly where Turner had set up his easel – to increase water levels in their cut. This blocked Boston's meander from the other end and now even his wharves were redundant. He took the commissioners to court again and won only a paltry sum this time, but also the right to insist on a lock in the weir, so that in theory at least barges could use his wharves. The commissioners built the lock, but in 1869 they removed it. In a fit of pique Boston built another weir at the lower end of the island and installed those eel-bucks. In doing so he privatised the river in front of his house – his real motivation, so everyone suspected – and it is a contentious annexation to this day: the only 'private' reach of the main River Thames. The most recent court hearing, the *Environment Agency* v. *Mrs Rowland*, was heard in 2003. I can't find a record of whether the new trade in silver eels replaced Boston's lost income, or if it was ever a viable business. By the second part of the nineteenth century freight trains were replacing barges anyway and so both the commissioners' cut and Boston's eel-bucks were follies of sorts. Now the eel-bucks are gone and the commissioners' cut is used only by pleasure boats.

All this might seem of only passing relevance and yet the vignette of commerce and rivalry is at the heart of the story of the eel. It's exactly how structures like weirs and sluice-gates became grand-fathered into the landscape: through water-use and access wars. The scene that Turner drew is not available now, not on any part of the Thames. There are no shallows that cattle can wade in. From Oxford to London the river is a staircase of weirs, a linear boating pond and home to an armada of pleasure boats that can go where they want because the river is wholly navigable. This probably makes it a nicer thing to potter along, or live beside, but the change is made at the expense of native wildlife like salmon and eels and sturgeon. It needn't be that way.

Taunt took another photograph of Lord Boston's weir from the other side, then he punted upstream to the commissioners' weir and photographed that too. I had to walk to the other end of the lock cut to see it. Unlike Boston's, Odney Weir is still there. Without it, boats would have as tough a time getting past this bend as the barges had before 1830. But there's a difference. In Taunt's photograph Odney Weir looks insubstantial compared to the modern monolith. It is made from dozens of oak hatches and it leaks like a sieve. Water simply cascades through the weather-worn timbers. Of course it would have been an instant barrier to salmon, but by 1837 the Thames salmon was extinct anyway. Eels, on the other hand, which would also have better tolerated London's outpourings of toxic pollution than salmon, would have been able to get through this leaky nineteenth-century structure. Not now. The twenty-first-century version is made of steel and concrete and the water does not cascade, it falls in vertical sheets from the lip of the weir.

John and Gary, for all their lack of PhDs on the subject, had it pretty much taped. Bit by bit we've closed and bolted the door on our eels.

Then, amongst laudable attempts to reduce all anthropogenic impacts on eel mortality to zero, we've drawn our bead on the wrong target: the artisanal eel trade. For all sorts of cultural and historical reasons this is a shame. It may yet prove to be a shot in the foot, because it's pretty clear that the only way to judge the real status of our eel population is by using decade-spanning catch data supplied by people who can actually catch eels. As the fishery is phased out, that data set is vaporising. If we ever restore numbers, how will we know? How will we even target our efforts? Meanwhile 'conservation' stocking gives the appearance, both to actors and audience, of doing something positive, though it may not do anything at all, it may make things worse and it certainly takes the impetus away from doing something more permanently substantial ... like unblocking rivers. Worst of all, as millions upon millions of elvers are fished from the Bay of Biscay the cloak of this already questionable conservation exercise is draped across a much darker and wholly unsustainable trade.

'Out there' are global problems: their resolution requires time, political will and whatever technology will save us all from suicide by carbon emissions. Back home there are 16,000 structures across England and Wales that eels and elvers cannot get through.

4. WEST

A SPARK TOUCHING A FUSE

I was fourteen years old when I first saw a salmon: in Ireland again, as with the eel. Before that summer my innate passion for fishing had been sustained, God knows how, by a pond near the Star and Garter gate in Richmond Park or by the Thames under Twickenham Bridge or crabs in a muddy harbour in north Norfolk. Crabs were easy to catch on scrags from the village butcher. I caught sticklebacks in the pond. The only fish I saw in the Thames was a half-dead bream covered in lesions. Ecologically south-west London was more or less dead in the 1970s. So, I watched *Out of Town* every week and dreamt of wilder places.

At boarding school the pond called Stinkers was rumoured to have fish in it. I never saw them. Most of my early letters home referred to Stinkers, but usually because someone had been thrown in and never because anyone had caught a fish. Mum wrote back once suggesting that the following summer we might go salmon fishing in Scotland with friends of hers. She must have hoped it would cheer me up, but one way or another that holiday didn't happen. Not then, anyway.

It was Ireland that gave me my first taste of the wet and the wild during those teenage summers when I went to stay at my godmother's house with Simon and Nicky on the west coast. I remember the very first time, how the three of us had to climb out and walk so that their father's asthmatic little French car could make it over the hill between Coolea and Kilgarvan. We'd been cooped up in the back since the ferry and this was the first time my feet had touched Irish soil. I'd never really seen landscape like it before, but the walk up that glen to the Top of Coom amongst the heather and wind-stunted birch trees felt like a kind of homecoming. I was not over-dosing on Yeats, not quite yet, but Thin Lizzy's 'Roisin Dubh' was the soundtrack of our summer and something in me related to all that sodden greenery, mist and myth.

We stopped at the top for crisps and a Coke at the 'highest pub in Ireland'. There were chickens in the bar. Then, just as Simon and I did on bikes the next year, we pretty much free-wheeled it from the pub downhill to the sea at Kenmare and beyond. We started to cross rumbustious little rivers that tumble quickly off those west-coast hills: the Roughty, then the Finnihy, the Blackwater, and finally the beautiful little Sneem River. It was on one of these that I saw a salmon jump a waterfall. The memory still plays like a film in my head: the salmon catching the top ledge of the fall, thrashing its tail like an outboard until it was swallowed by the tea-stained water of the river above. If I wasn't bewitched already, I was then. Strange that with both salmon and trout, my first encounter should be this leap from their dimension into mine (the trout jumped out of a chalk-stream in Normandy): a spark touching a fuse.

The fuse had been set by a book I'd been given for Christmas: the *Collins Encyclopedia of Fishing*. I almost lived in the pages of that book. The 'game-fishing' part ('game' refers to fish like salmon, trout and grayling) was written by an angler named Reg Righyni. A handful of photographs illustrated the text and even in its two-dimensional form the salmon already had its spell on me. That black-and-white photo of a fresh cock-fish: with its enormous jaw and menacing eye, it looked like an armoured, medieval war-horse. Or the fisherman straining at the pull of what must have been a vast salmon lashing at the surface, far out across the river. These two photographs and a few others of the flies used to catch salmon, ornate concoctions of tinsel and exotic feathers with names such as Thunder and Lightning or Green Highlander, evoked to me a world of chivalric, knightly combat. The rod, a lance. The heraldic flies. The armour-plating of the fish.

Better than the photos were the drawn illustrations of the salmon in all its life stages: as a finger-barred juvenile 'parr', as a silver 'smolt' migrating to sea, as a chrome-plated 'fresh-run' salmon returning from the sea, as male and female salmon in their spawning colours, and finally as the spawned-out 'kelt'. Again this costume drama fed the romance. All fish vary in appearance, but none has quite the martial pomp of a salmon, and none are as drop-dead beautiful. Nature was having a good day, the day the salmon was made. A salmon is awesome and majestic: that must have gripped me, even before I'd seen one for real. As for the living fish, you'd have to be hard-hearted not to feel something profound at the sight of a salmon leaping a waterfall.

I didn't catch one, however, not that summer or the few that followed. The closest I got was when I hooked a fresh, silver fish in the River Inny further round the coast. I dragged it as far as the shingle but the fish – a small salmon perhaps, but more likely a sea trout – flipped on the stones, came off the line and was gone.

Nevertheless, Ireland was where I first caught brown trout and taught myself to fish for them with a free-lined lobworm, and that plays a part in my love affair with salmon. They're very closely related, trout and salmon: subtle mutations crystallised by habitat and life cycles might have forged two species from one many aeons ago, but even now they will sometimes hybridise and amazingly sometimes those hybrids are fertile. And when the trout goes to sea – as many do – grows fat and turns silver, the two species are very hard to tell apart. Sea trout never swim far, unlike the salmon whose journeys are vast, but it's almost certain that if you fish for one, you'll fish for the other and the ways you catch them overlap too.

We started fishing for the trout in the little loughs above Waterville: in the peat-stained tub over Eagle's Hill, which was called Coomrooanigl, and along the necklace of loughs which curl back into the mountains above Lough Derriana: Tooreenbog and Adoolig and the three nameless loughans above, all the way up to a sheer rock-face where a stream tumbling from the mountains above crashes on to fern-covered rocks. These loughs were easy to fish with a spinner: a bar of shiny metal which looks like a tiny fish. The trout were small, sometimes not much bigger than the spinner they had attacked. But they were hungry and aggressive and we never left without a creel-full.

Then we found our way to the little stream at Castlecove: a tiny beck that drains the hill above Staigue hill fort. This stream was so overgrown it was almost impossible to flick a spinner there without catching up on a tree or a rock. But it was the nearest river to my godmother's place, an easy cycle ride away. So, we persisted. We dug worms in the garden for bait, returned with a tin-full and learned how to fish running water. We started with a ball of lead on the line, anchoring the worm to the river just like we did with lugworms in the sea. Soon we discovered it was more effective and much more fun not to use a weight at all, just to flick the lobworm on a free line into the pools and runs and let it drift and roll on the current, until a tappety-tap that told you a trout was on the end.

We haunted the Castlecove River and all those streams nearby: the Sneem, the Inny, the Finglas and the rivers above Lough Currane. Though we never caught a salmon, we did catch lots of trout and what I learned free-lining with a worm became a large part of what I now know about fly fishing.

Yeats's fly-fisherman had by now climbed to a place 'Where stone is dark with froth' inside my own daydreamy self-imaginings: 'the down-turn of his wrist / When the flies drop in the stream'. I'd seen the fly anglers go out in boats on Lough Currane too, and watched their mesmerising casts swishing back and forth through the air. Then there were Reg Righyni's esoteric descriptions of the science of it all, intriguing me with the idea that fly fishing might be a more sophisticated, arcane and rewarding version of what I was already doing. One way or another I was bound to pick up a fly rod. That long-promised trip to Scotland was the catalyst.

Every summer, Pat and Dee, two friends of my parents from university days, took a lodge called Braelangwell on the River Carron, one of several famous salmon streams that flow into the Kyle of Sutherland. It being a fun and relatively informal fishing party for friends and children, they had asked us to join them several times before. My parents weren't anglers, however, and we'd never quite made it work. It must have been my growing enthusiasm, nurtured in Ireland, that made the difference. In 1983, the year before I went to university, Mum and Dad finally accepted the invite.

I knew that I'd have to fly-fish on the Carron. We had some ancestral cane rods and reels in the attic, so I strung one up and for a few weeks before we left I practised a rudimentary cast on the back lawn. I made all the basic mistakes: dropping the rod too far behind me, not giving the line enough time to straighten, trying too hard. But eventually I worked something out, at least to the point that I could – without lassoing my head too often – flick the line up behind me and chuck it out again, straight ahead.

The first morning of our week Pat got me out of bed before breakfast. I dressed, pulled on some rubber waders and followed him to the home pool, where he took me through the basics of the tackle, the line, the flies. I had the longer of our attic's cane rods, a fourteen-footer that weighed a ton and had probably last seen action between the wars. The Napoleonic ones. The fishing world had moved on to fibreglass and graphite and this weapon was retro in the extreme. Pat was polite though. He studied the pole, shrugged and said it would toughen me up. Then he showed me how I should start at the top of the pool, casting across and slightly down the river and let the line swing round in an arc until it was straight below me, that I should then lift and cast again, taking a few steps downstream between casts.

After all that rock crawling in Ireland this felt like something between fishing and a slow-motion military parade. But I did what Pat told me to do, pacing my way down the pool, while he sat on the bank and watched. When I had finished he told me to run through it one more time, but to take my time about it and then he left to get back to his guests and his kitchen. My casting was haphazard. Often I needed the pull of the river to straighten the line after it landed. Once or twice I caught the grass behind me. But gradually I got the hang of what I was doing. My casts got longer and I began to cover the water. I couldn't, however, see how this would get me a fish. It felt too mechanical, and it felt like I was using a broadsword when, on the little streams in Ireland, I had been used to an epée. I went back to the house with nothing in my creel.

After breakfast the fishing was divvied up amongst the adults – there were only so many 'rods' that could be fished at any one time – and I didn't get another turn until the evening.

The fishing was slow for everyone. It hadn't rained for a week or more. Salmon are more aggressive after a downpour: they run upstream on the rise in water and then as the river settles, so do the salmon in whatever pool they have reached. There they await the next rush of fresh water when they will push on upstream. For a few hours or a few days after rain their bodies are still brimful of the hormone that made them run and during that time if a brightly coloured fly swings past, they'll snap at it. Fish that are fresh in from the sea are aggressive too. That all wears off in time and without rain the salmon become more and more lethargic. Eventually they lie comatose on the bed of the river and the lure which a few days earlier might have got the salmon to bite, does absolutely nothing to stir them. You can send out the most perfect casts. You can swing the fly over their heads until you drop. It won't make any difference. This is how it was on the Carron. No fish had been caught by lunchtime. No fish had been caught by supper. I wandered down at about five o'clock and had another go on the home pool and the pool below. Although my casting was improving, nothing took hold of my fly.

Tuesday was much the same, but Pat must have noticed how hard I was trying during my dawn and dusk raids and that I was restless for more, because he suggested I try a tributary upstream, beside which he had barracked his younger teenage children and their friends from school. Built by Thomas Telford to house the rector of Croick Church, the handsomely shabby manse was more bothy than fishing lodge, with hay bales and pallets for furniture, jars of damp sugar and teabags and a box of matches by the fire. Most of the time it was a way-station for trekkers crossing Scotland coast to coast. But it was set beside the River Blackwater – or less catchily the Abhainn an t-Strath Chuileannach – a Carron tributary which salmon ascended in dribs and drabs. A mile or so of fishing came with the weekly lease.

I drove up there after breakfast, along a winding single-track road, hemmed by stone walls and birch trees. I came to a junction where a phone box stood sentry in a dark wood. The sign beside it read Croick Church 1 mile. Beyond the wood the gently pastoral order of the strath gave on to wilder ground. At the foot of the valley lay a staircase of white water and tea-stained pools lost under alders. Then around a bluff I found the half-acre of tree-shrouded gravestones and the manse beyond, white-washed and streaked with moss under broken gutters. I parked by the manse, crossed the wet hill. Here the river fell over a high waterfall, boiled in a dark cauldron of granite, and slipped over an apron of rocks to fan out into a wide pool.

I was back in Ireland!

I hurriedly set up the short cane fly-rod, the one I had practised with at home, threaded an ancient fly-line through the rings and tied on a fly called a Blue Zulu. Back in touch with what I was doing, I started to hunt the stream for fish, flicking the fly any old how into the places I would have thrown a worm. It didn't take long for something to strike at it. The rod jagged down with more violence than I was used to and a silver sea trout jumped clear of the water, the first I'd ever hooked on a fly. Others followed and over the next few hours I winkled three more sea trout and a half-dozen of their brown-trout cousins from out of that pool and the gorge below it. Meanwhile the odd salmon splashed lazily at the tail of the flow. Every once in a while a more lively fish would fling itself at the waterfall above, catch the water if it was lucky, or a rock if it wasn't and in either case bounce back down to where it had come from. A few of the fish that had been in there too long wore the scars of these futile attempts at the falls. They were stale, listless fish and though I tried teasing the Zulu across the water above them, none came close to taking the fly. I returned with a creel that was reassuringly heavy, but without a salmon.

We ate my catch that evening as a starter shared out amongst the whole party and I went to bed chuffed to have caught something. I soon woke again, haunted by the thought of those fasting salmon at the manse. I got up, tiptoed through a sleeping house, found the keys to my parents' car and drove back up the valley through the midsummer dawn to try again.

The manse was only recently asleep – a fire smoked gently at the edge of the lawn; the stale after-glow of cigarettes and beer hung about the motionless, dawn air – and the pool was quiet too, but for the sound of the cascading water. For the sake of form I lengthened a fly-line across the water, fingered and thumbed the Blue Zulu over the likely lies. Still no fish stirred. After a few minutes I stopped casting, sat on a rock at the head of the pool and studied the currents more carefully. My attention was caught by a seam of still water between the main flow and an eddy which curled along the underside of the bank. Here the foam had coalesced into a gently spinning spiral. Just beyond, a boil on the surface suggested a submerged boulder.

I found the scruffiest fly in my box, stripped off the feathers and tied it on the line. Then I turned over a rock. Nothing. Another. Nothing again. A wet hill. Poor soil. I wondered briefly about trying near the bins back at the manse, but didn't want to wake anyone or draw attention to my nefarious plan. Then under the third or fourth rock I found what I was after: a worm. One wouldn't be enough, however, because I had to flick the bait out as far as that dead water. So, I hunted on until I'd clambered over most of the hill and had a ball of worms wriggling on the hook.

Crouching at the edge of the flow, I swung my Medusa bait like a pendulum, back and forth, trying to build up enough momentum. My first cast was hopeless. My second, not much better. Too far and the worms swung round in the current and hung up like a flag in the wind. Too close and they did the same, only in the other direction. Eventually they plopped into the target, splatting a tea-stained hole into the foam. Now, I had to hold the line just so, making sure that neither the up nor downstream currents pulled my bait out of position. The worms sank and held, by my reckoning in the dead water just to the side of that midstream boulder.

It didn't take long. First there was tremor on the line. A heartbeat. Then a steady pull. It stopped. Then another. I lifted the rod, taking up the slack line. The next, longer, more determined pull cut a dark stripe across the white froth. That's when I struck.

The line went solid. Was it a rock after all? It must be a salmon. The pulsing Morse code of the fish's tail telegraphed up the line. I lifted harder. The line tightened through the rings, cut sideways across the run, stopped and held the far side of the flow. I'd hooked a salmon all right.

I lifted the rod. The fish yielded. I leant back again, only this time the fish turned and charged downstream. The rod bucked. Tectonic energy turned to volcanic. My rod snapped straight, the line fell limp. Before I could think where my salmon might have gone next, something fizzed into the air under the alders and landed with a crash. The line had wrapped around a rock and the fish was jagging at the resistance. If it ran hard again now all would be lost.

Nothing for it. I waded in as water gushed over the tops of my thigh waders, staggered drunkenly across the cobble riverbed and walked the rod around the rock, trying not to set off the next explosion. Too late. The fish bolted at the first change in pressure. A rooster-tail of spray chased after it. A bow wave surged at the tail of the pool and my fish was gone, over the lip and downstream.

As the reel ratcheted angrily, I realised a rock-strewn run was all that lay between the bolting salmon and the gorge below. I clambered back to shore and lifted the rod top to reveal a cat's cradle of fly-line looped here and there and wrapped around rocks all over the river. It took a moment or two to follow the mess, but there at the end of it my salmon had run itself to ground and was impotently flailing on a rocky shallow, half in, half out of the water. My fish was one flap away from getting off the line, so I lolloped inelegantly down the bank, my waders sloshing with water, and jumped in again, scooping and scrabbling at the stricken fish until I'd got it far enough up the bank that I was sure it couldn't get away. Then, both of us exhausted, I knelt down and admired my first salmon.

It was not exactly fresh off the tide but I wasn't going to let it go. I found a rock and killed it and took it back to the lodge looking for praise that I knew even then was not my due. I never told anyone how I'd caught it, except my father who suggested that I wrote in the record book that I'd used an 'Umsundululu fly'. Unless the keeper could speak Xhosa, no one would be any the wiser, said Dad.

These might not have been the most dignified or honourable minutes of my fishing life, but they were the start of a love affair, chasing salmon 'through hollow lands and hilly lands', the start of something that now goes far beyond fishing. I like to think I've made up for things since, that I've managed to leave some rivers better than I found them. My mother had looked at the dead fish and said something about what a shame it was that this animal had survived so long at sea and forged its way upstream only to be killed by a fisherman. Her sentimentality irked me sometimes. But as is the way with mothers, the comment smarted and stuck and perhaps it became the start of something too, a way of at least trying to approach this privilege of wilderness by giving back as much as I take.

Over the next few years we returned to Scotland for a week each summer. Mostly we messed about on lochs or trout-filled tributaries. I didn't often get to fish a beat where there was a real chance of salmon. Even so, I winkled another from the Einig – that Umsundululu fly again – and another out of the River Shin. I put the Einig fish back – it was stale, like my first – and kept the Shin fish because it was fresh and I'd caught it properly. But I had watched the conifer forests going up around Loch Ailsh. I'd seen the head-waters of the Oykel and Carron choked with silt after rain, inklings then of what I know too much about now: the insidious and innu-merable threats to the salmon's survival.

I was about to write that the Shin fish was the last salmon I killed, though I have now caught hundreds over the years. Scrolling back I can recall others: a nice fish – one of four – from the River Almond the year my son was born; another on the River Coquet on a family holiday. There have been a few, though not many. It is never straightforward. More than any other fish, salmon force me to question my ethics: of killing them, and also of not killing them. The famous American angler Lee Wulff wrote that a fish is too valuable to be caught only once. As conservation this is unarguable. But there's something about the salmon's life cycle and journey that is so awe-inspiring, moving even, that to interrupt it by catching and then releasing the fish feels gratuitous. Perhaps, then, there is a feeling that this very occasional but primal act of killing a salmon is fundamental to it all, that it is some kind of necessary, but necessarily occasional, observance that ... keeps me honest.

Why don't I agree with my mother in the end? Partly because everyone, without exception, has a negative impact on the natural world. Sentimentality does not exonerate you. Mostly because without fishermen there might be no salmon at all: certainly not in the parts of their kingdom where they are most under threat. Fishing might be a visceral and contradictory mix of passion and exploitation, but almost without exception the people who do the most to combat the threats to wild salmon – and there are many threats – are the people who enjoy catching them. And setting them free again. It's too simplistic to say that our motives are only selfish. Even if they were, would that matter? Results matter. As it is, this relationship with wilderness, wild fish and rivers is much more complex than that.

I had caught only those three salmon, on the Blackwater, the Einig and the Shin, before I left university in 1987 and applied for a job teaching Art in Dorset. It was my mum who spotted that the school where I was hoping to work was set beside a river. Rob, the head of Art, was a fisherman too and after I joined his team we became known as the Fishing Department. At break times through my first few weeks there Rob and I would stroll to the river and watch the tail of the weir for rising fish. There was, it turned out, a dim hope for Rob that one or other amongst the many rise forms would one day be made by a trout. But it never was. I was more surprised by this hope of their presence than the fact of their absence, because to me trout – like salmon – had always been fish of wild uplands, not pastoral, lowland or even suburban England. But Rob had actually caught a few over the years he had been there. More than that, as the teacher who ran the fishing club he kept hold of the school record book which went back to before the 1950s and this showed that trout had featured not just occasionally but regularly in the schoolboy catches of twenty or thirty years before. As had salmon. If the hope of trout had surprised me, the one-time existence of salmon here amazed me. We were on the edge of the Bournemouth and Poole suburban sprawl. Traffic jammed the roads outside the school gates every rush hour and weekend. And yet, said Rob, once in a blue moon the salmon did still show up.

It was warm that September and early October. Then the Indian summer broke and that infamous storm of 1987 rolled over England. Millions of trees and a lot of rain fell. The river rose high and brown. Never mind trout, there were no fish of any sort rising at the tail of the weir. Our cathartic break-time strolls had come to a natural end. Rob and I were in the Art Department when one of the boys came rushing in a few days later and breathlessly announced 'Salmon!' One had been trapped beside the weir. Dropping whatever we were doing we followed the messenger and found a huddle of boys at the edge of the river. One of them held a large, coppery salmon by the tail, cradling its belly with the fish head-on to the current. The salmon, they said, had jumped and missed its mark and was found floundering on the mossy concrete sill. One of the boys had rushed to fetch a net and had managed to catch it. The appearance of Rob precipitated an excited babel of entreaties, some to kill it, others to let it go again.

'It's massive, sir. We could stuff it!'

'No! We should put it back above the weir.'

'Please, sir!'

'Please, sir!'

Rob looked at me. I shrugged and joked that it might look good in the Art Department's goldfish pond. It was a proper salmon, fifteen pounds or more. Whether we kept it by killing it, or just held it in the net forever, universally I think there was a feeling that we didn't want to let this miracle go. Rob was emperor of this weir pool, however.

'I think we should help it on its way, don't you?' Rob said.

The revived salmon was placed back inside the net, lifted from the water by its gaggle of pall-bearers and ferried along the bank to the wooded island above the weir. The boy who'd held it before, took the wrist of the tail again and with one arm under the fish's belly he lay down on the bank and at a full arm-stretch lowered the salmon into the water. The fish felt the flow and with a flick of her tail was gone.

We might all have felt we'd never see another. But others followed. For a fortnight they jumped at the school weir trying again and again to power against the flow that pressed out from underneath the sluice gates. It seemed impossible to believe. An explosive force of nature. Every chance I could I went back to see if they were still there. The same fishing-mad schoolboys were invariably there, just as bewitched as I was by the awesome spectacle, by this *rus in urbe*.

It was hard to say if we were seeing the same few fish over and over, or if this amounted to something like a run. Eventually, when the flow had subsided enough to allow it, the sluice gates were closed and the salmon turned to the fish-ladder. I saw one or two jumping this watery staircase, but it presented no kind of obstacle and soon our salmon were gone.

I might almost have said forever, but there was one more magnificent echo. The following spring the boys found another trapped in the mill race: an enormous, spawned-out cock salmon. It weighed thirty-six pounds, though it was thin as a rake and taller than the boy who discovered it. It must have weighed over forty, or even forty-five pounds when it came into the river as part of that same Great Storm run. The last giant of the Stour? It was unlikely to survive, we thought, but such a fish deserved whatever chance we could give it, so it was taken across the island to the main river and released.

In 1991 we lit a candle to that fish's progeny. I had met Simon Cain, a concert cellist from Tobago via Coventry, who had given up a career in the concert hall to pursue his passion for rivers. From a blacksmith's forge beside the River Avon – the Stour's more glamorous sister – Simon was now pioneering something called river restoration: part science, part history, part landscape art. A few visionary river-keepers, men like the late Ron Holloway who had spent his life creatively tending the River Itchen, had set the trail. But Simon was working on a scale no one had yet attempted, battering against government agencies still locked inside a land-drainage mindset. His work, and my interest in it, was born out of this zeitgeist: that our landscape had been taken to the brink of a drear, dystopian lifelessness. Simon remembered the Coventry bomb craters, and the shivering awfulness of arriving there from a tropical paradise. Four salmon-less Octobers on the Stour had been added to the sooty grime of my 1970s London childhood. In the name of a 'modern', self-sufficient future our rivers had been made into straightened, entrenched canals, full of farmed fish, while the idea of the wild had been consigned to national parks or the Celtic fringes of the British Isles. We were pissed off about it.

Simon came down to the school and talked to the kids about the work he had been doing on the River Wylye: how he had narrowed the stream to compensate for the fact that over half the flow was now lost to water abstraction, and how he had replaced the gravels where salmon and trout once spawned, gravel which had been dredged out after the war by land-drainage engineers bent on turning water meadows into wheat prairies. Fired up by his hellfire fervour we got to work on that millstream spawning bed: we removed all the abandoned bicycles and skateboards and radios, we brought in fresh gravel and narrowed the channel to flush out the silt, hoping that at least a pair of Stour salmon would come and procreate where their parents had.

The candle burned in vain. That enormous salmon was the last I ever saw in the Stour, though I worked at the school until 1995 and stood watch every autumn. Very rarely I hear of another salmon seen somewhere in that river, but one always wonders if it will be the last.

I doubt salmon have ever been quite free of their tormentors, not since we started netting them for food – and that was a long, long time ago. But salmon had always survived. Had I known it then, these Stour fish were almost the last of their kind. They had come upriver on the hem of a great storm while the species itself was caught in a perfect one. Parts of that storm originated in the landscape crimes that Simon and others had started to protest against. Other parts were more distant, more potent, perhaps less reversible.

KING OF FISH

As long ago as 1527 the philosopher Hector Boece described in his *History of Scotland* this remarkable species of fish that went to sea as silver juveniles and came back only a few weeks later many times bigger but with no food in their stomachs. He might have severely overestimated the growth rate, but in a credulous age his observation was at least half right. Salmon are anadromous, meaning they migrate to sea to feed and return to fresh water to breed. The opposite of the catadromous eel. Less secretive than the eel, the salmon's migratory lifestyle has also been broadly understood for much longer, though it is no less of a wonder. And that's not to say the salmon is entirely known, either. Even within the last few years some remarkable aspects of its life cycle have come to light: the evidence that in places salmon kelts – the few fish which survive spawning and return to the sea to feed again and eventually to breed again – will wait in the estuary and escort young salmon on the early stages of their migratory journey from fresh water to salt; or that salmon recognise their relatives by scent and travel in family groups; or that the magnetite in their bodies may explain their unerring navigational skills.

The natural-history miracle of this king of fish begins with that on-form day of creation which occurred something like 100 million years ago. The salmon is part of a family of relatively primitive fishes called teleosts: like herring and smelt, they have a light bone structure and they store fat evenly throughout the muscle tissue, both of which aid buoyancy in types of fish which hunt prey in the surface layers of the sea. But weirdly the salmon has double the number of chromosomes of its immediate ancestors, making it something of a chancy, genetic aberration. To get this double set, the proto-salmon must have evolved from two separate species of euryhaline (an ability to live in fresh water and the sea) smelt which had themselves been interbreeding and hybridising. The hybrids might have had traits that boosted their ability to survive and thrive in the conditions at the time, but without a lucky pairing of two hybrids with the exact same double set of chromosomes, they would not have spawned successfully. And yet somehow this million-to-one miracle occurred and a fertile salmon-like fish was created.

A double set of chromosomes is rare in nature, but not unique: where it occurs the 'polyploid' plant or animal tends to grow quickly and to grow larger than usual. The theory, therefore, is that this euryhaline polyploid was able to take advantage of the relative sanctuary of fresh water for breeding and the abundant food of the ocean to boost growth, fertility and egg size. At various points in time different members of the salmonid family have split off from this common ancestor: the grayling (which has kept hold of the smelt's distinctive cucumber scent) and whitefish, the different species of Pacific salmon (coho, sockeye, chinook, cherry, pink, chum) and Pacific trout (rainbow and cut-throat) and the charrs (the American brook trout, the European Arctic charr). The common ancestor of our native Atlantic salmon and brown trout split quite recently – only a few million years ago.

It's likely that this double chromosome facilitated adaptability, and that this explains how there are so many subspecies of salmonid occupying distinct niches all around the northern Pacific and Atlantic basins, from the jewel-like cherry salmon in Japan, to the monstrous Mongolian taimen, which can grow up to six feet long, or the Danubian huchen, which is not much smaller. The other defining feature of this strangely adaptable genetic accident, the proto-salmon, now taken to an extreme in our Atlantic salmon, is an inclination to reproduce in the exact same place the fish was born.

All salmonids tend to do this, meaning that distinct strains and subspecies evolve relatively quickly, adapting to the particular conditions of that place: the north-west Atlantic versus the north-east, or at a smaller scale Lough Mask versus Loch Leven, say. Atlantic salmon spawn with a more intense geographical fidelity than most, by imprinting as juveniles on the scent of the rocks they nested in. Not only do salmon belong to particular catchments – the Tay versus the Spey – they also belong to individual rivers within those catchments, to particular parts of those rivers, to particular spawning burns or even pools.

The trait is an evolved survival trick. If spawning has worked in a given place, then it is more likely to work there again than in some randomly chosen different place. For Atlantic salmon, which breed only once at the end of their lives, the choice of spawning bed is a binary one: get it right and the offspring of that fish may survive to breed themselves. Get it wrong and they won't. Perhaps this explains the supreme accuracy of the salmon's homing instinct? The effect over time is that distinct populations or tribes of salmon adapt through natural selection to local conditions: they might run to sea at different times, choose distinct migration routes and return to their natal river at particular ages and times of year. Overall the Atlantic salmon must have adapted incredibly well: its natural range extends from the Iberian Peninsula, all the way north through Atlantic Europe – France, Germany, England, Wales, Ireland, Scotland and Scandinavia – to the northern tips of Russia and Norway, across the North Atlantic to Iceland and on round to eastern Canada, Newfoundland and New Brunswick, down the eastern seaboard of North America, as far south, once upon a time, as Connecticut.

The salmon is, on an evolutionary time scale, still adapting. Whether the species will keep up with the pace of change we are now throwing at it is another thing.

I first watched salmon spawning when I moved to Glenalmond College in Scotland in the mid-1990s. They ran the River Almond late in October and were into the spawning burns before Christmas: tiny little streams these vast fish could hardly turn round in. The redds – hollow nests and mounds in the gravel cut by the hen salmon – might have accounted for all the pools and riffles in that burn opposite the college: it was as if someone had gone down the stream setting off grenades. I must have counted two dozen fish in there. Some bolted at the sight of me, or sidled deeper under the banks. Those lost in the oblivion of the spawning act didn't seem to care who was watching. The male salmon stood out a mile: by mid-winter they had morphed from sea-silver into a shoe-leather brown, intensely peppered with crimson-red spots, and they glowed like drowned blowtorches. As they rode the currents above the redd and from time to time glided up to the glassy surface, it was possible to see their kyped jaws, like a Tudor codpiece, and the fleshy adipose fin just ahead of the tail, swollen into a flag of vigorous maleness.

The hen salmon by contrast were a dull, slatey grey. The pigments (which come from the shrimp that salmon gorge on at sea), which ignite the skin of the male fish, have in the hen salmon travelled from the muscle inwards to her ovaries.

To dig the redd where she sheds her eggs, a hen salmon turns on her side and violently fans her tail, lifting the stones on the bed of the river so that they roll and settle into a mound. The pulsing motion of the redd-building tells the cock fish that the female fish is ready: he holds close, guarding his mate. Other, smaller cock salmon will try to get a look-in. A big fish might see them off, but he cannot do anything about the swarming hordes of immature male parr, little salmon that haven't even gone to sea yet, who throng to the orgy when the hen salmon finally shivers out her load of bright, orange eggs. This precocious sexualisation of the juvenile fish is just one of several survival traits the salmon has developed: if immature cock salmon, which don't need the food-rich ocean to grow their seed, are able to fertilise a hen's ova, then only one returning female salmon is all it takes to keep a family alive and the species has doubled its chances.

Later, I took photographs of the grizzly beauty-in-death of this class of '96 salmon, their worn-out bodies returning to the amniotic river, giving life through decay to the next generation. For salmon the spawning act is usually a final one, especially in more barren, upland landscapes and nutrient-poor rivers. Given that precocious parr can fertilise eggs, one cannot help but wonder whether the real function of the marine phase for so many of the cock fish that do not find a mate is simply to carry nutrients from a place of abundance to a place of scarcity: life begetting life for 100 million years. It is all so beautiful.

Roughly 300 degree-days after the eggs are shed (300 divided by the average temperature of the water: therefore sixty days if the water is five degrees centigrade), those that haven't been eaten, or smothered in silt, or washed away in floods, will hatch into alevins. Tiny fish, barely recognisable as salmon, they carry yolk sacs like shopping bags and live in the gravel where they hatched, emerging into the open stream only at night. For now the alevins are small, protein-rich prey for a host of predators: dragonfly larvae, trout, dippers, kingfishers, mergansers. With every incremental increase in size and agility they reduce their chances of being eaten. Survival depends on claiming and holding territory, which must increase in tune with the growing appetite of the young fish, and there is nowhere near enough room in the burn for all of them. As nature intended, only the strongest survive. Their bright, finger-barred markings are a sign of territorial dominance, but scent and the salmon's highly developed sensitivity to it play a role too. Catlike, they mark and imprint on the stones in their patch and they defend them fiercely.

And thus they live or die, survive or thrive – for a year or so in Spain, for up to seven in the frozen north of Norway, for three of four through most of the British Isles – until the toughest are large enough to go to sea as 'smolts'.

The name for the young, sea-bound salmon comes from the word molten and describes the silver sheen the fish acquire as they migrate downstream. The markings that hide salmon-parr so well amongst the marbled, mahogany colours of their nursery streams would stick out like a sore thumb in the sea: so the hormonal changes which trigger migration also trigger the development of silvery, reflective guanine crystals over the surface of the fish's skin. The salmon becomes a mirror.

Timing is everything. The smolts must reach the sea as the torch is lit – by the lengthening days and warming sun – on the gunpowder trail of their food supply: a spring bloom of plankton, feeding sand-eel larvae, feeding salmon. To survive they must quickly grow their way up the food chain. Young salmon will eat more or less anything they can get their mouths around: windblown insects, sprats, sand eels, the larvae of young fish and shrimp.

The ocean does not offer equal feeding opportunities, however: its fertility depends on nutrient supply, which is locally influenced by rivers and estuaries, by depth of water and the influence of tides, currents and storms which stir up the seabed. The seas around the British coast, the North Sea especially, are very rich. Rich enough for sea trout. Nevertheless, salmon swim right on through them. The salmon are heading for somewhere better still, and much further away: one of the richest feeding lanes in all the world's oceans, a vast meander curve on the planet's oceanic conveyor belt which stretches from Newfoundland, across the base of Greenland to Iceland and on to the Norwegian and Barents seas.

Here, the frigid winds of the Arctic condense and cool the surface layers of the sea forcing the cooled water to sink. This in turn stirs nutrient-rich water back to the surface. In the continual daylight of summer along this subarctic thermohaline, nutrients and sunlight feed algae, algae feeds zooplankton, krill, amphipods, whitefish and capelin: and all of this feeds salmon. This part of the North Atlantic is the Harrod's food hall of the oceans. Salmon know it and have known it for millions of years.

Not only is the length of journey extraordinary, so is the precision of the salmon's internal compass. Exactly how they find their way is still subject to research and speculation. Scent must be part of it, especially close to shore and in fresh water. At sea, temperature bands and relative levels of salinity have been thought probable navigational aids. But more recently scientists studying the Moray Firth have recorded young salmon completely ignoring these invisible contours. Through the North Sea and beyond, the smolts – those that take this route – appear to track the continental shelf with an accuracy that still puzzles the scientists studying them: the young fish are at the surface and yet the physical features which define this transition between shallow sea and deep ocean lie fathoms below. Perhaps then the particles of magnetite stored in the fishes' lateral line make the salmon into a sort of living compass, sensitive to the earth's magnetic fields. However they do it, smolts follow distinct oceanic pathways until they reach their feeding grounds, where they swim with the gyres of circulating current, busily feeding and growing until after one year or several, hormonal triggers drive the fully grown salmon home again.

If salmon knew exactly where they were going, their destination was a mystery to man until deep into the twentieth century.

In the late eighteenth century the German ichthyologist Marcus Bloch had cited eastern princes fastening rings around the tails of salmon, thereby proving a link between the Caspian and northern seas and the Persian Gulf and, in the absence of better ideas, it was much quoted, including by Mrs Beeton, that salmon feed in Persia. If Bloch's anecdote was based on anything real it was almost certainly the Caspian sea trout, an enormous subspecies of trout that is almost extinct now.

Richard Waddington, the inventor of one of the most successful salmon flies in history, had another theory: he was sure that salmon followed a paper trail of eels as far as the Sargasso Sea and back again, navigating like a kind a kind of predatory Theseus. Weirdly, he published this theorem in 1959, two years after scientists had actually stumbled on the beginnings of the truth: that salmon feed on the edge of the polar front, near Greenland or in the Norwegian Sea.

Every once in a while over the years Greenland longliners had caught salmon when they were chasing cod. It was an odd bycatch because Greenland is, with one exceptional river, too cold for salmon. These fish were assumed to derive from that exception, the River Kapisigdlit. Then in 1953 a scientist called Jorgen Nielsen actually studied the scales of one of these fish and discovered that it wasn't from Greenland at all, that it had spent only three years in fresh water when salmon parr in the frigid Kapisigdlit are almost twice that age before they go to sea. It must have come from somewhere else. A couple of years later a tagged Scottish salmon was caught near Maniitsoq, west of Greenland. A few years after that a fish from the Canadian River Miramichi was caught in the same waters. These two fish had carried their number plates halfway across the North Atlantic and unlocked a mystery of the natural world.

Over the following decades thousands of salmon were tagged off Greenland's west coast: the same tracking trick in reverse. A tiny number were ever seen again, but these did tell a story. Twenty-eight were recaptured in Canada, forty-four in Great Britain, sixteen in Ireland, two in France and three in Spain. In the 1970s salmon were also tagged in the Norwegian Sea and north and south of the Faroes. Most of the salmon from the Norwegian Sea were recaptured in Norway and Russia. Most of the southern Faroese fish returned to Scotland, Norway and Ireland, although three were later caught again off Greenland. The northern Faroese fish were mostly Norwegian, with a smattering of Scottish, Irish and Russian fish too.

If the North Atlantic is their prairie, it was becoming clear that salmon feed in herds tracing ancient oceanic pathways, carved over millions of years. The most amazing, but sadly now the most perilous of their journeys, that of the southern European fish from Spain, France, Ireland and Great Britain which swim all the way to western Greenland, is so enormous because the Atlantic has grown by the width of one fingernail every year they have been doing it. The time span is so long that Canadian and European Atlantic salmon are growing apart genetically, and yet still they share the same dining room, one which also moves with the sometimes expanding, currently shrinking polar ice caps. It's like one wing of their house has slipped down a very, very long hill and yet still the occupants trudge to the top of it for dinner.

It's also a long meal: their time away is counted in sea-winters, and as at every other stage of their life cycle, salmon stagger their habits. Some spend only one winter at sea. They are are known as grilse or single-sea-winter fish and they don't travel as far: most of those southern Faroese fish were grilse from Britain. They leave fresh water in the spring weighing only a few ounces, and return home the following year many times the size, having grown, in the fisheries scientist Richard Shelton's words, at a rate 'rivalled by few other cold-blooded creatures'. The rate does not slow for the fish which stay longer. These are the true salmon: 'multi-sea-winter' fish or MSW to use the fishery acronym: they travel further too. Our MSW salmon are the fish that trudge to Greenland. While a grilse might weigh anything between about four and eight pounds, true salmon weigh ten pounds or more. Sometimes much more.

A STORY TOLD BY GIANTS

The largest strictly verifiable salmon ever caught with a fishing rod in British waters weighed sixty-four pounds. That's four and a half stone, or about half the size of the woman who caught it, Georgina Ballantine, a ferryman's daughter who was fishing from a boat with her father on the River Tay in 1922 when the monster took hold of her spinner. She took two hours to land it and her record still holds almost a century down the line.

In 2007 Fred Buller published the wonderful *Domesday Book of Giant Salmon*, the result of a lifetime's research chasing down dozens of stories of monstrous fish. Fifty pounds was the entry point for a citation. Mrs Ballantine's fish is nowhere near the top of the 'any-method' list, although most of the eighty fish that stand between hers and the largest ever caught were from Norway and all the British ones were caught in nets. Outlandish fish caught in British rivers include the largest Atlantic salmon ever recorded, a behemoth of 104 pounds caught by poachers in the River Forth.

Then, the very year Fred Buller published his work Donald Milne rewrote it with a fish from the River Ness that was dubbed by the astonished press the 'true Loch Ness Monster'. It was far too big for the scales Donald had with him and was therefore never weighed. In Ballantine's era this fish would almost certainly have set a record because Donald would have killed it. But it is a sign of the times – and of the man – that Donald put his fish back to complete its life story. Its measurements were quite literally off the charts: fifty-six inches is one inch beyond the limit of the standard 'Sturdy' scale (that equates salmon length to weight) and is beyond the scope of every other length-to-weight scale I can find. A fifty-five-inch Sturdy fish would weigh just over seventy-one pounds. By the time a fish is that big every inch is worth five or six extra pounds: so we could say the Ness monster weighed seventy-seven pounds or so, a stone more than Miss Ballantine's record-breaker. But Donald photographed his fish and it was almost as round as it was long. Most people who've seen the photographs think Donald's monster was much bigger than this, that it must have weighed something like eighty-five pounds.

Fish of this size come along once in a generation. Those of the dimensions that merit an entry in Fred Buller's lists are still very rare indeed: 469 are listed between 1700 and today, although most

254

of those date from after 1875 as records gradually became more comprehensive and reliable. They are rare genetically: not many fish are programmed to spend so many winters at sea or are capable of feeding so hard, growing so well or living so long. They are rare because the longer a fish spends at sea, the more it runs the risk of being eaten by a dolphin, otter, or seal ... or netted by a fisherman. Giant salmon must be the canaries of all canaries in the coal mine of the Atlantic salmon life cycle. If anything is going to tell a story, surely these fish will.

Perhaps the most interesting list in Fred's book, therefore, is the one that shows how many truly giant fish (sixty pounds plus) were recorded in any given quarter of a century from 1850 – when rod-and-line angling for salmon became a truly popular pastime and when fishery records took on a meaningful level of thoroughness – to the present day. Starkly different from any other period was the first quarter of the twentieth century, which yielded almost double the number of monster salmon than any other.

I thought this odd: over four of those years most salmon anglers were at war, while in the aftermath of that conflict the world was gripped by a terrible flu that killed millions more than the bullets and bombs had done. The surge in numbers could not, on the face of it, correlate with a surge in the gentle pastime of angling. Moreover, surely the documentation of enormous fish would only have improved over the subsequent decades?

I wondered briefly whether this was a similar phenomenon to how both world wars allowed a temporary increase in cod stocks while the trawling pressure slackened. Maybe four years of conflict had allowed salmon stocks to recover? But in the 1920s the salmon's high-seas feeding grounds had yet to be discovered – so they weren't netted at sea – while Buller's list included fish caught by inshore nets anyway. Something else must have accounted for the scale of the anomaly.

Maybe I should have been looking at not so much a surge in numbers as the comparative slump that followed. In the first quarter of the twentieth century most people were still quoting Bloch's daft story about Caspian princes. By the latter half of it we had discovered the salmon's El Dorado and we pillaged the place. The infamous Greenland drift-net fishery began in 1959, almost immediately upon the discovery of the salmon's feeding grounds. Greenlanders were joined by Faroese, Norwegian and Danish drift netters too. Their annual catch rose quickly, and peaked at 2,689 tons in 1971. That's almost half a million fish, or about 5% of the total global population of Atlantic salmon at the time. In one year! At the peak of the slaughter over one-third of all the fish feeding to the west of Greenland were being caught and killed each year. But these were multi-sea-winter fish: they might naturally have stayed at least two years, if not longer. The chances of any given MSW salmon making it back from Greenland during those years were slim. The toll on salmon as a whole must have been massive. Then consider that these west Greenland feeding grounds belonged to a distinct geographical grouping of salmon: ours. West Greenland is where the bigger British fish migrate to feed, along with fish from France, Spain, Ireland and Canada. The Greenland drift netting would certainly help explain a comparative nosedive in the numbers of big salmon from these places, if not so much from Norway. But even if it did, the netting ended over twenty years ago. Still our stocks of big fish haven't recovered.

What else, then, could explain that early-twentieth-century glut of giants, or the scarcity of them since? The temperature of the North Atlantic is now known to influence the survival and growth rates of salmon. With this in mind I looked for information on the Atlantic Multidecadal Oscillation (AMO), the natural phenomenon whereby the temperature of the North Atlantic oscillates between warmer and colder periods on a cycle that spans decades. Then I went through Fred's index of 469 monster salmon and noted the year each one was caught. The correlation was spooky. The more frequent historic catches of giant salmon appeared to exactly coincide with cooler phases of the AMO: the first quarter of the twentieth century witnessed the lowest sea surface temperatures (SST) since the middle of nineteenth century and up to the present day. While there was another cooling between the 1970s and 1990s the SST then dipped only as low as the high of the late-nineteenth-century warm period. It is well known that AMO either exaggerates or disguises more general trends in global warming. While there was a relative increase in the numbers of large salmon caught through the late 1970s and on into the 1980s and 1990s, not nearly so many were caught then as through the 1920s. This must have been part of it then: the fluctuating North Atlantic temperature. The observation isn't new, but Fred's list is just telling the same story in large letters: vast salmon are more abundant when the ocean is cooler. So, was this why 1987 was the last year I saw salmon in the Stour, a southern river renowned for its big fish?

Partly. Perhaps.

It is probably a mistake to look for any one cause, because what Fred's list of monster salmon really showed was both a fluctuation *and* a decline. Much of our recent knowledge acquisition – the tracking of the smolt migrations, for example, fingerprinting the DNA of distinct salmon populations, research into the composition of the salmon's diet – has been driven by an urgent need to understand what is happening to a creature that has simply defied all our attempts to conserve it, or to understand what we need to do to conserve it. Wild salmon are no longer commercially netted or for sale. Their freshwater habitat is generally improving: although there are stark local exceptions. Anglers now release most of the fish they catch. But still the numbers plummet. The total estimated population of Atlantic salmon in the sea has fallen by about three-quarters in the last few decades. And that is probably nothing to how far they have fallen in the last few centuries.

Natural populations of wild animals vary considerably anyway, from one year to the next, or over longer cycles. The breeding success of haddock can vary a hundredfold, for example. Salmon are naturally more stable, because of the way they stagger and hedge-bet the times they run to sea, how long they stay, the times they return. Even with salmon the natural cycles that do exist – which we're only just starting to understand – complicate and mask the impact mankind has had and is still having. The decline in our salmon is one thing after another through the centuries. It gets hard to unpick cause from effect.

It's also difficult to judge these things without any real idea of what natural abundance would once have looked like. Atlantic salmon are of 'least concern' on the IUCN red list. This must be some kind of anomaly when they are actually extinct across 15% of their native range. Globally, Atlantic salmon might be holding on: they have strongholds in Russia and Iceland. But indigenous strains no longer exist in rivers like the Thames or the Rhine. Those are gone for good.

Recently scientists have attempted to quantify what our European population of salmon was like before any fisheries existed: for this purpose the 1959 onset of Greenland's fishery is seen as some kind of ground zero. A paper published by the North Atlantic Salmon Conservation Organisation (NASCO) describes how scientists used historic 'catch data, estimates of exploitation rates, unreported catches and other information' to arrive at an estimate they called pre-fishery abundance (PFA). While the numbers describe a plunging decline from a global population of about 8.6 million in the late 1960s (regarded as a period of abundance) to one-third of that now, with even more severe declines in some parts of that stock like British and southern European salmon, the PFA itself surely describes what is called 'shifting baseline syndrome'.

With our precarious global population of 3 million salmon we look back on the 1960s as some kind of Edenic time when the fish were three times as abundant. If only we could get back to that! It's just the same with eels and cod: we have lost touch, have never really been in touch. Neither memories nor data can look back far enough to know for sure what we have lost, or therefore, what we have yet to win back.

The nominatively determined fishing writer Anthony Netboy stated in his 1968 book *The Atlantic Salmon* that 'the turning point in the history of the English and Welsh salmon was the onset of the Industrial Revolution'. It's a frequently repeated refrain, that salmon were truly abundant until the furnaces started burning at the end of the eighteenth century. While the Industrial Revolution was undoubtedly *a* turning point, and while it was the final death knell for many individual runs of salmon, the idea of a pre-Industrial Revolution 'abundance' is really just another baseline shift, just like the IUCN red-listing, and just like our new 'PFA'.

THE ROCKS BENEATH

I read an interview many years ago with the palaeontologist Richard Fortey, circled a quote in it and then lost the cutting. I had wanted it for an epigraph in my last book and three years too late I found it again – when I wasn't looking of course – marking page 414 in Auden's collected poetry and his poem 'In Praise of Limestone' the theme of which is much the same: 'Far from being the driest of sciences,' Fortey had written, 'geology informs almost everything on our planet and is rich with human entanglements. The rocks beneath us are like an unconscious mind beneath the face of the earth, determining its shifts in mood and physiognomy.'

In 1815 William Smith published the first and still the most beautiful geological map of Britain. It looks random at first glance, a marbled swirl as if someone had stirred a rainbow pot of pigments. But there is a beautiful symmetry and staged order. Smith used pink

and purple to describe the harder, older layers of igneous and meta-
morphic rocks and the older sedimentary rocks which stretch all
across the south-west peninsula and up through Wales, across north-
west England and into Scotland. And in bands fading through shades
of blue, yellow and green he described the progressively younger
layers of softer sedimentary rocks which cover south and eastern
England. There's a discernible change from one spectrum to the
next along a line which runs from eastern Devon straight through
the Black Country and north, north-east to the southern edge of
the Yorkshire Moors. This division, which marks the transition from
Triassic to Jurassic also marks an approximate change in topography
between a more generally upland and a lowland Britain.

Overlay on to Smith's map all the rivers that still hold salmon
today and the border between their presence or absence would almost
exactly trace the division between the pink areas and the blue, green
and yellow. In other words, the rivers that still contain salmon are
mostly upland and are made of harder, older rocks. Only one
meandering line of a river with salmon in it bisects the whole of
the younger 'sedimentary' yellow and green of south-eastern England:
the River Thames. Even that line is, in terms of indigenous salmon,
an aberration. It might not be there at all without the efforts of
another nominatively determined fish lover, Sir Hugh Fish, who led
a lifelong campaign to restore salmon to the River Thames and
finally succeeded in 1985. The few fish that run the Thames today
might be the descendants of that campaign, they might be strays,
but they are not native Thames fish. The same is true of the River
Trent, which drains the Midlands north to the Humber: that river
was restocked in 1998. Not a single other stream holds salmon or is
marked on the map between Portsmouth and Hull: the coastlines
of Sussex, Kent, Essex, Suffolk, Norfolk and Lincolnshire, the Home
Counties, most of the Midlands and the east coast as far as North
Yorkshire are a salmon desert. Only on the very edge of the green

at the south coast are there any post-Jurassic sedimentary streams which salmon still run – the rivers Itchen, Test, Avon, Stour, Frome and Piddle in chalky Hampshire and Dorset – though they are only just holding on. The Piddle and the Stour reported no fish at all in 2015. The other four between them reported just 781.

You might suppose from this that salmon just don't get on well in the rivers that drain those sedimentary landscapes of the south and east. They've been absent for so long I sometimes wonder if this isn't what people think now: that with the exception of the Thames, salmon were simply never there in the chalk-fed rivers of eastern Yorkshire, Lincolnshire, Norfolk, Suffolk or Kent, in the brackish streams of the New Forest, or the Sussex Ouse, Arun and Rother. Or the Medway.

Trout still thrive in these chalk, clay and greensand rivers. The Thames, which once produced salmon 'in such plentie' as no other river in Europe could rival, is fed by dozens of tributaries that are just the same and these are where the Thames salmon would have spawned: rivers like the Windrush, Evenlode, Kennet, Pang, Wye, Colne, Ver, Misbourne, Chess, Lea, Mirmam, Beane, Stort, Wandle, Darenth and Cray. If salmon ran these rivers, there's no geological reason why salmon would not once have run similar rivers all across the south and east. Even if the pattern of their absence *appears* to be geologically determined. Geology being 'rich with human entanglements' there will be other maps or sets of data that could be revealingly overlaid. Density of population, for example, would have an inverse relationship with salmon distribution. As would some kind of map of land drainage, farm payments and intensive arable production. They'd all tell a story that starts with geology. They'd all reveal something about landscape and salmon.

One of the first chapters in that story would open with a map of early medieval watermills. Margaret Hodgen drew one for her 1939 paper 'Domesday Water Mills', published in *Antiquity*. In the accompanying text she described how the staple cereal crops of Saxon England were rye, barley, oats and millet, occasionally wheat, and how these cereal crops were ground by hand with a quern, which was part of the hearthside equipment in every Saxon farmstead. Grinding corn by hand in this way would have been a laborious daily chore but there is no evidence that the technology the Romans had almost certainly brought to Britain – the remains of a Roman mill on the River Fleet lie under the pavements of Farringdon Street, for example – survived their retreat. Through the Dark Ages water-milling remained dormant in small pockets of southern France and in Italy, from where it re-emerged about the year 500 and spread rapidly in what historians have described as a power revolution, but should be called a resurgence. The earliest evidence of a post-Roman watermill in Britain is from a 762 charter referring to a monastic site near Dover, suggesting the technology came back from the continent. Just over 300 years later in 1086 William's auditors counted 5,264 mills in his newly conquered kingdom. Like sedimentary rocks, these mills when marked on a map are also mutually exclusive with present-day salmon either side of that geological divide between the Triassic and the Jurassic.

Medieval watermills. Twenty-first-century salmon. They are bound together in mutual opposition by geology because the sedimentary, lowland landscapes to the south and east of that line are more malleable, homely and fertile than those to the north and east. They were well suited to human habitation and to farming sheep and corn. The rivers that rise in them are benign too. They are spring-fed and so their flows are reliable and equable: ideal qualities for the harnessing of water power to grind that corn.

It's not as if there were no watermills in the harsher, harder landscapes to the south-west and north. But the land was not as fertile, so there were fewer. These were spread out across many, many more miles of river, so the density of mills was a fraction of that in the south-east. And because these upland rivers are prone to violent flooding, the early watermills in the north and west were constructed to the side of the main rivers and were fed by diverted 'mill leats'. Moreover, the mill wheels were the more basic 'Norse' type which sit horizontally in the flow. Norse mills neither impounded nor blocked the rivers they were built on.

In the south and east, mills were built across the main stem of the streams because they *could* be and because this was how to get the best out of the gentle but constant flows of these spring-fed rivers. Here the mill wheels were 'Roman'. They harnessed the energy of the river more efficiently than the Norse mills because gearing was used to flip a vertical rotation of the waterwheel into a horizontal rotation of the grinding stones. But the Roman mill relied on a 'head' of water, created by blocking the river. The three types of mill – undershot, breastshot and overshot – describe the evolution of the technology and where the water hit the wheel: across the bottom, in the middle or on to the top. The efficiency of the Roman mill, therefore, increased in proportion to the height of the blockage.

On the Wycombe Stream in Buckinghamshire, a tributary of the Thames, there were twenty Domesday mills like this on a river only a dozen miles long. The Mole, another Thames tributary, also had twenty mills. On the Colne there were thirty-three. These were the streams Thames salmon had used for spawning: the chalk and lime-stone tributaries and headwaters. Around the coast where I live in Norfolk – a county no one would associate with salmon because they have been absent for so long – the rivers Burn, Glaven, Stiffkey, Babingley and Nar all had a Domesday mill just above the tide, with several more at intervals above. The River Wensum, Norfolk's longest chalk river, had thirty-three mills when William invaded. These rivers all continued and still continue to hold trout, the salmon's first cousin, because trout do not *have* to go to sea. But every one of these mills would have formed a more or less impenetrable impediment to salmon.

It's the same picture in every other county of that salmon 'desert'. Most rivers, certainly most of the tributaries, were at mill-saturation – the point where you simply can't fit any more in – by the year 1086. If by some miracle any salmon had managed to circumnavigate the steeplechase of barriers, their chances of spawning successfully in the sluggish, silty flows would have been vanishingly small.

With salmon it has been one extinction after the next. That the Thames held on to its salmon runs for so long was a function of its size more than anything. Even if the smaller tributaries and headwaters were largely blocked, enough spawning ground remained accessible in their lower reaches, or below weir pools on the main stem – which being so wide was impossible to block completely – to furnish a run of salmon, albeit a steadily diminishing one. At least until the next big wave of destruction in 1780. By then the baseline had already shifted.

It had been shifting since the tenth century, and long before that no doubt. The history of salmon and the British landscape is nothing if not a palimpsest. Scroll back a few thousand years and the Neolithic deforestation is still discernible in our floodplains which were raised by the suddenly increased silt loading in the rivers. Britain's covering of native woodland was cut in half before the year 2500 BC and as rivers warmed and flow regimes became more violent the impact on salmon would not have been slight.

By the Middle Ages every town had a tanning yard for leather. They were all built beside rivers and not much will have survived downstream amidst the horns, hooves and guts slung over the wall; the salt and dung washed off the hides; the lime used to dissolve the hair (lime or an intense distillation of urine, whichever was easier); the liquor which that became then washed into the same stream, to which was soon added the blend of dog shit and fermenting barley which was used to make the hides flexible, followed finally by the tanning liquid itself: acrid, stained water. The civic authorities of medieval York fought long-running battles with the tanning yards located *upstream* of the town.

As they did also with the butchers. The war got so bad that in 1372 the friars of York Abbey asked the king to help lift the siege of offal that had poisoned the air in their church, which was now full of flies and devoid of worshippers. The king tried to help and ordered butchers not to dispose of their offal within 200 feet of the monastery. The butchers carried on regardless.

So it rumbled, down through the decades, the same in Norwich as in York, the same in London, Chester, Winchester, Colchester and every other medieval town, no doubt. The idea that our waterways were pure before 1780 is as incorrect as that the salmon were still at prehistoric abundance or that our landscape was an Edenic wilderness minus a small degree of benign pastoral incursion.

If the mills hadn't blocked all the spawning streams of south and eastern England already, a surge in the development of navigable waterways over the centuries of the Middle Ages will have driven more nails into the lowland salmon's coffin. The Romans cut the first navigable channels, the Car Dyke in East Anglia, the Foss Dyke in the Midlands. As with other innovations and technologies our landscape bought a 500-year reprieve when the conquerors left for home, but the medieval period saw a rebirth. With navigation came dredging, to flatten the gravel shallows that are a natural part of river morphology (on which salmon spawn) and thus allow the easy passage of barge traffic. In 1424 an Act of Parliament facilitated the dredging of the River Lea funded through a tax on boat owners. The Lea was the site of Britain first 'pound locks' too, established there in the late sixteenth century, an innovation that revolutionised the transportation of goods around the lowland English landscape, but yet another barrier to migratory salmon, on sturgeon, shad and lamprey. As the Victorian naturalist Frank Buckland had observed: by converting rivers into navigable waterways 'the salmon's nest became a pike pond'. John Constable's gritty but Romantic views of Dedham Lock and Flatford Mill on the Suffolk Stour depict the transformation.

Constable liked to paint mills too: Parham, Gillingham, as well as Dedham and Flatford over and over again. So long as they conformed to his Romantically bucolic aesthetic. Over the centuries mills proved adaptable: corn mills became fulling mills became paper mills. Constable might have painted any of these. But he wasn't much into the more contemporary incarnations, powering urban industry. Nor was Turner, though his skies might have been inspired by the airborne effects of the changes that now ravaged great swathes of the British landscape. If anything Constable's Romanticism, and the movement itself, was a response, an antidote to the dehumanising and ecologically destructive impact of the Industrial Revolution. Enclosure Acts had cleared the landscape of people. Technology gave them employment in Britain's new and burgeoning cities. Thus we invented hell.

Constable's paintings harked back to, or insisted on the continuance of, a more innocent pastoralism. Set against the infernos now lighting soot-blackened skies, these clacking mills of Suffolk seem as benign a presence as could be imagined. It took an artist like Philip de Loutherbourg to see the terrible beauty in the twilit birthplace of British industry: *The Ironworks at Coalbrookdale.*

William Blake's line about dark, satanic mills, is probably the best-known lament (it was inspired by the Albion Mills near where he lived in Blackfriars, steam-powered flour mills that were a marvel to some, a devilish invention to others) but the art critic John Ruskin was more direct and explicit. Describing the view from his bedroom window in Croydon – a name that hardly calls to mind a rural idyll nowadays, but was once a perfect slice of English countryside and the source of the Thames's most celebrated trout and salmon tributary – he wrote:

> my bedroom window commanded in the morning what was once a very lovely view over the tower of Croydon Church to the woods of Beddington and Woddon. But no fewer than seven newly erected manufactory chimneys stood between me and the prospect, and the circular temple of the Croydon Gas Company adorned the centre of the pastoral and sylvan scene. There is not the remotest possibility of any success being obtained in any of the arts by a nation which thus delights itself in the defilement and degradation of all the best gifts of its God; which mimics the architecture of Christians to promote the trade of poisoners; and imagines itself philosophical in substituting the worship of coal gas for that of Vesta.

John Ruskin led what might be described as the first river restoration movement when he tried to breathe new life into the expiring and defiled springs that fed his beloved River Wandle. He was the first to foresee climate change as a result of industrialisation, the first to champion green belts. He was one of a few lonely voices: the dissenting artists and commentators. Most were too busy getting rich or working the shirts off their own backs.

The Industrial Revolution brought with it not only more bloody dams, bigger, imposing and sturdy enough now to assail the energetic rivers of the uplands, the north and west, but two interrelated forms of river pollution, both familiar menaces now greatly magnified – sewage and industrial waste. The combined effect of these exaggerated physical, chemical and biological barriers was to slam the door for good on salmon in the Thames and the Trent and bring a brand-new purgatory to rivers that had until this time been relatively free of demons: rivers like the Tyne, the Mersey, the Don.

The first true factory was built in Derby in 1718. It was a water-powered silk mill set over the River Derwent, which at the time was still a bountiful salmon stream. Mill technology had come a long way since 1086, and the powerful rivers of the north were no longer untameable. Fifty years later Richard Arkwright adapted his spinning wheel from horse-power to water-power and opened his first water-powered spinning mill at Cromford. Jedediah Strutt then built his own cotton mill at Belper. Both were also on the Derwent. The Darby family, who had pioneered the production of cheap pig-iron using coke-fired furnaces, built their ironworks at Coalbrookdale on a swift-flowing tributary of the Severn, also a notable salmon river. Over the next few decades, growth of the cotton, iron, steel and manufacturing industries filled the formerly 'green and pleasant' valleys of middle England and south Wales with blast furnaces, forges, smelting works, mills, machine sheds, chemical plants and manufactories of various kinds, all spewing noxious waste into the sky or the rivers beside which they were inevitably sited. Coal mines fed the furnaces with raw material and a depopulating countryside supplied the labour.

In one sense that was good for rivers: the socially unjust clearances have probably contributed, in the long term, to a defiantly rural and comparatively wildlife-rich countryside in spite of the fact that our small islands now house 60 million people. That's because most of us live in cities. Many of these cities were born, or grew exponentially, during the late eighteenth and early nineteenth centuries: Manchester, Liverpool, Leeds, Sheffield, Newcastle. Row upon row of Lowry housing: bricked-up yards, alleyways, miserable, damp, jerry-built housing, one-up one-down, end-of-row for the posh ones, millions of chimney pots sending smoke into the sky and millions of chamber pots filling the drains, ditches and rivers. 'Myriads imprisoned by the English Minotaur of lust for wealth,' wrote Ruskin, 'and condemned to live, if it is to be called life, in the labyrinth of black walls, and loathsome passages between them.'

This English Minotaur spared as little thought for the working classes as for salmon or the rivers. The River Mersey is just one example of a formerly clear-watered salmon stream that by 1850 was biologically dead. A bewildering 750,000 tons of ash, colliery waste, rubbish and sewage was tipped into the Mersey every year in the middle of the nineteenth century, so much that it accumulated into islands in the stream, islands wreathed by a poisonous, fetid liquor in which nothing could live, let alone the king of fish. Engels described the River Irk in Manchester in 1844 as 'a long string of the most disgusting, blackish green slime' and its 'pools from the depths of which bubbles of miasmic gas constantly arise and give forth a stench unendurable'. One wonders if it didn't become for him a metaphor for all the ills of early, rampant capitalism.

Urban sprawl soon overwhelmed the capacities of cesspits, soil-boxes and nightmen. Latrines overflowed into the streams workers drank from. Cholera was rife. Bit by bit civic authorities – when they could be bothered or were forced to pay for it, for few in authority had much minded a stench they didn't live beside or the cholera they didn't suffer from – diverted household waste to former rainwater sewers and the word sewage was born. Unfortunately for salmon it went straight into the rivers. The bacterial activity of faecal decomposition saps a river of oxygen. Rivers can handle a small amount of it. But in the quantities that poured in, untreated, from the mid-nineteenth century onwards, very little could survive.

The past might be another country, but this legacy didn't go away quickly. In fact it hasn't gone away at all. I can remember the stink of the Tyne in Newcastle in the 1970s. The Thames was devoid of fish and biologically dead from London downstream until well into the 1960s, as were the urban reaches of many British rivers, rivers that had once held salmon. But we still allow raw sewage to pour in ungoverned quantities into rivers all over Britain. In 1877 Archibald

Young assembled a list of British salmon rivers seriously impacted by industrial pollution, mining, sewage, dams and weirs: the Axe, Camel, Dart, Dee, Dove, Eden, Exe, Fowey, Kent, Ogmore, Rhymney, Ribble, Severn, Stour, Tamar, Taw, Torridge, Tees, Teifi, Teign, Towy, Trent, Tyne, Usk, Wear and Wye were all on it. The Mersey, Don, Aire and Calder were already devoid of salmon. As, of course, was the Thames.

In the war to save this fish we are mostly losing ground: the chemical barriers of industrial pollution might have been lifted only to be replaced by agricultural pollution and acid rain, while sewage still poisons our rivers and all across Britain the physical barriers of obsolete industry remain. Given half a chance salmon can and will find their way back: as they have most famously into the Tyne and the Taff, and most heart-warmingly into the Mersey and the Aire and the Calder and the Don. But the indigenous salmon of East Anglia, the Midlands and the south-east are long gone. On the south coast a half-dozen chalk-fed rivers in Hampshire, Wiltshire and Dorset might hold the last lowland native-salmon runs in the country, but they are teetering on the edge of survival. Only the Thames carries a hope – and it is the faintest glimmer – of what could come again.

While I worked on this chapter in 2017 I spoke about our lost salmon runs with Paul Knight, director of Salmon and Trout Conservation UK, and asked whether he thought salmon might ever reoccupy the extinct rivers of the south-east, if only we could get rid of all the barriers and properly restore their dredged and canalised courses. Paul thought it possible. He told me that most of the salmon now running the Thames (there aren't many) are not descendants of the 1980s restocking programme but strays from the River Itchen's wild stock. It is an exciting prospect to think that rivers from which the salmon has been shut off may recolonise in this way. The salmon returns to its natal river with almost unerring accuracy, but a few do go astray – quite deliberately one suspects – and thus they colonise new places or recolonise places once lost. Of course it has happened before. Across vast tracts of northern Europe the Atlantic salmon has been shut off by ice sheets for many thousands of years at a stretch and has recolonised that ground again when conditions allowed.

In the grander scheme of things this fact rings one bright and one sinister note: it suggests that all is not lost, and yet underlines the significance of what still might be lost.

Across the geological time scales that measure the ebb and flow of ice sheets and indigenous races of salmon distinct to given rivers, the 1,000 years that have elapsed since mankind started to block salmon runs with watermills is put into some kind of perspective. The Devensian glacial epoch – we tend to call this one the last Ice Age, though technically we are still in an Ice Age, only an inter-glacial phase of it – occurred between 17,000 and 71,000 years ago, and the Anglian between 424,000 and 478,000 years ago. Before and between those major glaciations there is evidence of many other phases of glaciation, of the ice sheets breathing in and out over the European land mass and across the centuries.

The Atlantic salmon survived them all.

Our south coast, which is now on the southern margins of the species' range, became at those various points in time their extreme north, while Spain, the extreme south of their current range, became a salmon stronghold equivalent to Norway or Iceland today. There were almost certainly Atlantic salmon running the rivers of North Africa, where there are still relic populations of wild trout in the Atlas Mountains of Morocco. After each phase of glacial retreat Atlantic salmon reconquered territories that had been lost to them for tens of thousands of years at a time. We know this because otherwise there would be no salmon now in northern England or Wales or Scotland, let alone Norway and beyond.

A line called the glacial maximum marks the furthest extent of the ice in each of these periods. In the Anglian period, ice fields reached what is now the north coast of Devon and Cornwall and traversed the country in a mazy line between Gloucester and Chelmsford. The Midlands were buried under almost 1,000 metres of ice. In the most recent glacial maximum, the Devensian, the ice fields curved in a vast bow across the country so that our Midlands were locked in an arid permafrost, while every estuary north of a line from the Severn to the Wash was under ice. And thus every British salmon-river north of that line must be populated by a race or family of salmon that is, in terms of how salmon adapt to their natal rivers, less than 17,000 years old. If the rivers from which our salmon have been lost can possibly recolonise sometime in the future – when we finally listen to the heartbeat of the planet and manage it accordingly – then maybe no one will much mourn the loss of a few thousand years?

But our southern chalk streams, along with the thirteen remaining south-coast salmon rivers to their west in Devon and Cornwall, are the only British salmon rivers that *weren't covered by ice at any time during all these glacial phases of the current Ice Age*. Our south-coast salmon – like the barely extant salmon of Normandy, Brittany and Iberia – have occupied these streams and evolved in them since the Atlantic salmon itself evolved as a species. The race of salmon I watched running the Stour, where they are now close to extinction, have been running the River Stour – or at least a version of it – for millions of years, not thousands. They are one of our oldest native vertebrates. This fact puts that schoolboy fish-rescue into perspective.

The River Stour, the Test or the Tamar didn't look then as they do now. With so much of the earth's water locked up in ice, the sea had retreated beyond the tips of Brittany, Cornwall and western Ireland. The North Sea was not a sea at all but a vast land-based ice field frozen solid as far south as Lowestoft. This wall of ice blocked the northwards flowing alignments of the Rhine, Seine and Thames, which flowed instead into a vast glacial lake, the overspill and eventual destruction of which cut the straits of Dover and made Britain an island. Our present-day south coast was hundreds of miles inland and all of these rivers along it, from the Thames to the tip of Cornwall, were periglacial or tundra headwaters – comparable to the river systems in present-day Iceland, or northern Russia – in a vast catchment which included the Rhine and Meuse, the Seine and the rivers of Belgium, the Somme and northern France too. Its salmon migrated to and from an estuary now lost under the waves somewhere between Penzance and Brest and up what is known as the Channel River.

Perhaps the alignment of this sub-sea river and its estuary explains why salmon from our south coast and from Ireland follow the same, long-distance migration paths as Spanish and French fish, and why our east-coast salmon, from Yorkshire north to Scotland, migrate to the Norwegian Sea instead. Rivers like the Tay and Tweed, when they were intermittently released from under that ice, flowed north-east across the bed of the North Sea towards a deep gulley called the Norwegian Trench. Are these lost river courses the same routes young salmon take today? Do they still migrate 'downstream' even when they are at sea? It wouldn't surprise me. I'm reminded of the more pathetic story I was told about ducks in High Wycombe which persist in wandering through the town along the course of the buried stream. Or what Gary told me of eels in the lakes he nets which still follow the course of the streams lost fathoms beneath his punt.

SISYPHUS THE FISHERMAN

If the map of Britain marks this battleground of territory lost, of isolated divisions barely holding on, one river is a present-day Western Front: the River Wye in the borderlands between England and Wales, one of the great British salmon rivers, famous for its one-time vast runs of vast fish, second only to the Tay in Fred Buller's lists of mammoth salmon. Twice in the last century has the Wye salmon run teetered on the edge of extinction, twice has it been pulled from the brink.

The Wye rises on the bleak, eastern slopes of Plynlimon in the heart of Wales, only a few miles from the Irish Sea. It flows south and west, its serpentine 150-mile course the perfect fractal of a single meander sequence, to run into the sea at Chepstow in the Severn Estuary. It's a Welsh river as far as Hay-on-Wye, becomes English through its middle reaches from Hay to Symonds Yat, is Welsh again for another short loop, until for its last few miles as if to settle its identity once and for all it becomes the border proper. The way it traverses the ground could be a metaphor for its history, and its salmon: from one state to the next and now on the border between them.

The Wye, whose name derives from the Celtic Gwy – shared with rivers near and far, the Conwy, the Gowy, the Teifi, even the Medway in Kent – was covered by Anglian glacial ice, but not wholly by Devensian. Its race of salmon, therefore, may have belonged to that indecisive river-course for almost half a million years. This is the legacy we have hold of in these rivers that run the border between survival and extinction: a continuity of natural history reaching back across epochs of time.

Thank God, then, for fishermen.

As J. Arthur Hutton wrote in his 1949 book *Wye Salmon and Other Fish*, 'They are the only people who take an active and intelligent interest in the welfare of our salmon fisheries, and who are prepared to give up their time and money for the work.' Hutton was not describing his own efforts – though these were considerable. He was telling the story of what had happened fifty years before, of how a single-minded body of fishermen and one man in particular – John

Hotchkiss – had possessed the foresight and determination to resurrect the Wye's salmon runs. How they had brought the Wye back from the point where even its netsmen had stopped bothering, to become in the first half of the twentieth century the most productive salmon river in England or Wales. As if to prove that we never learn anything, two decades after Hutton commemorated those efforts – the 1970s – the Wye fell off a cliff again. Two decades after that and almost exactly one hundred years after Hotchkiss 'saved' the River Wye, a different single-minded body of fishermen, and one man in particular, put the collective shoulder to the rock and began to roll it, one more time, back up the hill.

While I have caught English salmon, I haven't caught many: one on the River Test (my only south-coast salmon), two on the River Coquet, three on the English part of the Tweed. I have never caught a Welsh salmon and I have never caught a Wye salmon, English or Welsh. This was starting to feel like an omission, so I wrote to this latter-day Sisyphus, Stephen Marsh-Smith, and asked if he could help me catch one. At the same time I hoped he might tell me the story of his beloved river and what he was doing to save it. I would be welcome, said Stephen. He suggested June and a beat he fishes every Tuesday called Wyesham, an hour or so downstream from where he lives. Though the river flows past his garden, the fish are rarely there by June. He then mentioned – as if in passing – that he had caught two fish so far that year: one just a few days after the start of the season which had weighed about forty pounds, the other a few weeks later, which weighed twenty-seven.

The Wye has always been a big-fish river. Anything over thirty pounds is a huge fish. Over forty, it's front-page news in the fishing world. I have never caught a salmon that weighed more than twenty. Yet back in the day, when Hutton wrote his paean to the river Stephen's catch would not have raised many eyebrows. The Wizard of the Wye in those days was Robert Pashley. Over almost forty years between 1908 and 1947 Pashley caught 9,122 salmon in the River Wye. In his best year, 1936, he landed 678 which represented over 10% of the total rod catch for the river. Even had he fished for six days a week for six months, that's still almost five a day. He can hardly have done anything else but hook and land fish, but he was also a district, county and parish Councillor, an alderman, a member of the Wye Catchment Board and chairman of the Board of Wye Conservators. Hutton describes a man whose 'heart got rather badly strained by the First World War', by which I think he was trying to show, in an understatedly English way, a man trying to heal through the catharsis of fishing. Of those several thousand attempts to wipe from memory the horrors of war, twenty-nine were 'portmanteaux' – the Wye-side word for enormous, once-in-a-lifetime fish of the class Stephen began his 2016 season with. Pashley's ranged from forty to forty-eight and a half pounds. That's a lot of once-in-a-lifetime fish. Pashley was fortunate as well as skilful: he might have begun his fishing career at a nadir of the Wye's fortunes as a salmon river – and in his early seasons he didn't catch *that* many fish – but this start exactly coincided with the first manifestations of a turnaround in the Wye's fortunes, and later, when he came home from the war, Pashley enjoyed the river's new heyday, the 1920s.

By the late nineteenth century Wye salmon runs had declined to such an extent that only a few hundred fish were caught each year, when once it had been thousands. The laws of supply and demand had devolved the fate of the nation's industrialised salmon rivers to the unpolluted River Wye. As salmon runs collapsed in those polluted waters, so the demand for salmon from elsewhere went up, and up. Exploitation rose in line with prices and prices in line with increasing scarcity. With a brace of fish worth the same as a pig they had become their own poetic cliché: salmon were, literally, bars of silver.

To mine this trove 11,000 wicker 'putcher' and 'putt' salmon traps were stationed in the Severn Estuary – with the tide out it must have looked like the trenches. A barricade awaiting the diminishing battalions of salmon vainly trying to make it home to the rivers Usk, Wye and Severn.

Upstream on the Wye was an almost unbroken barricade of netting from the estuary, all the way up the river to Hay-on-Wye, a distance of almost a hundred miles. Hardly anything got through to spawn, and any fish that did were speared or gaffed on their spawning beds. If by some miracle a few survived to procreate, their progeny were sold in the local market, as 'Wye whitebait': 'banknotes sold at 8d a pound' as Charles Dickens described the wantonly destructive trade.

Against the headwind of this onslaught, the Wye Preservation Society formed in 1862. The society employed watchers to protect the spawning beds, but the work was almost impossible and made worse by sympathetic magistrates who barely discouraged the poaching. There was an aura of romance about poaching, then as much as now: it righted ancient wrongs (the Enclosure Acts) and was one in the eye for the landed gentry. In reality, there wasn't much that was romantic about 'sunning' the river, poisoning the water so that every fish in it came dead to the surface. There were an almost limitless number of spawning brooks to cover and a tireless swarm of well-armed salmon bounty-hunters to contend with. The society made little impact. There was just too much money in salmon and not enough to support any easy means of policing the thievery.

As if things couldn't get any worse, in 1890 Messrs Miller Bros, a very proficient Scottish netting company, acquired the lease of netting rights across most of the lower river. Salmon runs were tumbling precipitously but Miller Bros knew what they were about and set about extracting the most they could from the new deal. In the first year they sent 9,000 salmon by train from Chepstow to London. Two years later, techniques refined, tides and running times understood, their catch peaked at about 12,000 salmon. From then on the fatal toll of this professional netting operation made its full impact. Miller Bros' catch tumbled as they overexploited the resource: sixty-one tons of salmon became fifty-four, then thirty-six, then twenty-two and finally in the year 1900 only fourteen tons of fish were caught. Meanwhile the rod anglers were increasingly failing to bother either. Netsmen, poachers and 'whitebait' hunters between them had run the river into the ground.

In a strange twist of fortune the overexploitation of the dwindling stock created the opportunity for its revival. John Hotchkiss realised the netting rights were hardly worth much any more. When the Miller lease came up – having taken all the fish, they did not renew – the Duke of Beaufort sold his right to the Crown. The Crown leased the rights to the reconstituted Wye Preservation Society, now called the Wye Fisheries Association. The association, chaired by Hotchkiss, suspended all netting.

In 1902 a by-law was passed banning all netting further upstream too. The netting was worth so little that the owners of those rights were entitled to little compensation. Later, when the stocks picked up they got far more money back from rod anglers than they ever had from netting the river. Thus by the year 1902, when the salmon run had reached its lowest ebb, all netting in the river had effectively ceased. It never resumed again above tidal waters, except at the hands of poachers, of course. But even the poachers couldn't stop the turnaround. With its brakes off, the Wye came back from the brink. And how!

For a few years the rod fishermen gazed downstream and wondered if it had all been worth it. They were too impatient. Any salmon that hatched after the nets came off in early 1903 would not have migrated to sea before 1905. The earliest time salmon from that year-class might have returned would have been in the summer of 1906, when 468 salmon were caught. The multi-sea-winter salmon from the same year-class did not come back until 1907, 1908 or even 1909, when 1,424, 1,571 and 1,356 salmon were caught respectively. It takes a while to rebuild a salmon run.

By 1913 the rod catch of 3,538 was seven times its 1906 level. Meanwhile the nets had resumed on a more modest basis and in 1913 they trapped double that again. The Great War slowed the fishing down, but not the recovery of salmon. From then on and through the 1920s the catch climbed until by 1927 a record-breaking 6,145 salmon were caught in the River Wye on rod and line.

In annotating the history of these roller-coaster fortunes Arthur Hutton had noted a falling off in numbers over the next few years, one that was shared with other rivers in England, Wales and Ireland, 'but not to the same extent in Scotland'. Much as Hotchkiss had set the late-twentieth-century model for salmon conservation – his netting buy-out scheme was echoed on an Atlantic-wide scale in the 1990s – Hutton was on to something years ahead of his time. He noted that dip and then a second surge in numbers through the 1930s, the bumper years of 1935 and 1936 yielding almost as many salmon as 1927 had.

'These successive fluctuations in the runs of salmon are most extraordinary and are difficult to explain,' he wrote, 'but the fact that many of the ups and downs seem to have occurred simultaneously in so many different rivers and throughout such a wide area, indicates that they were not so much the results of local conditions but must be due to some factor, or factors, favourable or unfavourable, in the sea.'

After 1936 the numbers of returning salmon fell again and continued to fall until the time he wrote his book, 1949. In an attempt to unlock the mystery, Hutton took all the data he could get hold of from around the UK – from landings at Billingsgate, the weight of salmon carried on Scottish railways and steamers, etc. – and combined these with his Wye figures to arrive at average catches for England and Wales, for Ireland, for Scotland and specifically the River Wye. He then compared the catches from each year with the averages, how much a given year was above or below, and began to trace patterns on a graph. He found, for example, that the catches of salmon for the whole of Ireland marched exactly in step with those of the Wye, and that both showed more extreme variance between good and bad years than Scotland.

'One might suggest,' he wrote with lovely modesty, 'that our salmon harvests depend on two classes of fish, say West Coast or Atlantic and East Coast or North Sea salmon'.

Which is more or less exactly what our fisheries scientists have confirmed in recent years: a division evidenced by DNA, manifested through differing oceanic migration routes and feeding grounds and explained by the history of glaciation.

The general scarcity that Hutton gloomily noted right then in the late 1940s across the whole of the British Isles was certainly down to 'unfavourable' conditions at sea, though a resurgence of poaching hadn't helped. Perhaps, Hutton suggested, 'fluctuations in the Gulf Stream may have affected the supply of herrings, or of other forms of food on which the salmon depend'.

Basically Hutton, an observant and curious fisherman, had nailed it fifty years ago and long before science proved him right. What he had noticed – if only he had known – was the cyclical impact on salmon runs of the Atlantic Multidecadal Oscillation; the way the sea temperature influences not only the sheer abundance of food, but physically how far north the polar front is and therefore how far north the food is; and finally the differing manifestations of these impacts on what he had described as 'Atlantic' stock versus 'North Sea' stock.

Overlay that AMO on the salmon of the Wye and everything that Hutton had observed is at least in part explained by the temperature of the North Atlantic. Between 1885 and 1902 the Wye's salmon (and every other British salmon, though more acutely those from the 'Atlantic' stock) were caught between merciless overexploitation in fresh water and a warming Atlantic out to sea.

Fortunately for the River Wye and for the Wizard's catch record and Hotchkiss's dream of restoring his beloved river, from 1902 when the nets came off, the Atlantic also cooled and remained in a negative cycle until the early 1930s. The bounce-back, Pashley's red-letter decade of the 1920s and his twenty-nine 'portmanteaux' were down to those two brakes coming off simultaneously. The opposite of the perfect storm, it was the perfect summer: a cool one.

Then in the 1930s the Atlantic began to warm and by 1949 the rod catch had tumbled to about 2,000 fish. Through the 1960s the ocean entered a cooler phase. Catches on the Wye bounced back and were sustained at over 5,000 salmon per annum for over a decade. Then in the late 1970s as the sea began to warm again, the long-term average fell ... again. This time off a cliff. The Wye's salmon run hit rock bottom in the early 2000s when it was a case of déjà vu one century on, with annual catches of fewer than 500 salmon.

These trends are the same across the whole of England and Wales.

One temptingly easy conclusion would be that it makes little difference what we do to exploit or conserve the salmon: it's the Atlantic Ocean that sets the pace. This is too simplistic. Just as in recent decades all the evidence suggests that man is actually influencing the temperature of the North Atlantic too, the existence of background trends does not mean the way we manage our seas and rivers cannot influence, exaggerate or overlay those trends. It might be hard to tell which makes the bigger impact: excess exploitation and habitat destruction or the oscillating temperature of the North Atlantic; but we do at least now know that when the North Atlantic is in a warm phase we ought to be careful about adding storms of our own making.

With Atlantic salmon it has been one of these storms after another: early medieval climate change, surging population growth, defor-estation, watermills, urban pollution, industrial pollution, exploitation in fresh water and the sea, habitat destruction, dredging and canal-isation, dams and more bloody dams. In the face of this onslaught it would be easy to give up.

But what if we can make a difference? The proof, surely, would be to buck the trend, to lift salmon runs in a particular river, while others decline and in spite of a warming Atlantic? Hotchkiss's achievement was amazing, but it wasn't made into the teeth of the wind. In 1902 the Wye was on its knees, but it would have recovered anyway through the cooler decades of the early twentieth century. By 2002 the Wye's salmon catch had fallen again, this time to its lowest ever: 357 fish.

'That was the absolute pitch-black moment of the Wye's history,' said Stephen as we sat down with a glass of wine the evening I arrived. It's a long way from Norfolk to the upper reaches of the Wye, about as far as you can go in the British Isles in a direct line east to west. It was early June – as instructed – and although I was hoping for a salmon, I wasn't optimistic. High pressure had drifted over the country and was baking Wales with unseasonal, if themat-ically appropriate warmth. Outside Stephen's window the tea-stained river tumbled down a cascade of rocks, settled into a bouncing roil, then darkened over a shelving furrow in the riverbed. I watched a dipper flittering from one side of the stream to the other. The sun had left the water and the shadow of the hill was now slowly inching up the trees on the eastern bank. A few trout dimpled the surface, like forgetful rain. Stephen was telling me about the early days of the Wye and Usk Foundation, the conservation body he founded to resurrect the fortunes of the river.

'All through the 1960s up to the mid-1970s the numbers had been building. And after that, every decade that followed was a decline.

It didn't happen suddenly. It was forty years running steadily downhill.'

'What is it about the 1970s?' I asked. 'If you want to find the point when some creature started to tank towards extinction, the 1970s is the go-to decade. It's just the same with the poor old eel.'

'The 1970s was when the Common Agricultural Policy was born!' said Stephen, as if the answer was obvious. 'You take Radnorshire here. Its sheep population doubled once and doubled again. It peaked at 4.2 million! The streams were puddled to destruction, but worst all of the sheep explosion brought this terrible chemical, synthetic pyrethroid. Sheep dip. There's a stream here, just at the foot of the hill, the Sgithwen, famous for its native crayfish population. A farmer tipped his entire stock of synthetic pyrethroid into it. Everything … dead.'

That outrage spurred the Environment Agency – 'in the true fashion of a government agency', Stephen said wryly – to undertake a survey. The survey showed that 97% of Welsh rivers were polluted by sheep dip. Suddenly the complaints of the trout fishermen, that there were simply no insects any more, began to ring true. In the River Eddw they found a dead ewe. That sheep had killed every insect for seven miles.

'It was ridiculous with sheep,' said Stephen. 'You had to stock them to a certain density to get the farm payment. The farmers actually bred smaller sheep so that they could fit more into their fields! There were tribes of this tiny little Welsh thing all over the hills, dripping poison and the young salmon had nothing to eat.'

Stephen paused, taking a long sip from his glass.

'If I were to go through the full gamut of what happened in that decline. Gosh. Disease. Sheep dip. Acid rain. Weirs.'

Over the next hour or so Stephen and I gassed on and on, both aghast at and gloomily revelling in these stories of Orwellian dystopia, until the last of the sunlight had left the trees. As if to contradict our wine-fuelled foreboding, the dimples of rising trout in the pool below had become, in the gathering dusk, a steady patter. The river looked perfect. Then Stephen's wife Seren came through, her face and hands decorated with oil paint – she's an artist – looked impatiently at us and the clock and suggested we ought to eat soon and talk about something else.

'That's a better idea,' said Stephen. 'I'll take you through everything in order tomorrow. And you'll have caught a salmon by then,' he said.

We ate in the sun room. At about that point in the evening when the world beyond the window panes is on the verge of disappearing behind a veil of reflections I saw a salmon jump out of the water in the pool below: a dim burst of silver and then a silent, white splash. I stood up and pressed my face to the glass. Wobbling crescents of reflected sky washed against the rock, midstream. But by the time Stephen turned and focussed his gaze to the place I was pointing, it was as if the fish had never been there.

PHOENIX

We set off after a too-lazy breakfast, the sky an unwelcome blue, the day already simmering. It was a longer drive than I was expecting, underlining how long the Wye is, but also that there is no easy route from anywhere to anywhere else through Wales. As we drove Stephen told me how he got into fishing as a student at Bristol, fishing for brown trout in some reservoirs unprepossessingly named the Tanks. The 'disaster' came when a friend took him fishing on the River Wye. They went several times. It was all very casual, sauntering off in the morning, heading straight to the pub, splashing around in the river all afternoon, catching nothing. But then, one day, Stephen caught a salmon. It wasn't a big fish, about eight pounds but he was hooked too. It's been a long journey since then, much of it uphill.

Stephen's ancient Shogun diesel grumbled and yawed its way up an appropriately steep and meandering hedge-hemmed lane. It probably knew the way, he and it must have driven this route hundreds of times. With the river at our backs we were crossing the watershed into the valley of the Usk to the south. The shortcut. The River Wye, meanwhile, was taking a different route, a hundred-mile loop east through Herefordshire and back again.

Stephen had his Damascene moment during the second heyday of the river. There were huge runs of fish then. In 1973 anglers had already caught 2,000 fish by the end of March. At an average weight of twenty-one pounds! But then came a series of disasters and the start of a forty-year decline. There was a huge mortality that year, with a bitterly cold April, dry weather and a salmon disease called ulceral dermal necrosis (UDN). Then there was the 1976 drought. The weed had grown like crazy and then died in a hurry, sapping all the oxygen out of the river. Thousands of salmon died and every poacher for miles around was there hoicking out any that lived. Then Welsh Water, in an attempt to relieve the situation, let a load of water out of the Elan dam on to what were effectively very hot rocks. The river steamed!

It hadn't taken us long to get from happy memories to death.

'It killed bloody everything,' said Stephen. 'Then there was another disaster. They let go of some ferric nitrate, which is a cleaning thing. Dropped it into the river by mistake. Tons of it. That just about sealed it for the future of the Wye's salmon.'

'This was in 1976 as well?' I asked, amazed at the roll call of terror.

'No. This was a little later,' said Stephen. 'I'm just taking you through them all, one by one. I am going to show you this graph later, Charles,' he added as I made notes, remembering that he was getting ahead of things. 'The point is, I wanted to emphasise what the statutory bodies do in response to these disasters. They pass by-laws! I now describe it as Surrogate For Action. The problem is not lack of laws. It's lack of fish. The solution is restore the habitat.'

On we drove, the Shogun warming in the sun, cooking up a fug of wet waders and fishy landing nets. Soon enough Monmouth appeared. We turned over the bridge, and crossed the daisy-flecked River Wye. We drove another mile or so downstream and then pulled off to the side of the road, overlooking the river. I half opened the door and shut it again quickly at the sound of air brakes and the rushing pressure wave of a passing lorry. Stephen was out of the car already, chatting to an angler who was knee-deep in the river. By the time I caught up with them I learned that nothing had showed so far. The angler was just finishing and would head downstream, leaving this run to us. My host suggested I go first.

'Okay,' I said. 'I'll just be a minute tooling up.'

'Use my rod,' Stephen suggested.

I hesitated.

'It's ready to go. Start at the rock there. Short line at first. Then when you're past it whack over to the far side of the run. You don't even need waders. Cast off the bank.'

Almost forty years on from that morning at Braelangwell, I still hadn't learned that much about the conventional way of fishing for salmon with a fly, that slow-motion parsing of the water which, in the hands of those who are good at it, is so spellbindingly beautiful. It is called Spey-casting, named after the Scottish river. Instead of a clumsy overhead heave, the pull of the river is used to anchor the fly-line, so that when the angler powers the rod forward the spring of it loads against that resistance, builds and releases, lifting the line into a gracefully unfurling wave which flies out across the surface of the water, straightens and falls. It looks and feels great, but is technically tricky and needs practice.

I might also use a fly, nowadays, not a worm, but otherwise not much has changed in my approach since I caught that first salmon on the Blackwater. I winkle them out any old how, prefer to use a short rod and think more about the fishing than the casting. In the back of the car was the kit I needed to actually fish. At Wyesham in June and under Stephen's headmasterly eye, I saw that I was going to have to do it properly. Some casts went okay. Most didn't. Stephen's attention drifted – thankfully. But only because he had seen my huffing and puffing. He wasn't expecting anything to happen. And nothing did.

Except that every once in a while a salmon languorously rolled at the surface and further downstream one particular fish jumped out of the water as if set by a clock. I wondered if some kid was throwing bricks in until I caught sight of the fish hanging in mid-air for a fraction of a second before another enormous white splash engulfed its torpedo form and the river wobbled again, bank to bank. I reached the end of the run and Stephen suggested he have a quick go while I got my waders on. He had seen my casting and thought I'd find it easier if I was in the water.

I went back to the car while he walked to the top of the run. With two graceful licks of the line across the surface he weighted his first cast, lifted the rod, aimed and hammered. The line flew, an arrow-headed wave unfolding across the water, and the fly dropped with a plinky splash ten feet upstream of where one of those salmon had conspicuously rolled. Five more casts and Stephen wound in, walked down the bank and aimed another perfect cover drive at another particular target. I went back down and stood beside him.

'Ready?' he asked, winding in.

'As I'll ever be.'

My second run down was better. Once in the stream I was beyond reach of those line-grabbing nettles at the foot of the walkway and slowly my Spey-casting muscle-memory reanimated itself. Still the fish rolled and lazily kerthumped. But none took my fly. It was noon. The sun was full on the water and the warming air now shimmered over the green meadows and willow-lined riverbanks.

We tried another spot downstream, a gravelly shallow that deepened under overhanging bushes and a railway bridge. The place felt more fishy somehow. Especially when a salmon rolled tantalisingly close to the end of my fly-line. I braced myself for the pull of a fish, that 'brace' being a conscious relaxation. Salmon hook themselves, though the incorrect instinct is always to strike. Ideally you do nothing and then lift the rod into an – endlessly surprising – presence. I tried again. And again. I was on the exact border now between Wales and England, or rather I was in England, but the fish had rolled in Wales. I wondered abstractly which of the two countries I would have caught it in, had I caught it. Which I hadn't.

Stephen followed me down. His casting might have been better, but the fish didn't seem to care. We broke for lunch and joined a throng of anglers at the local pub, a pleasing mix of ages, backgrounds, tweed caps and baseball caps, none of whose owners had caught a fish either. Then a rumour wafted amongst us of a salmon taken before breakfast. A few moments later its captor arrived, a lightly built, elderly gentleman who said – as if everyone should have known better – that dawn was the only time to be fishing in this heat. He then ordered a pint and an enormous steak and kidney pie. I'm sure he planned to spend the afternoon asleep.

Perhaps we should have joined him. Instead we drove back to the river to try again. But then we found the keeper Joe Cobley brewing up a coffee in the fishing hut. A black Labrador lay across the doorway stirring motes of dust into the streaming sunshine with its tail.

'How you getting on?' asked Joe, spooning sugar into his coffee.

'Plenty moving, but nothing taking.'

'It's a bit warm I'm afraid,' he said, as if responsible for the weather and his uncooperative fish.

'So what would *you* be doing today?' I asked.

'Me? Sleeping. Till about seven o'clock.'

I stepped over the dog into the cool interior of the hut. This seemed as good a place to be as any. There really was no point in flogging the somnolent river. I glanced out of the window. Stephen was at the wheel of his Shogun, head back, cap over his eyes.

Joe put the kettle back on while I wandered around the hut examining the photos on the wall, a sun-bleached exhibition of trophy salmon and happy anglers from across the years, pinned and Blu-Tacked to the shiplap timbers.

'There's some lovely fish in these pictures,' I said.

'That's a thirty-pounder, that one there,' said Joe. 'That one below is twenty-eight.'

Joe told me that he'd been a ghillie his whole life. His father is a ghillie too and still works. He was always on the river as a boy, helping his dad. Then he got occasional work on another beat upstream, in the holidays and at weekends. As soon as he finished school he went up there full-time. He worked for that same family until he came to Wyesham four years ago. As Joe described it, his job is ghillieing and his hobby is fishing. It turned out that Joe's favourite holiday river was one I knew, the Easkey, in western Ireland. I'd fished it once, strayed on to some private water by mistake and caught a salmon there. My Irish guide found me unhooking it and led me away smartly, glancing back over his shoulder as we cantered down the bank.

'You were on the Laundry Pool,' said Joe, knowingly. 'And you weren't alone. There's a lot of poaching on that river. A lot of poaching.'

And thus we had meandered to the subject I had wanted to ask about, here on the Wye.

'There was a massive amount here too,' Joe admitted.

Not for the first time in the river's history either. Joe was talking about the 1980s and 1990s. Hotchkiss had tried to tackle the issue a century before. And in the 1930s it was like Piccadilly Circus again according to a report Stephen had shown me, crowds of poachers out every night in every valley, lighting up the riverbanks like fireflies. I had the impression that the Wye salmon had never been free of their crepuscular tormentors, hacking at them with gaffs across the decades.

It got so bad in Joe's day, he told me, that he and his fellow ghillies formed a sort of vigilante poaching squad. There was a lot of money in the game and the poachers were an intimidating crowd. Working together the ghillies made an impact. But it took a while. Eventually they were sworn in as special constables and made arrests. Three gangs in four nights one time, Joe said proudly. But those days are over, thankfully. Joe looked around for some wood to touch and tapped the chest of drawers beside him. The difference between then and now is the adjudged severity of the crime. Everything has changed now that the fish are seen not so much as pounds of flesh, but as a species in danger of extinction.

'The courts would once have said something like: "You had ten salmon, at an average of ten pounds, at £3 a pound, that's a £300 fine." And "Naughty boy, don't do it again." But when the numbers of salmon went down, well it changed. Then it was ten salmon at an average weight of ten pounds, and if each salmon would have laid 300 eggs per pound that's so many thousand eggs to a run that is classed as "at risk". Straight away the penalties went from a few quid to prison. That's what put a stop to it.'

Joe glanced at his watch. Stephen had woken and wandered in for a reviving coffee. For a few minutes the chat drifted back towards the oppressive weather. Joe was hoping for over 200 on his beat this season, but wouldn't see it at this rate. They'd topped 300 a few years ago, close to an all-time record.

I looked at Stephen as if to suggest we ought to go and try to do something about lifting Joe's catch return. It was too hot, of course, but we were never going to catch one chatting in the fishing hut.

We didn't catch one in the river either, though fish crashed and rolled all about us. We tried the run below the bridge and at every cast I was hopeful of the gentle but insistent pull on the line that signals all hell is about to break loose. Hell stayed where it was, although the water looked perfect and my casting was better for the lunch break.

The hot afternoon drifted into a cooler evening and at about the time that Joe would have been getting up from his armchair to try his luck, we shrugged shoulders, wound the lines in and set off back upstream. Stephen had booked a table at a Nepalese roadside café near Abergavenny where we ordered Gurkha curry, deliciously chilled pints of Felinfoel and with peacocks mewing from the rooftops above the garden, Stephen told me about how I had come to witness – if not to catch – all those salmon crashing about in a rejuvenated River Wye.

He placed his laptop on the table between us and showed me a graph. It wasn't the Greek economy, Stephen joked, but the collapse of the Wye salmon stocks. The point on it that Stephen wanted to draw attention to was the moment in the early 1970s when, after record returns of salmon had flooded into the river for the previous decade, the authorities built a hatchery to rear young salmon artificially.

'This was the whole failure of the river. Because once you had a hatchery nothing else mattered. You could let go of poaching: "Don't worry, we'll make up for it with the hatchery fish." Water pollution? "Don't worry, we'll fill it up with hatchery fish." The hatchery was going to solve it all. And from that point on, every time a new barrier went up the authorities said to themselves, "Oh great! Now we don't have to patrol that particular headwater." Plus you had the wild salmon being swamped with farmed fish. For young salmon territory is everything, so that wasn't particularly helpful either.'

The hatchery changed the mindset and blinded people to the real problems. Stephen had mapped these out on a timeline, each body blow to the river marked by a decline in salmon: the impact of UDN in the early 1970s; the 1976 drought which killed the run of adult fish that year, as well as one year-class of young salmon with a commensurate ripple effect over the next few years; the impact of acid rain on the survival of young salmon in the late 1970s; the sheep dip which killed all the insects that young salmon feed on; the damming of the feeder streams where salmon spawned; the onset of the Common Agricultural Policy and those 'woolly maggots' all over the hillsides nibbling and puddling riverbanks to their bare bones; and finally what the authorities did about it all, which was to rear hatchery fish and pass by-laws.

'That was the mentality! Always the authorities try to regulate themselves out of trouble. They didn't deal with the causes. And so finally,' said Stephen, clicking back to the Greek economy, 'in 2002, we got down to an all-time record-breaking low of 357 salmon.'

'So, what did you do about it all?' I asked.

Stephen realised that you fix the world, first by fixing your back yard. To counter the adverse impacts of things which are beyond local control (warming oceans) take direct action against things within reach (blocked rivers). With salmon a lot depends on the baseline amount of accessible miles of good spawning and nursery habitat. The greater the length the more young salmon a river can support. The number of salmon that return to a river is a percentage of the number that river sends to sea. Oceanic conditions might mean that percentage is more like 5% than the 15% of decades ago. But increase the number of fish going to sea and you *will* increase the number that return.

Stephen worked out how much of the River Wye catchment was inaccessible to salmon. Hutton had done the same in 1932 and estimated that a quarter of the catchment was behind barriers of one sort or another. The rest of the catchment was accessible and in comparatively good condition: there was no acid rain, no diffuse pollution, no dredging.

'And this is the situation when I started in 1997,' said Stephen. 'Half of the river is behind barriers. A steeplechase of weirs has gone up. Over a quarter is impacted by acid rain, sixty-two kilometres. Another quarter is trashed by diffuse pollution. And there are just these few streams, tucked away in quiet corners – the Dernol, the Llwyfen, the Marteg – which were holding the entire population of Wye salmon.'

Stephen tackled the obstructions. Clicking through a series of pictures he showed me roof-high blockages of fallen timber; water-falls with all the natural gaps in the rocks through which the salmon could otherwise have swum blocked up with sandbags and concrete; farm weirs; impassable culverts under roads and forestry tracks. And then the solutions: a baulk of concrete pinned with rebar across the face of a weir – the simplest fix of all, it gives just enough traction for the fish to get over – or concrete stairwells, or in a few instances jackhammers and dynamite.

'In total we've taken down twenty-one weirs and installed seventy-two fish-passes. Plus countless removals of timber trash-dams. At a rough estimate it adds up to about 821 kilometres of recovered salmon habitat: that's the size of the average British salmon river. We tackled the quality of the habitat too.'

More pictures: of rivers puddled to destruction, then the same view a few years later, lined with grass and willows, the stones polished clean, green weed wafting in the flows.

'We've installed miles of fencing to keep the sheep out, coppiced miles of overgrown alders which were shading out the streams, and stabilised mile upon mile of eroding riverbank. We've put lime in the headwaters to counter the impact of acid rain. We've bought off all the netting in the estuary. Not a single Wye salmon is taken in nets any more.'

Finally Stephen reached for the graph that marked out the last few years.

'So ... the enquiring mind asks: does it work? This is the Lugg tributary. Here are the surveys in 2003. The red dots are salmon. And this is it now ...'

Stephen scrolled on to the next frame and the Lugg catchment transmogrified from a bare tree in winter, to a baubled explosion of red dots. A decorated Christmas tree.

'There are young salmon all over the headwaters and that's getting better year on year. The number of salmon caught before the end of May, the big fish the Wye is famous for, has climbed from fewer than fifty in 2002 to almost 400 in 2014. This year is already looking better. And that, Charles, is the story of how you saw a lot of fish today, even if you didn't actually catch one. You'll have to come back for that.'

The numbers certainly tell a story, but what kind of story in the wider context? As Hutton had shown in 1949, the ebb-and-flow pattern of salmon runs is similar from river to river, year to year and decade to decade within broad geographical regions. The underlying determinant is out there at sea, where salmon die, survive or thrive according to cyclical temperature trends, food availability and the relative position of the polar front. Yet it is obviously possible to destroy individual runs of fish: salmon became extinct in the Thames or the Mersey, not because of the temperature of the Atlantic, but because man created barriers of pollution that killed everything. Is it possible, therefore, to restore them?

Stephen had to get up early the next morning for a breakfast meeting and went to bed saying he'd be back home sometime after nine. Since I had a lazy morning ahead I dug out my laptop and ate up the small hours hunting around online for recent salmon-catch data for England and Wales. I made a spreadsheet and, like Hutton had, I divided the English and Welsh salmon into a North Sea stock from north-east England and an Atlantic stock from south-west England, north-west England and from Wales. Then I plotted them on a graph. The Atlantic line showed the exact same quality of peakiness that Hutton had noted. The North Sea graph was steadier, though both shadowed each other in the timing of the rises and falls. The Atlantic trend-line showed a steady decline from just under 14,000 fish at the turn of the millennium to about 8,000 in 2015. The North Sea line was pretty much flat: 4,000 fish then, 4,000 fish now.

Then I plotted two rivers, the Wye and its neighbour the Severn. The Severn rises in the same Welsh uplands, takes a similar looping course through pastoral England and flows into the same estuary. Its fish take similar migratory routes and feed in similar parts of the Atlantic. It is a bigger river, however, and historically, carried more salmon than the Wye. Not any more. The Severn is troubled by barriers, habitat issues and acidification in the same way the Wye was. Only no one has (yet) done much about those things. The Severn's trend-line, was more or less flat, averaging a barely-holding-on 300 salmon. The Wye trend-line, however, was distinctly, defiantly uphill. Its run of fish *is* increasing at a time when English stocks, river by river *and* as a whole, are decreasing: 173% up versus 21% down.

Stephen and the Wye and Usk Foundation had shown that we can make a difference. A big one.

I woke slowly, but knew from the heat, the glint of light off the river outside my window, the heavy, oppressive air, that it was already another mid-August day in early June, that there would be no point at all in casting over an already lifeless river.

I was surprised when I drifted in to the sun room looking for tea to find that Stephen hadn't gone yet.

'What time were you supposed to be there?' I asked.

'Now,' said Seren, shrugging her shoulders helplessly. Stephen patted his pockets, turned over papers, tipped up boots. 'Take mine,' said Seren handing him her car keys.

With that and an instruction to me to try for a trout – there are loads of the bloody things out there nowadays, he said – Stephen left in a hurry.

An hour later Stephen had not yet returned. His short meeting must have turned into a long one. It was quarter to ten. I wandered outside and stood on the path overlooking the river. Bees hummed in the flowers, the air was busy with the electric chatter of birds. I leant into the warmth of a sunlit wall and watched the river drift by. It was a beautiful day to anyone but a salmon angler. After a moment Seren popped her head round the door and warned me that the decorator would arrive soon: he's lovely, she said, but once caught in a chat with him there's no easy escape. I glanced up the road. Still no Stephen. His salmon rod was leaning against a flowerpot by the back door. I guessed that it was parked there between outings all summer long. I might as well have a go, I thought. The walkway beside the river looked dry enough, so I went down in my shoes and started to pull line off the reel, ready to cast.

At the far side of the river towards the top of the run a boulder disturbed the flow more or less where I thought I had seen that salmon jump while we ate supper the night before last. I lengthened the line, surprised by how much easier it was today than yesterday. Within a few casts I had covered the rock, though nothing – and I wasn't in the least surprised by this – took my fly. Then on about the fourth cast, as the line swung across the stream, I saw a flash of light deep within the hollow of the pool, a breastplate of coppery silver briefly tilted at the sky. My line had disturbed that salmon.

I tried again, a few more casts. I carried on down the pool – as one must do with proper salmon fishing – and just as I lifted the rod for the final flick a slight jag registered, the line scythed left and right and a small, silver fish came skimming out of the water. On a fourteen-feet salmon rod a shad gives little account of itself, but even so I was delighted to get a close-up look at this rare alien.

There at my feet was … well, basically a herring, miles from the sea. Big-eyed, fork-tailed, oily and solid. It was difficult to tell whether this 'May fish' was a twaite or allis shad, though the allis are much rarer. Like sea trout they feed around the coast and spawn in fresh water. Like salmon and eels they are declining all across their native range, Morocco north to the Solway Firth. It is now illegal to fish for shad, so I carefully unhooked my accidental angling crime and slipped it back into the river, where it darted off across the shallow rocks, stirring a tracer of orange silt in its wake.

The salmon I had seen was lying deep in the pool. It was unlikely, now I came to think of it, to rise up to the surface on a bright day like this. Nor would it take anything big in such clear water. My problem, then, was how to get a small fly in front of it when all I had was floating line and Stephen's mysterious fishing rod. I nipped back up to the car, changed my shoes for wellies and grabbed a box of flies. Back at the head of the run I hunted for what I had in mind: a fly I had used in Iceland a few years before with a brass, bullet-shaped head. There! I had one and it looked right to me, small and spangly, like something you'd hang on a bonsai Christmas tree. I tied it on my line and threw it out. Remembering and ignoring Stephen's advice of a day before, I threw a few 'mends' into the line – loose upstream bows of line that take the tension off and allow the fly to sink. Even so, I still didn't feel the fly was swimming deep enough, so the next cast I threw the line not just square to the bank, but upstream and across. Then I threw mend, after mend, after mend into the cast. This was more like it: I was back in Ireland! Again.

As the line floated past me and began to draw tight I glided the rod-tip back upriver. Basically I wanted that fly to come off the bottom and take a sky-bound swing right past the nose of the fish. No salmonid on earth, no grayling, no trout, no salmon, can quite resist the sight of a glinting bauble springing off the riverbed in front of them.

Except that this one did. I passed the spot where I had seen the flash of silver. I tried again. Reluctantly, I stepped on down, thinking I ought at least to fish to the end of the pool. I heard the sound of a car slowing on the road above and then moments later the gate latch at the top of the driveway. Stephen was back. Quickly, I cast again, the same inelegant upstream flop, then mend after mend. I couldn't do this once Stephen was watching. The cast straightened. I lifted, picturing my gaudy fly dancing in the dark. Suddenly the line slammed tight and the rod bucked heavily. A semaphore in silver flashed violently from deep within the tannin flow, brighter with every passing moment until there, thrashing at the frothy surface, was a salmon!

Now all my thoughts were focussed on not losing it. Daft I know, but somehow my entire story – or at least the positive note I hoped it might end on – hinged on this one fish: a symbol of what can be regained. And I needed to touch it: that messy, contradictory, visceral passion again. I shouted out in case anyone up at the house might hear me. The salmon jagged like an untrained dog on a leash, surged into a sprint and jumped. I shouted again. Then I heard Seren's voice.

'My goodness. Have you got one?' she called out from the path by the back door. Then 'Stephen! … Stephen! A salmon!'

Bit by bit I was winning. Stephen's impossible-to-cast-with-rod was good at least for playing a fish: every angry head-buck and roll was countered by its remorseless pliability. The fish was almost in by the time Stephen appeared at my shoulder.

'Bloody hell, Charles. Have you got one? How the hell did you do that?'

'I don't know exactly. But I think it's a sign.'

I had the salmon in the shallows now and on its side. I stepped into the water and gently but firmly got hold of the wrist of its tail. The fish was officially landed.

'That's incredible,' said Stephen, as delighted as I was. 'It's twenty-six degrees, for God's sake!'

'She's fresh too. Quick photo?'

Seren had come down with a camera, but on this scorcher of a day I wasn't going to subject my first Welsh and Wye salmon to much of a fashion shoot. I lifted her quickly, grinned like a Cheshire cat and set her back in the water: a twelve-pound hen salmon that had been to Greenland and back, and was now on her way home to build the next generation.

EPILOGUE: HOME AGAIN

ENOUGH FOR A FEED

I never did get out fishing with Dick Thurlow, though I tried each autumn. In 2015 Dick was away in Hartlepool. That was when he told me the shoals normally appear off Winterton in October. But when October came around the fish were thin on the fishing grounds. Then a series of easterlies one after the other kept him off the water. The last I heard that year Dick was still hoping the fish would appear in November.

The following season played out the same: I was away or he was away or the weather was no good. I was thinking I'd never get out there when at the start of October 2017 I got an email from Dick, no text, just pictures of him and his brother unloading a catch of herring on the beach at Caister. I recognised the lifeboat station in the background. One photo showed a glittering pile of fresh herring heaped up on a blue tarpaulin.

I wrote back asking when he was going out again, a little disappointed to have missed the voyage. A few days later – about 12 October now – I got another message saying there were good shoals about, that they'd just landed 300 stone of fish, but that he was now away on a survey project. His son would take me out, he said. He'd pass on the number. I wrote back saying I was ready to drop everything and jump in the car. It was true. I had the yellow wellies lined up beside a raincoat and hat in the back hall.

'Okay,' wrote Dick. 'I'll let him know.'

That was the last I heard. It was like a radio beacon had suddenly died.

I waited for a week or so longer, and then tried another, now more desperate trawl of the internet. The name Paul Williams came up on a fishing news website. I chased around the search engines and found out that he ran a fish shop in Great Yarmouth and still used a small boat to catch his own stock of herring. He went to sea single-handed, two or three days a week to drift his nets off Scroby Sands. I called the fish shop, but Paul wasn't too upbeat. The price of herring was at rock bottom right now, he explained, no more than 30p a kilo. It was hardly worth going any more.

'As you can imagine, you'd have to catch a lot of fish to make that pay,' he said. 'People just don't want to eat herring now.'

I asked if he knew why not.

'I was on the herring drifters in the 1970s,' said Paul. 'I was there when the ban came in. It was only a three-year ban, but it might as well have been a hundred years. All the people who used to eat them, they just stopped. Now that generation are dead anyway and their sons and daughters, well ... they don't eat herring because they didn't grow up with herring.'

The same old story again and again: if the stock collapses, the market collapses: as do livelihoods, culture. Without the market all that history becomes just that ... history. Even if the fish stocks recover.

In spite of all that Paul said he would take me out ... if he went out.

'It'll take you two hours to get here, but getting two hours' notice out of me isn't easy. Try calling on Monday.'

I did, several times. I let the phone ring and ring.

Meanwhile, I was talking to anyone who might have an idea. That's when I heard that Jim Temple from Morston also goes out

to catch herring in the autumn. As with Dick and Paul, Jim's operation is ad hoc and mostly aimed at putting a few fish on his own
kitchen table. When he's not fishing he runs seal-watching trips for
tourists. I'd been on one with my kids a few years ago. I rang Jim.

'I heard you might be calling,' he said.

I told Jim that if I didn't get out to sea and actually catch a herring
I might never believe they really existed. He laughed.

'They're out there all right, but the water's a bit sheer just now,'
he said. 'You want a wind to stir it up a bit, otherwise they see the
nets. But ...' – he was looking at the forecast as we spoke, I could
hear him tapping keys – 'Sunday looks good. It's gonna blow over
the start of the weekend, then settle. I'll give you a call.'

I'd heard that before. I had my yellow wellies ready, but I didn't
have my hopes up. Sunday's daylit hours came and went. It was
already dark when the phone went. I'd just made a cup of tea.

'Is that Charles? We think we might go out now. It's a lovely
evening. How soon can you get here?'

Twenty-eight minutes was the answer. I left my tea on the kitchen
dresser. The winding coastal road was quiet, the tarmac was dry and
I wasn't going to miss this trip for anything. It must have been about
six o'clock when my car headlights picked out the triangle of grass
and the little sign pointing left to Morston Quay. I hardly recognised
the lane in the dark, the cropped hedges and bungalows, until the
track opened out, more or less as I remembered it. As I drove over
the flood bank and through an empty car park my headlights
skimmed across a plantation of masts, tangles of rigging, little flags
fluttering in the breeze and the hulls of boats beached for the winter.
I had no idea where to find Jim or his boat, so I meandered through
the maze until I saw a flash of light. Something was moving out in
the channel.

I stopped on the highest hummock of land I could find – the
tide was lapping hungrily at the gravel track – and climbed out into

a breezy, fresh night. Was the boat leaving? I fumbled and stumbled into my wellies at the back of my car, shouting hello into the darkness to let them know I was here, though they couldn't have failed to see my headlights strafing across the harbour and salt marsh. By the time I got to the jetty they were mooring up and cursing the outboard.

'Are you Jim?' I asked a shape in the dark.

'I'm not. He is,' said a voice.

'Evening,' said another, darker shape at the far end of the boat. 'Bloody thing.'

I wasn't late. They'd just been out in one dinghy to fetch another and now they had to swap the boxes of nets over. This gave me a few minutes to get my coat on and fiddle with my wellies – which were all bunched up under my trousers – dancing on one leg at a time around the rising water, all the while trying not to get run over by their teleporter, which had cranked into smoky life and was gunning back and forth.

'When's high tide, exactly?' I asked when the din had died away.

"Bout now. You'll be all right parked there, I reckon. Jump in.'

We pushed off into the silky dark, all lights off. Only now did I notice the moon, which was glowing with a fierce silver light from behind a skein of clouds.

'This is Charlie,' said Jim, introducing me to his crew of two, both faceless silhouettes from where I was sitting. 'And this is Tone and this is Dump. Andrew really, but we call him Dump. Charlie's writing a book about ... what is it you're writing about?'

'Fish,' I said.

'Hi Charlie,' they said quietly, one after the other. They had noticed the moon too. It had edged out from behind the clouds and suddenly the salt marsh was glowing.

'What a fabulous night,' said Jim, as if it was the first like this he'd ever seen.

As we thrummed down the channel, the four-stroke outboard having overcome its ailment, our wake slid away then folded with a sloppy hiss on the mudbanks. Dump was at the front of the boat with a spotlight, picking out buoys that marked the safe passage. Every so often he called back an instruction and we'd steer one way or the other. We passed the brooding hulks of sailing boats, anchored and silent. Not a thing stirred except our small boat, the engine, the wake. The place was emptying, Jim said, now winter was more or less on us. I asked about the route we were taking, that it seemed unduly cautious to be navigating so precisely in this vast expanse of water. They laughed. A few feet that way and you could walk the rest, said Dump, nodding towards the darkness. Jim explained that a wrong turn would have us stuck on the mudbanks in pretty short order.

After a ten- or fifteen-minute run we pulled up alongside a much larger fishing boat and I realised – with some relief – that we wouldn't be going out to sea in the dinghy. We had to swap boxes of nets once more, bass nets out and herring nets in, before finally we cranked up the engine on the bigger boat and headed out.

'What a beautiful, night,' Jim said again. 'What a beautiful place.' He'd worked here all his life and still he was in love with the sea.

As we cut out through the narrow gap in the dunes the boat kicked up over the first line of waves and then settled into a steady rise and fall. I felt the breeze stiffen. The spotlight was still on, hunting the darkness. Tone and Dump were trying to find a buoy whose light was broken and another which marked a wreck. Suddenly the latter appeared around a headland of dunes, a single north star attached to the tip of a rusty mast.

As I stood in the doorway to the cabin I noticed that Jim's face was visible for the first time, dimly lit by the glow of instruments. Peering at his navigation screen, Jim explained the route. We wouldn't be going far. You don't have to for herring.

'Reckon we'll run up parallel to the shore and drift back down to where we've come from. We found them here before,' he said, tapping the screen.

I watched the winking triangle of our boat bob across a pixellated sea.

We motored for twenty minutes or so, the dark lump of coast to our left, the faintest glimmer of night sky and the endless sea to our right. Jim slowed every so often, hesitating over whether to stop or take our drift a bit further. Eventually he cut the engine to idle. Immediately the boat started to bob on the swell and I started to feel ill. I pressed my back against the cabin wall and stared hard at any fixed point I could find on the horizon: a light on a windmill, the dim solid line where sea met sky.

'Which way are we pointing?' asked Jim, disconcertingly. 'Where's my compass?'

I could see the lights of a town on the horizon and asked if it was Skegness. No, it was Wells. Of course. But, if that was Wells then north must surely be to our right and perpendicular to the lights? I hadn't even said it out loud when Jim and his crew realised the same thing. I wondered briefly if we'd make it home, but at least we knew which way to point the stern. The crew placed a sack over the gunwale and slid the net box into place, while Jim positioned the boat.

'You ready, Tone?' asked Jim.

One on each side they started to pay out the nets as Jim gunned the engine. This was a far cry from the steam drifters: but for our diesel motor, we were herring fishing in the early nineteenth century. As we lurched forward Tone's and Dump's hands criss-crossed to a blur. Red and white floats flew like tracer bullets off into the darkness, the ghostly white net fading away like a vapour trail.

'Whoa, whoa!'

A scramble of hands as the last of the floats flicked out of the box and away, before Tone reached out at full stretch and grabbed the end of the rope.

'Thank fuck for that,' he said.

Jim slowed and then cut the engine. 'Well done.' Then, into the new silence he added: 'All we need is enough for a feed. That's all. Then I'll be happy.'

It was the first time he'd set the nets this year. As we settled into our bobbing drift I told Jim about Dick Thurlow's success round at Caister, 300 stone of fish.

'Bloody hell,' said Jim. 'We don't want that many! I wouldn't know what to do with them. Anyway, the water's too sheer for that kind of catch, I reckon.'

I wondered if the full moon was a problem too, but Jim thought not.

We hadn't been drifting more than ten minutes when Dump asked how long ago it was that we had set the nets. He was dreaming of the supper he had waiting for him when he got home. 'Toad in the hole,' he said, lovingly.

'How fast we drifting, Tone?' Jim asked.

''Bout one and a half knots, I'd say.'

'What's that then? ... In an hour we'll have gone about ... a mile and a quarter. If we caught just fifty herring that would be bloody lovely. We'd all get a feed. 'Cos we can always come again. I love it, I really do. I love coming out here in the day too, when you can see what you're doing. But the water's got to be really dirty for that. Christ, you don't have to be out long. They can be like whitebait, sometimes, herring can. We had some good whitebait in the summer, didn't we lads?'

The 'lads' murmured in distracted agreement. Both were on their mobile phones, texting, watching YouTube clips.

'I bloody love whitebait,' Jim continued. 'You've got to have a decent size, mind. But cor we had some good ones in the summer off the end of the point.'

'Whitebait and a pint of Wherry,' I added dreamily, the thought of this prince of suppers arguing with my growing nausea.

'Bit of hollandaise sauce, too,' said Tone, looking up from his phone. 'They do bloody good whitebait and Wherry at the Anchor.'

'Hell, I've got an appetite now. If we don't get any herring I'm going to be so pissed off,' said Jim.

I asked how he cooked his herring. Jim used to dip them in flour, then fry them, he said. Not any more.

'Me mate old Bernie said there's only one way: you got to grill 'em on tin foil. Turn it low. Cook 'em slowly, right through. Then turn it up and crisp the outside. Gor blimey! Bloody lovely.'

He cold smokes them too, to make kippers – ''cos some of those herring are plump little buggers' – but it took him a while to get the hang of it. He wasn't sure how to salt them. So he went down the coast to see an old pal at the Cley Smokehouse.

'Mike. He's the most lovely, soft-spoken person. Ever so well bred. His brother's a lord. "Hello, darling boy," he said, 'cos that's how he speaks, "what can I do for you?" I told him I was trying to make kippers, but I didn't know how much salt to use in the brine. "My darling boy," he said. "Much as I love you, I can't tell you that. It's the Cley secret, our own recipe." Well, you could have knocked me down with a feather. I went home totally dejected. But then, within a fortnight my daughter's boyfriend got a job there. "Clippy," I said, "you know when you make up the brine? How much salt do you use?" "That's easy," Clippy said. "You put a potato in it and keep adding salt till the potato floats." Well, I was away after that!'

For an hour our chat drifted like our boat, this way and that. Seals. Mullet. Which Norfolk beer is best. Which baked beans. I wondered what we might look and sound like to someone on the shore, our disembodied and dimly lit faces bobbing past, our laughter carrying across the water. Would they guess that this small boat and its crew of fishermen, it and a handful like it, were more or less all that was left of an industry and culture that had built and defined the east coast?

This was the last fishing trip on my tour. I'd released my salmon in May 2016, and had written most of my book, waiting all the while for a chance to catch some herring. If I'd learned anything on my journeys, I reflected as I tried to hold back the seasickness by staring at the lights on the offshore wind turbines where most trawlermen work nowadays, it was that a sustainable and vibrant future for our fish and fisheries must surely include, must depend upon, this: fishermen on a boat, passionately in love with where they come from, with how it is faring, knowing what it used to be like, caring about how it will be in the future.

Sadly, my innumerable trawls of the internet, all the books and papers I'd read and all the chats I'd had with cod skippers and eel men and salmon anglers, had suggested to me that this scene of impassioned, informed localism is under threat more or less every-where. Fishermen have given up or been forced out for many reasons: market forces; legislation that is either bewildering or inadequate, unenforced or draconian, often all at once; a subtle but inexorable annexation of marine and freshwater management by the academy and government agencies and politicians; and by rose-tinted or sentimental or just plain uninformed public opinion: and often, of course, by the fishermen's own lack of restraint.

It's easy to blame fishermen alone and we often do, academics and conservationists especially. It was fishermen, after all, who drove our North Sea cod stocks so close to oblivion, herring likewise, and many of the other commercial stocks I haven't written about expli-citly. It's fishermen who toss perfectly good fish over the sides of their boats, who use damaging trawling gear and echo-sounders and ever more capacious boats and powerful engines in the pursuit of ever greater catches. Of course they do. This lack of restraint has been the inevitable result of the dysfunctional systems of fishing rights, management and exploitation that fishermen have always worked under. Out at sea it was, for centuries, a free-for-all. Fishermen warred over the resource, but for a long time the wide oceans and fertile North Sea could more or less withstand the pressures they exerted using hand lines and hemp nets and fishing under sail (though there were complaints even in Tudor England about the damage caused by newfangled trawling). Once the technological advancements of the Industrial Revolution kicked in and trawlermen began to feed a rapidly expanding population, then everything changed. Over the next hundred years we competed for fish until the seas were empty.

The precedent of territorial waters established valiantly by Iceland promised some kind of reprieve, at least until the UK joined what we called the Common Market and our fisheries became the entry ticket. Many of the pioneering voices calling for a more sustainable way to manage sea-fisheries had been British. Cautionary good sense had been aired since at least the late 1800s. The British government was slowly waking up and had been pressing for a cessation, or at least a slowing down, of the herring fishery; only no one was listening amidst the clamour to catch the very last one in the sea and turn it into pet food. With our accession to the EEC the faint possibility of forbearance, made possible by the prospect of controlling a sovereign reach of sea, vanished as quickly as it had appeared. Our sea fishing rights became one of those de facto components of ever closer union. Except there has been little union and little appetite, nation by nation across Europe, for scaling back fleets and catches.

I have been told that my diagnosis of the EU's fisheries policies is too gloomy, that we have made huge progress in recent years. I thought the same until my head-spinning week on Dave's trawler. In fact a small uplift in cod stocks is just the start of what ought to have been possible. Our seas and rivers which used to abound with fish (and which could support thousands of fishermen if we could find a way to fish sustainably) are so sparsely populated we have lost touch with what they once were like, or with what they could be like again. Scientists build targets around levels of 'abundance' that are shadows of true abundance. Fishermen, where they manage to eke out a living, are still racing each other to the last fish in the sea. Even if we win a bit of ground back, as we have with North Sea cod, it is progress from a low base via measures imposed from above and which therefore are not owned by those whose behaviour they try to govern. If you don't own the regulations you cheat them, or grouch about them. The merest blip upwards in the fish count results in cries for whatever controls brought about that uplift to be removed.

Is it too mad to imagine instead a rejuvenated coast, where fishermen working in a sustainable way make a living selling good fish to a public who are fussy about where they come from and how they are caught; or to imagine a future where we have vast marine reserves; or an inshore fishery where artisanal fishermen can also make a good living too, because there are plenty of fish in the sea and we have discovered how to keep it that way; or to imagine a fishery where the fishermen 'own' the resource to the extent that they have a stake in exclusive rights that will make them good husbands of that resource; or a fishery managed by fishermen and scientists working together, owning the regulations equally? Is that all really such a pipe dream? They've more or less done it in Iceland.

Back here, cod stocks might have recovered, but there are still massive contradictions at the heart of the system, and meanwhile all the little fishermen have given up or are really struggling. The boats making fortunes in Peterhead are the massive pelagic hoovers, as big as ferries, sucking the food chain out of the North Sea. Whether Dave made any money or not, on any given trip, depended very largely on whether or not, in the days before he returned, the market had been flooded with frozen Norwegian cod caught on a massive scale. The entropic drift is still towards the bigger, the more powerful. And thus our coast, our island, is losing its history.

Somewhere out there in the dark waters of the North Sea a small number of herring were – if we were lucky – becoming caught in our nets. I had no idea how many we'd get but felt sure we'd get a few. Each herring would strike our net at a particular point in space and time, though it had taken the whole ocean and several years to get there. This thought alone ought to realign our sense of what a fish is worth, what it is a distillation of. It is what my mother was trying to express when she mourned my first salmon: its magnificent journey had ended, and I had ended it. More fundamental, however, is the question posed by this collision of the global with the local: to whom do wild fish belong? Who is responsible for nurturing them? Or for exercising the self-restraint needed to ensure their future?

The keepers of early carp ponds built the habitat, stocked the fish, gave them time to grow, caught what they needed, put the others back, left ponds fallow, rotated the harvest over a four-year cycle, and so on: an effortlessly simple system of diligent husbandry and measured, abstemious harvest. A system that works if you own the ponds, the water, the fish. Michael Graham and Edward Russell were reaching for something like this when they suggested that commercial fishermen would do better if they fished less: here the sea does the husbandry and the fishermen take only what the sea can sustainably give. Unlike the carp pond, however, the sea isn't owned by anyone, or at least it wasn't when Graham and Russell were writing, and we have shared ours, one way or another, ever since. That appears to make all the difference in the world. No one listened to Graham and Russell because to do so would have been to put one's own nation, or boat, at a disadvantage relative to other nations or skippers who might not have been so conscientious.

314

Forbearance is eroded in exact step with the growing feeling that whatever you leave behind will be taken by someone else. Diligent husbandry is eroded if someone else hogs the rewards of your work.

Somehow we need to build systems of ownership and management that combine the self-interest of localism, which vest ownership, passion, husbandry and self-restraint in the fishermen who harvest the resource, with the globalism that fosters co-ordination and co-operation in the management of the sometimes vast natural systems our fish inhabit and depend on. Should we look to government to impose this order? Government track record suggests maybe not. Take one fish: salmon.

Salmon are in decline nationally and fading away with them is a rich seam of British cultural and natural history: nowhere is this loss more stark than on the west coast of Scotland where real salmon have been replaced, one for ten, with ersatz, farmed salmon you oughtn't even give to your cat. For twenty years the salmon-farming industry has denied any link between the salmon farms, their infestations of parasitic lice and crashing declines of wild salmon and sea trout in the rivers and lochs of the Highlands and Islands. The Scottish government has been complicit all the while and turned a blind eye to the damage because the industry brought jobs (how many were Scottish jobs?), revenue and taxes to a part of Scotland where there was little other full-time, well-paid employment. But at what cost? Sainsbury's Taste the Difference smoked salmon is marketed with a picture of a lonely pine, and a castle on the shores of a mist-draped Scottish loch; Marks & Spencer's smoked salmon is from Lochmuir where no doubt the glens echo to the cry of the osprey: if only Lochmuir really existed. Peat and heather, oak and applewood, Scottish this, Scottish that. The real picture is of a lifeless seabed, billowing tides of excrement, dead shellfish for miles around, and lorries full of ruined salmon, cooked in an ever more toxic brew of chemicals in an effort to rid them of increasingly immunised lice. From Tesco to Waitrose, it's all sold under a banner of something the product has destroyed: Scottish natural heritage.

TENURE

On the other coast, the English 'north-east drift net' fishermen still catch about 15,000 to 20,000 salmon a year, fishing more or less as we were now fishing for herring: with a curtain of nets held high in the water and close to the shore, or sometimes with beach nets, intercepting fish which are homeward bound on their spawning run. Working from small boats in all weathers or on foot between the tides, the drift netters are part of our fisheries heritage. Like other artisanal fishermen I have written about, they also feel as if they are under siege. Ned Clark, chairman of the north-east branch of the National Federation of Fishermen's Organisations, is one of their spokesmen. Just a few days before my herring trip he had described in an NFFO newsletter 'a period of great uncertainty for the salmon fishermen of the Northumberland, Durham and Yorkshire coasts': the Environment Agency had published an assessment of English salmon stocks, with proposals about what could be done to halt their inexorable decline. For the drift netters it was the latest salvo in a one-sided campaign to abolish their way of life. Ned called the science spurious, and claimed that the precautionary approach has been overused in order to downgrade rivers into 'at risk' categories that need enhanced measures of protection: a curtailment of netting amongst other things. For thirty years – as Ned saw things – anglers and landowners had coveted the salmon caught in these coastal fisheries, had wanted to claim them for rod-and-line angling in rivers. There was something mean-spirited and vindictive about their campaign, he wrote in a letter to the *Berwickshire News*, 'to extinguish the small-scale net fishery for salmon and trout in the north-east of England'.

I read all this with difficulty. I was one of those anglers who thought Ned's fishery unsustainable. How could I square this with the opposite thought that a vibrant future for our fisheries ought to include fishermen like him? It seemed a contradiction that undermined the whole spirit of what I was trying to reach for – the preservation of fish and a simultaneous preservation of culture. A preservation of fish *through* the preservation of culture.

Although I could see things from Ned's point of view – this was his livelihood and history, after all – he used his rhetoric and facts judiciously: the survival of salmon at sea has nothing to do with the netting, he said; the proposed closure of the nets treats a symptom not the cause; and rivers like the Tyne are experiencing record runs. All true. Survival at sea is the main problem, and the Tyne is doing well, having recovered from near extinction. But the more particular issue is that the north-east drift net is a mixed-stock fishery which intercepts salmon heading home to spawn in a number of east-coast English and Scottish rivers, some of which might be able to take the loss of salmon from their spawning stock, some of which cannot. Salmon anglers have been arguing against mixed-stock fishing for years, because it is indiscriminate. For marginal or recovering rivers it is potentially disastrous. It seemed a shame that the issue had become so polarised. Both salmon anglers and netsmen must want the same thing, after all: an abundance of wild salmon. The anglers' campaign is not vindictive; it is not even about having more fish to catch with a fishing rod. It is about how we hold on to, or even reverse the decline of an endangered fish.

The International Council for the Exploration of the Sea estimates that there are only 200,000 English and Welsh salmon in the sea (a *total* global population also described as 'pre-fisheries abundance', though the use of the word abundance could be ironic). That's less than half of the 1970s total and Lord knows what fraction of salmon numbers before the nineteenth century, or the ninth. If those figures are correct, fourteen English netsmen catch (and kill) almost 10% in any given year: a scary proportion, surely?

Salmon anglers catch their share: about 12,000 on average in recent years. Traditionally, the salmon is a fish one catches and kills: in the 1970s the rod-catch and the net-catch figures would have been comparable because *all* the salmon were killed. Nowadays of the 12,000 salmon caught by anglers about 9,000 are released to spawn. There's an argument to say even the 3,000 killed is 3,000 too many. If anglers want netsmen to stop killing salmon, my feeling is that we ought to stop killing them too.

But that's not to mention the efforts put in by anglers and land-owners to preserve and restore the salmon spawning and juvenile habitat. Even Ned conceded that the answer lay in habitat restoration, along with improving the survival rates of salmon smolts in rivers and at sea. Indeed it does: in order to send more smolts to sea, which in times of poor marine survival is our best answer, we must take responsibility for their husbandry: a responsibility netsmen and rod-and-line anglers could share equally, surely?

Back in Scotland, things have recently moved to the point where these distinctions I'm trying to sketch out have become academic. For years the Scottish government ignored – defied even – the entreaties of the salmon-conservation lobby to end mixed-stock salmon netting. In 2010, they even lobbied the EU for a £100,000 grant on behalf one of the principal fisheries, to help develop its facilities. I remember being copied on a letter from Niels Jacob, chairman of Laksaskip, the Faroe Salmon Fishing Association, to Alex Salmond, then First Minister for Scotland. Niels was appalled by the grant and pointed out that since the time his fishermen had voluntarily forestalled their fishing operation in 1991, an estimated 1 million Scottish salmon (and 4 million Norwegian) had been spared and allowed to return home to spawn. 'It was with great sadness,' wrote Niels, 'that we recently learned that over the same period of twenty years Scottish netsmen have killed 969,234 salmon off the coast of Scotland.' The Faoroese salmon fishermen were seriously considering reclaiming their rights. If they had, so too would the Greenlanders. Yet even with the pan-Atlantic treaty under threat, the Scottish government did not end the netting, or even compel a shift of the netting operations to a catchment-specific basis, which is so much more sustainable.

This Scottish intransigence and the polarised argument in north-east England are microcosms of how and why fisheries management fails.

In an attempt to force the Scottish issue, the Salmon and Trout Association (now Trust) lodged a complaint with the European Courts that the Scottish government had failed to put in place sufficient controls to protect Atlantic salmon in Special Areas of Conservation. The complaint was upheld, the Scottish government was finally forced to do what they had long been asked to and now we have lurched to the other extreme and there is no salmon netting at all anywhere in Scotland. Worse, there must now be a grievance amongst the netsmen and a sense of being cheated.

I had recently spoken to Andrew Wallace trying to understand, how things had got to this point. Andrew was a good man to ask: he is fisheries director of the Fishmongers' Company, vice chairman of the Atlantic Salmon Trust, he sits on the Association of Salmon Fisheries Boards in Scotland, and is chairman of the Rivers Trust for England and Wales and the Rivers and Fisheries Trusts of Scotland. He agreed that the dialogue on both sides had got out of kilter. It had become a sort of 'toffs versus the horny-handed sons of toil', which wasn't a true reflection of the issues.

'There is no reason why you can't have sustainable netting within a catchment,' Andrew told me. 'The problem with mixed-stock fisheries is that they defy the common-sense idea of every fisherman having a stake in the conservation of the fishery. The north-east drift nets have no particular stake in any given river: they're catching as many fish as they can. It was the same in Scotland in the Montrose Basin. Traditional netters like Bob Ritchie on the Esk, who is the ultimate expression of a low-key, sustainable netsman, one who anglers and river owners are very comfortable to see continue: these guys are members of the Fisheries Boards, they pay a levy to the Fisheries Boards. Conservation is in their long-term interests. There is a good argument for local, river-by-river netting, if a given river can withstand it. Sadly that might all be beyond us now in Scotland, because the argument became so polarised.'

The long-running, contentious debate between drift netters and rod-and-line anglers shows how much we need to find a better way to manage our fisheries. One where everyone concerned owns a stake in a fishery's overall welfare and therefore is incentivised to fish sustainably, or even to stop killing fish until things improve.

'It's all about tenure,' said Andrew, helping me towards the thought I was struggling to put words to. 'Whether at sea or in fresh water or in between. Lack of tenure was a failure of the Common Fisheries Policy as much as it was with everything that preceded it. The Common Fisheries Policy had a sort of European tenure, but that just didn't really do the job either for stock management or for communities. With fisheries of any sort you just have to give the confidence to the fisherman that if they manage their fish stocks sustainably and responsibly they are not going to be impacted by others who haven't done so and come in to screw it all up for them. Rights-based fisheries are the only way you can possibly hope to proceed.'

It sounded so simple, when it is obviously anything but. At present we are in danger of heading the other way: to curb the excesses of overfishing, to address larger-scale issues of conservation and environmental change and damage, we are more and more looking to government and scientists and tenure is being taken away piecemeal. We do this at our peril, because when all that passion and history has gone who will really know or care about the state of our rivers and sea? After the netsmen have been compulsorily stopped, what next for the anglers?

'It's a sort of psychological mind-shift,' said Andrew. 'Because you're in conflict with the idea that this is some great, natural and public resource. But there are really exciting emerging solutions to this conundrum round the world and some very clever people working it out. Iceland is a shining example. And the great thing is, when you get the tenure right, when you find a way round the "tragedy of the commons", then you get a very quick response from fisheries.'

ABUNDANCE

I have dedicated this book to Orri Vigfusson. An Icelander. I very much wanted Orri to read it, had hoped for his approval. But Orri died of lung cancer in 2017. It was typical of Orri that I didn't even know he was ill. I'd written to him a few times in the months before, noticed that his replies were more tardy than usual, but had assumed that was simply because he was busy cutting another deal with salmon netsmen or politicians somewhere around the North Atlantic. With Orri, that could have been New Brunswick or Spain or any point in between. He mixed equally and easily with fishermen and presidents, celebrities and royalty. Whatever it took to get the deal done.

Orri was born in Siglufjordur, a small port tucked away in an icy fjord on the north coast of Iceland. In 1942 the sea was the only way in or out. Even when I first went there at the start of this century it was a dead-stop at the end of a long gravel road under precipitous slopes. There's a tunnel and tarmac now and the place has a bustle to it in summer: there are cafés on the waterfront and brightly coloured fishing boats stud mirrored reflections of mountains and sky. On a knoll of rock and grass a thousand plastic knives are suspended on taut strands of nylon inside a wooden frame the size of a small barn: kids find it irresistible, mesmerising. They touch the restless shoal as it shimmers in the breeze. On the waterfront and back across the road are the remnants of the herring trade this silver shoal commemorates: sagging wooden jetties, a warehouse, barrels and gutting benches, offices with their ledgers and Bakelite telephones, boarding rooms for the herring girls, wooden beds, clogs, and hair-brushes, all preserved as if the fishermen and clerks and herring girls had only just moved out at the end of summer. Less human in scale and quite sinister are the rendering boilers where the herring were processed into oil and fishmeal and fertiliser. Orri never lost sight of his background in the herring industry. He would talk about how his family were involved in the overfishing and the collapse of herring stocks in the 1960s and how this played on his mind when he saw the same thing happening to salmon twenty years later.

The catalyst for Orri was a nosedive in salmon stocks in the early 1980s. Orri started to talk to salmon fishermen all over Iceland and found they had noticed the same thing: catches had halved in only a few years. Meanwhile, the Greenland drift-netting operation was at its peak and all across the North Atlantic salmon stocks were being exploited unsustainably. Orri had seen where that road led to. An intergovernmental body had been formed – the North Atlantic Salmon Conservation Organisation (NASCO) – and a treaty had been signed a few years earlier in 1984, but Orri was always deeply cynical of government or intergovernmental initiatives. They didn't work in general and in particular the NASCO treaty didn't apply to coastal waters where most salmon netting took place. Rather than relying on or waiting for governments to legislate over fisheries – something they repeatedly fail to do either properly or at all – we should, Orri argued, get on with it and take responsibility ourselves. This is exactly what Orri did in 1988 when he established the North Atlantic Salmon Fund.

Orri was already a successful businessman. He had made good money selling vodka to the Russians and he used some of his own wealth and all of his connections to raise a pile of cash with which he intended to pay salmon netsmen to stop netting. The Faroese fishermen were the first he spoke to and it helped of course that Orri was a fisherman too, that his family had fished for herring, that he was steeped in the same frigid, wind-swept North Atlantic waters. They met in Oslo in December 1989. The fishermen listened to his ideas. Eighteen months later Orri had an agreement.

'It takes time,' explained Orri in an interview years later, after receiving another one of the many conservation awards he was given during his later years. 'Because we don't just give cash over the counter. We try to help the fishermen into other jobs so that everyone can be a winner.' Often the fishermen were reluctant to give up their rights for good. That didn't faze Orri at all. He would cut the deal for two or three years, giving the fishermen a chance to see how things went. Orri found that they rarely sat idle through that time, that they would spot other fisheries opportunities and pursue those instead. He called what he did 'green capitalism'. Fair compensation was his motto. More than fair. Orri believed that you had to be generous, that you had to recognise and respect the fishermen's right to earn a living, that there was history and personal pride at stake. He wanted everyone to leave the negotiating table feeling as if they had been fairly treated.

Most importantly, Orri's methods worked. A few years after the Faroese deal he struck another with the Greenland drift netters and he helped them to divert their efforts towards the production of lumpfish caviar. He helped to broker agreements off north-east England (there were sixty-eight fishermen catching 44,000 salmon a year there before 2003; now there are fourteen and the catch has more than halved) and Ireland. Over twenty-five years, Orri brokered some 2,500 different netting agreements covering about

85% of the salmon's native range. Literally millions of salmon have been spared by Orri's pragmatic, commercially minded, but very human diplomacy.

I got to know Orri when he invited me to Iceland to write about a trout fishery he was helping farmers to develop. While we were discussing these ideas he told me how he had helped one farmer, who owned salmon-netting rights, to open a cheese shop. Orri never stopped. He'd be there at supper, gone in the morning and back again by evening, having driven halfway across Iceland to take a celebrity fishing and persuade them to give his fund more money. I suspect he dreamed of saving salmon in the few hours he ever slept.

One afternoon Orri's daughter drove me across the north coast to spend a few hours fishing for salmon in a little river that flowed near his childhood home. I caught (and put back) four salmon in as many hours. I had never known salmon fishing like it, really: the fruits of Orri's work. These were salmon which probably would not have been there otherwise. After that trip Orri started to copy me in on the endless salvos of letters he fired from SS Iceland into the bunkers of various intransigent European governments. So I got to read about the advert he took out in the *Irish Times* saying that if a child could understand these issues of conservation, then why couldn't the Irish government; I got to read letters to the Russians explaining to them exactly how many of their salmon the Norwegians were taking; or letters to the BBC complaining that Greg Wallace's eulogy to smoked salmon at Christmas had utterly failed to inform the British public of the damage caused by salmon farms. He was tireless.

A few years later Orri drove me up the valley of another salmon river that he managed, the Sela. When Orri had taken on the fishery, he explained, its salmon were netted and the river catchment itself was only partially accessible to migrating fish. About 300 salmon were caught on the Sela each year. Orri and his colleagues opened up the spawning tributaries and called off the netting. They built salmon ladders around the steep waterfalls. Within a few years the catch had climbed to 900 fish and by the time Orri took me on that tour, it had trebled again to 2,700. The Sela had become one of the most prolific rivers in Iceland.

'It's all about abundance,' Orri said to me as he stood in his green wellies on a bluff overlooking the river. 'It's not good enough just to have a few fish, a run of salmon barely holding on, or these minimum spawning targets, above which scientists think everything is okay. Salmon were once truly abundant and my goal is to make them abundant once again. On this river, I feel we could treble the annual catch one more time.' I looked at Orri, open-mouthed: 9,000 salmon! Was he serious? Orri smiled. 'Then we can think about the great rivers of Europe, the Rhine, the Seine, the Thames.'

Orri dared to believe that the apparently impossible was possible. Then he proved that it was. That is one big part of his legacy. The others were his get-on-with-it approach and the philosophy of responsibility that he insisted was the foundation of progress. Just as Andrew Wallace had said. It is all about tenure. Governments don't really own rivers and seas and fisheries. People do.

It was almost time to pull the nets in: Jim didn't want to drift down as far as the crab pots he knew peppered the sea beyond Morston Point.

'They're shit-bags in the dark,' agreed Tone.

Dump looked at his watch, rubbed his hands and reminded us all that he had toad in the hole for tea. There was just enough time for an argument about the best type of ketchup before Jim called the drift to an end. As he did so a cascade of fireworks burst silently into flowers of orange and red in the sky above Morston, reminding us all what night it was.

For me at the end of my fishy journey there was symbolism in those celebratory explosions, though I didn't dare share it with my shipmates. They'd have thought me fanciful and no doubt a touch soft. It wasn't that the silent starbursts were signifying that all will be well in the world of fish and men. It was more that they suggested we've never had a better chance to try to make it so.

Tone and Dump quickly spread a canvas sack over the gunwale. One took the weighted side, the other the floats, and together they started to pull, while Jim lit the incoming net with his searchlight.

'I bloody hope there's some herring for us tonight,' he said.

And in they came, hanging silver in the torchlight. By the time we had all the nets aboard, fifty or sixty lay in the folds on the deck.

'Enough for a feed,' said Jim. 'Bloody lovely.'

ACKNOWLEDGEMENTS

I owe thanks to Vicky for everything, as I always do.

I owe thanks to more or less everyone mentioned in this book, to the fishermen, conservationists, authors, scientists, ghillies, bailiffs and river-keepers: I couldn't have written it without them.

I owe particular thanks to:

David Milne and his crew: Jake, Jakey, Richard, Michael, Frankie and Johnny for all welcoming me on board *Adorne*. DG for his expletive soliloquys. Charles Clover, Mike Park and Clive Monk for their help and advice.

Chris Yates for taking me to his secret lake. Jim Ellis for finding me a carp. John Andrews for sharing his knowledge and passion.

John Spalton and Gary Lee for revealing to me the secret world of the eel man. Andrew Kerr for inducting me in the ways of 'Green Terrorism'. Chris Bailey for putting me in touch with a real Fen Tiger.

My godmother Mary and her son, my one-time fishing pal Simon Etherton for bringing me to the west coast of Ireland all those years ago. Pat and Dee Castell for my first ever salmon. Stephen Marsh-Smith for my first Welsh salmon and for showing me all the marvellous things he and his team have achieved on the River Wye. Richard Shelton, Paul Knight, Ken Whelan, Simon Evans, Andrew Wallace, Joe Cobley, Lynn Cobley and George

Woodward for sharing with me their passion and knowledge. Patrick Lloyd for all his opinions.

Jim Temple, Tone and Dump for a magical evening afloat on the North Sea and, of course, for the herring.

Dick Thurlow and Paul Williams.

Alison Locker, Jonathan Lee and Jamie Stephens.

Lucy Luck and Juliet Brooke for encouraging and helping me to get this book started.

Rowan Yapp and Chris Wellbelove for encouraging and helping me to get this book finished.

Jim Babb and Henry Hughes, my good friends from across the pond, who always read, edit and advise so generously.

All my good friends who fish and who care for our rivers and seas with passion: you have all inspired this book.

FURTHER READING

While researching this book I read a vast number of books and papers, magazine articles and news reports, far too numerous to list. Below are some of the most relevant and useful books for anyone who wants to research further, along with some of the most relevant academic papers that I came across.

BOOKS

COD

Charles Clover, *The End of the Line, How Overfishing is Changing the World and What We Eat*, Ebury Press, 2004

Michael Graham, *The Fish Gate*, Faber & Faber, 1943

Paul Greenberg, *Four Fish, A journey from the ocean to your plate*, Penguin, 2010

Mark Kurlansky, *Cod: A Biography of the Fish That Changed the World*, Random House, 1997

William McIntosh, The Resources of the Sea, CJ Clay and Sons, 1899.

Redmond O'Hanlon, *Trawler*, Hamish Hamilton, 2003

Callum Roberts, *The Unnatural History of the Sea, The Past and Future of Humanity and Fishing*, Gaia, 2007

George A. Rose, *Cod: The Ecological History of the North Atlantic Fisheries*, Breakwater Books, 1948

Edward Stuart Russell, *The Overfishing Problem*, Cambridge University Press, 1942

CARP

BB, *Confessions of a Carp Fisher*, Eyre & Spottiswoode, 1950

Dame Juliana Berners, *A Treatyse of Fysshynge With an Angle*, 1496

Kevin Clifford, *A History of Carp Fishing*, Sandholme Publishing, 1992

Christopher Dyer, *Everyday Life in Medieval England*, Hambledon and London, 1994

Jack Hilton, *The Quest for Carp*, Pelham Books, 1972

Maurice Ingham, *The Carp Catchers' Club*, The Medlar Press, 1998

Leonard Mascall, *A Booke of Fishing with Hooke and Line*, 1590

Richard Walker, *Carp Fishing*, Angling Times Ltd, 1960

Izaak Walton, *The Compleat Angler, or the Contemplative Man's Recreation*, 1653

Chris Yates, *The Secret Carp*, Merlin Unwin Books, 1992

EELS

Roger Castle, *An Eel's Tale*, Janus Publishing, 2017

Tom Fort, *The Book of Eels*, Harper Collins, 2002

Ernie James, as told to Audrey James, *Memoirs of a Fen Tiger*, David & Charles, 1986

Christopher Moriarty, *Eels, A Natural and Unnatural History*, David & Charles, 1978

James Prosek, *Eels*, Harper Perennial, 2011

Richard Schweid, *Consider the Eels, A Natural and Gastronomic History*, Da Capo Press, 2004

SALMON

Roy Arris and Malcolm Greenhalgh, *The Atlantic Salmon Atlas*, Silver Run Publishing, 2003

Fred Buller, *The Domesday Book of Giant Salmon: A Record of the Largest Atlantic Salmon Ever Caught*, Constable, 2007

H. A. Gilbert, *Tales of a Wye Fisherman*, Methuen & Co. Ltd, 1929

Malcolm Greenhalgh and Rod Sutterby, *Atlantic Salmon, An Illustrated Natural History*, Merlin Unwin Books, 2005

J. Arthur Hutton, *Wye Salmon and Other Fish*, John Sherratt & Son, 1949

David Montgomery, *King of Fish: The Thousand-Year Run of Salmon*, Westview Press, 2003

Anthony Netboy, *The Atlantic Salmon: A Vanishing Species*, Faber & Faber, 1968

Richard Shelton, *To Sea and Back: The Heroic Life of the Atlantic Salmon*, Atlantic Books, 2009

Michael Wigan, *The Salmon: The Extraordinary Story of the King of Fish*, William Collins, 2013

HERRING

Frank Castleton, *Fisher's End*, True's Yard Museum, 2000

Sally Festing, *Fishermen: A Community Living from the Sea*, David & Charles, 1999

Patricia W. Midgley, *The Northenders: A disappeared community*, Lanceni Press, 1987

Donald S. Murray, *Herring Tales: How the Silver Darlings Shaped Human Taste and History*, Bloomsbury, 2015

Christopher Unsworth, *The British Herring Industry: The Steam Drifter Years 1900–1960*, Amberley, 2013

SCIENTIFIC PAPERS

COD

Carmel Finley, 'Fish Unlimited: How Maximum Sustained Yield Failed Fishermen', in *The Solutions Journal*, 2011

James H. Barrett, Alison M. Locker and Callum M. Roberts, 'The Origins of Intensive Marine Fishing in Medieval Europe: the English Evidence', in *Royal Society Open Science*, 2004

Walter Garstang, The Impoverishment of the Sea, in Journal of the Marine Biological Association, 1900

Michael Graham, Report on the North Sea Cod Fishery, 1934

Michael Graham, Modern Theory of Exploiting a Fishery, and Application to North Sea Trawling, in ICES Journal of Marine Science, December 1935

William Hutchinson, Mark Culling, David Orton, Bernd Händling, Lori Handley, Sheila Hamilton-Dyer, Tamsin O'Connell, Michael Richards and James Barrett, 'The globalisation of naval provisioning: ancient DNA and stable isotope analysis of stored cod from the wreck of the *Mary Rose*, AD 1545', in *Royal Society Open Science*, 2015

Ruth H. Thurstan, Julie P. Hawkins and Callum M. Roberts, 'Origins of the bottom trawling controversy in the British Isles: 19th century witness testimonies reveal evidence of early fishery declines', in *Fish and Fisheries*, 2014

CARP

James H. Barrett, Alison M. Locker and Callum M. Roberts, 'Dark Age Economics Revisited: the Fish-bone Evidence AD 600–1600', in *Antiquity*, 2004

Christopher K. Currie, 'Fish ponds as Garden Features, *c.*1550–1750', in *Garden History*, 1990

Christopher K. Currie, 'The Early History of the Carp and its Economic Significance', in *Agricultural History Review*, 1991

Richard C. Hoffmann, 'Environmental Change and the Culture of Common Carp in Medieval Europe', in Richard C. Hoffmann, *A Brief History of Aquatic Resource Use in Medieval Europe*, online by Springer-Verlag and AWI, 2004 and in *Helgoland Marine Research*, 2005

Adrian Franklin, 'An unpopular food? The distaste for fish and the decline of fish consumption in Britain', in *Food and Foodways*, 1977

Dolly Jørgensen, 'Local government responses to urban river pollution in late medieval England', in *Water History*, 2010

Alison Locker, 'In Piscibus Diversis; the Bone Evidence for Fish Consumption in Roman Britain', in *Britannia*, 2007

EELS

Daniele Bevacqua, Paco Melia, Marino Gatto, and Giulio A. De Leo, 'A global viability assessment of the European eel', in *Global Change Biology*, 2015

Sandra Casellato, 'European eel: a history which must be rewritten', in *Italian Journal of Zoology*, 2002

Benjamin Geffroy and Agnes Bardonnet, 'Sex differentiation and sex determination in eels: consequences for management', in *Fish and Fisheries*, 2016

A. James Kettle, Dorothee C. E. Bakker and Keith Haines, 'Impact of the North Atlantic Oscillation on the transatlantic migrations of the European eel', in *Journal of Geophysical Research*, 2008

Jose M. Pojular, 'Conclusive evidence for panmixia in the American eel', in *Molecular Ecology*, 2013

Johannes Schmidt, 'The Breeding Places of the Eel', in *Philosophical Transactions of the Royal Society*, 1923

Joshua A. Starry, Thomas C. Pratt, Guy Verreault and Michael G. Fox, 'A caution for conservation stocking as an approach for recovering Atlantic eels', in *Aquatic Conservation: Marine and Freshwater Ecosystems*, 2015

Thierry Wirth and Louis Bernatchez, 'Genetic evidence against panmixia in the European eel', in *Nature*, 2001

SALMON

Kevin D. Friedland, Julian C. MacLean, Lars P. Hansen, Arnaud J. Peyronnet, Lars Karlsson, David G. Reddin, Niall O Maoileidigh and Jennifer L. McCarthy, 'The recruitment of Atlantic salmon in Europe', in *ICES Journal of Marine Science*, 2009

Andrew M. Griffiths, Jonathan S. Ellis, Darryl Clifton-Dey, Gonzalo Machado-Schiaffino, Dylan Bright, Eva Garcia-Vazquez and Jamie R. Stevens, 'Restoration versus recolonisation: The origin of Atlantic salmon (*Salmo salar* L.) currently in the River Thames', in *Biological Conservation*, 2011

Margaret T. Hodgen, 'Domesday Water Mills', in *Antiquity*, 1939

Richard C. Hoffmann, '*Salmo salar* in late medieval Scotland: competition and conservation for a riverine resource', in *Aquatic Science*, 2015

C. Ikediashi, J. R. Paris, R. A. King, W. R. C. Beaumont, A. Ibbotson and J. R. Stevens, 'Atlantic salmon Salmo salar in the chalk streams of England are genetically unique', in *Journal of Fish Biology*, 2018

Jonathan R. Lee, 'Cool Britannia – from Milankovich wobbles to Ice Ages', in *Mercian Geologist*, 2011

H. J. R. Lenders, T. P. M. Chamuleau, A. J. Hendriks, R. C. G. M. Lauwerier, R. S. E. W. Leuven and W. C. E. P. Verberk, 'Historical rise of waterpower initiated the collapse of salmon stocks', in *Scientific Reports*, 2016

Malcolm L. Windsor, Peter Hutchinson, Lars Petter Hansen and David G. Reddin, 'Atlantic salmon at sea: findings from recent research and their implications for management', NASCO, 2012

Malcolm L. Windsor and Peter Hutchinson, 'The Work of NASCO 1984 to 2012', NASCO, 2012

HERRING

Marcus Bloch, 'Natural History of the Herring', in *Belfast Monthly Magazine*, 1809

D. H. Cushing, 'A short history of the Downs stock of herring', in *ICES Journal of Marine Science*, 49: 437–43, 1992

D. H. Cushing, 'The decline of herring stocks and the gadoid outburst', in *ICES Journal of Marine Science*, 1980

D. H. Cushing and J. P. Bridger, 'The stock of herring in the North Sea, and changes due to fishing', in *Fishery Investigations*, 1966

Mark Dickey-Collas, Richard D. M. Nash, Thomas Brunel, Cindy J. G. van Damme, C. Tara Marshall, Mark R. Payne, Ad Corten, Audrey J. Geffen, Myron A. Peck, Emma M. C. Hatfield, Niels T. Hintzen, Katja Enberg, Laurence T. Kell, and E. John Simmonds, 'Lessons learned from stock collapse and recovery of North Sea herring: a review', in *ICES Journal of Marine Science*, 2010

INDEX